STUDY GUIDE

ECONOMIC PRINCIPLES & POLICIES

SIXTH EDITION

RYAN C. AMACHER

HOLLEY H. ULBRICH

Prepared by

PATRICIA PANDO
Houston Baptist University

SOUTH-WESTERN College Publishing

An International Thomson Publishing Company

Acquisitions Editor: Jack C. Calhoun
Developmental Editor: Alice C. Denny, Dennis Hanseman
Production Editors: Sue Ellen Brown, Rebecca Roby
Production House: Shepherd, Inc.
Cover Design: Sandy Weinstein/Tin Box Studio
Cover Illustration: Jane Sterrett

HB67FD
Copyright © 1995
by South-Western College Publishing
Cincinnati, Ohio

ALL RIGHTS RESERVED
The text of this publication, or any part thereof, may not be reproduced or transmitted in any form or by any means, electronic or mechanical, including photocopying, recording, storage in any information retrieval system, or otherwise, without prior written permission from the publisher.

ISBN: 0-538-83851-5
 2 3 4 5 6 7 MZ 0 9 8 7 6 5
Printed in the United States of America

 This book is printed on acid-free paper that meets Environmental Protection Agency standards for recycled paper.

International Thomson Publishing

South-Western College Publishing is an ITP Company. The ITP trademark is used under license.

PREFACE

This *Study Guide* is your guide to the basics of economics; it is meant to be used. You may have read a travel guidebook before you took a vacation. A travel guide points out important things you should see and explains details you might not have known or understood. However, reading the guidebook is not the same thing as taking the trip!

In the same manner, this *Study Guide* will help you get the most out of your study of economics. You should refer to it and work in it often. However, it is not a substitute for reading the text book or going to class; it is a complement to those activities. Students who have done well in introductory economics courses frequently report that they reviewed each chapter in the Study Guide before the material was presented in class. Because the students were already familiar with the material, they were able to ask questions about troublesome parts while the chapter was being discussed in class. If you try this, you should find your grades improving.

Each Chapter of the *Study Guide* is divided into several parts:

Checking In summarizes the important points of each chapter in a few paragraphs. You may want to read this section before you read the chapter in the text, and you will certainly want to read it before your instructor discusses the material in class.

Trying Out the Terms allows you to match the new terms from each chapter with their definitions. Do this as soon as you finish reading the textbook chapter. Understanding all the terms will make the questions and problems easier for you..

Testing Yourself lets you check how well you understand each chapter. You should complete this part after you have mastered the new terms. This section contains true/false statements, multiple choice questions, and problems. Many problems are numerical applications of theories discussed in the textbook, and working with them will make the theories easier to understand. If you have difficulty with any part of this section, ask your instructor to review the material. If you are a member of a study group, your group can use these questions as a review and as a springboard for discussion. You will want to rework this section before your examination.

Taking Another Look presents a new application of or a different way of looking at some of the timely issues discussed in the textbook. This section does not appear in every chapter.

Checking Out gives you a last look at the important topics in each chapter. Use this section as a self-test; if you cannot explain an item, go back and review it in your text or class notes. This section is a good place to begin your review for an examination.

Answers to the Trying Out the Terms and Testing Yourself sections follow Checking Out.

Exercises end each chapter. Your instructor may assign the exercises as homework or as an in-class activity. If they are not assigned, you can complete them as a review. Ask you instructor for a copy of the solutions.

The *Study Guide* was prepared with you in mind. Its purpose is to help you understand and enjoy economics and also to help you earn a better grade. If, in your studies, you find some parts of the Study Guide more helpful than others, or if you come up with new methods of studying that you think will help others, please let us know. We will try to incorporate your suggestions when the Study Guide is revised.
Good luck!

Patricia N. Pando
Ryan C. Amacher
Holley H. Ulbrich

CONTENTS

Chapter	1	Economics, Economic Methods and Economic Policy	1
Chapter	2	Markets, Governments and Nations: The Organization of Economic Activity	19
Chapter	3	Supply and Demand: The Basics of Economic Analysis	33
Chapter	4	Unemployment, Inflation and Economic Fluctuations	49
Chapter	5	The Measure of Output, Income and Economic Growth	61
Chapter	6	Aggregate Demand and Aggregate Supply	75
Chapter	7	Classical Macroeconomics and the Keynesian Challenge	89
Chapter	8	The Keynesian Model	101
Chapter	9	Taxes, Government Spending, and Fiscal Policy	115
Chapter	10	Budget Deficits and the National Debt	127
Chapter	11	The Role of Money in a Market Economy	137
Chapter	12	Banking and the Federal Reserve System	149
Chapter	13	Financial Markets and Interest Rates	163
Chapter	14	Monetary Policy in Theory and Practice	175
Chapter	15	Current Issues in Stabilization Policy	185
Chapter	16	Aggregate Supply, Economic Growth and Macroeconomic Policy	197
Chapter	17	The Challenge of Economic Development	207
Chapter	18	Policy Applications of Supply and Demand	217
Chapter	19	Elasticity: The Measure of Responsiveness	231
Chapter	20	Demand and Consumer Choice	247
Chapter	21	Firms and Production	267
Chapter	22	Costs and Profits	283
Chapter	23	Perfect Competition	297
Chapter	24	Monopoly	313
Chapter	25	Monopolistic Competition and Oligopoly	331
Chapter	26	Regulation, Deregulation and Antitrust Policy	345
Chapter	27	Marginal Productivity Theory and Labor Markets	359
Chapter	28	Organized Labor in the United States	371
Chapter	29	Rent, Interest and Profit	389

Chapter	30	Poverty, Inequality, and Income Redistribution Policies	403
Chapter	31	Market Failure and Government Intervention Policies	415
Chapter	32	Government Failure and Public Choice	429
Chapter	33	Policy Studies: Cities, the Environment, and Health Care	441
Chapter	34	Trade Among Nations	451
Chapter	35	International Finance and Exchange Rates	463
Chapter	36	Economies in Transition	479

STUDY GUIDE FOR

ECONOMIC PRINCIPLES & POLICIES

CHAPTER 1

ECONOMICS, ECONOMIC METHODS, AND ECONOMIC POLICY

CHECKING IN

You are about to begin the very interesting subject of economics. Economics is the study of the ways in which people and institutions make decisions about producing and consuming goods and services, or how they face the problems caused by scarcity.

The study of economics is generally divided into two parts; both are concerned with these problems of scarcity. Microeconomics considers the interactions of producers and consumers in individual markets. Macroeconomics looks at the economy as a whole; it is concerned with aggregates, or quantities whose values are determined by adding up values for all of the individual markets.

Economics is usually classified as a social science. Economic theory is an abstract way of thinking that allows the development of models and tools that can be used to study social problems.

Resources are finite, but human wants are unlimited. In dealing with the problem of scarcity, people must make choices. They cannot produce everything, so in order to get more of one thing, they must give up something else. The value of the alternative given up is the opportunity cost. The principle of increasing opportunity cost says that the more of one good people have, the greater the amount of other goods they must sacrifice to obtain one more unit of that good.

The importance of opportunity cost is illustrated by the production possibilities curve. This model not only demonstrates the importance of opportunity cost, but also is useful in describing unemployment, economic growth, and the benefits of specialization and exchange.

The approach that most economists take is to make positive statements rather than normative ones. Normative statements suggest what *should* be done. Positive statements say "if this is done, then that will happen," without saying whether it *ought* to be done.

Economists assume that people act out of self-interest: that people always try to make themselves (or their firms or institutions) as well off as possible. Economics stresses how individuals respond to incentives (self-interest), so economists tend to rely on the market to solve many problems that they analyze. They attempt to clarify the options available to the decision maker and consider all possible costs. Economists also consider alternatives or substitutes that are available.

Policy analysis involves five steps: stating the problem, applying the relevant economic model, identifying solutions, evaluating solutions, and choosing and implementing solutions. Most economists' disagreements are over policy choices rather than economic theory. In general, economists agree much more than they disagree.

Economists depend on graphs and algebra to assist in their analysis. The Appendix to this chapter reviews some techniques you will be using in your study of economics.

TRYING OUT THE TERMS

Match each of the following terms with its definition, and then check your answers. If you are having trouble, go back to the text and find the definition there.

Part I

_____ 1. microeconomics

_____ 2. self-interested behavior

_____ 3. testable hypothesis

_____ 4. model

_____ 5. theory

_____ 6. normative statements

_____ 7. increasing opportunity cost

_____ 8. unlimited wants

_____ 9. scarcity

_____ 10. resources

_____ 11. macroeconomics

_____ 12. aggregates

_____ 13. economics

_____ 14. *ceteris paribus* assumption

_____ 15. social science

_____ 16. opportunity cost

_____ 17. positive statements

_____ 18. production possibilities curve

A. The study of how people and institutions make decisions about production and consumption and how they face the problem of scarcity.

B. The study of individual market interactions, focusing on production and consumption by the individual consumer, firm, or industry.

C. The study of the economy as a whole or of economic aggregates, such as the level of employment and the growth of total output.

D. An academic field that studies the behavior of human beings, individually and in groups, and examines their interactions.

E. Quantities whose values are determined by adding across many markets.

F. The central economic problem that there are not enough resources to produce everything that individuals want.

G. The needs and desires of human beings, which can never be completely satisfied.

H. The value of the other alternatives given up in order to enjoy a particular good or service.

I. A graph that depicts the various combinations of two goods that can be produced in an economy with the available resources.

J. The principle that as production of one good rises, larger and larger sacrifices of another are required.

K. A set of principles that can be used to make inferences about the world.

L. An inference from a theory that can be subjected to real-world testing.

M. A set of assumptions and hypotheses that is a simplified description of reality.

N. The assumption that everything else will remain constant, used for most economic models.

O. A basic assumption of economic theory that individual decision makers do what is best for themselves.

P. A set of propositions about what is, rather than what ought to be.

Q. A set of propositions about what ought to be (also called value judgments).

R. Inputs used to produce goods and services.

Part II

These terms are found in the Appendix to the chapter.

_____ 1. coordinates

_____ 2. *y*-axis

_____ 3. scatter diagram

_____ 4. tangent line

_____ 5. *x*-axis

_____ 6. bar chart

_____ 7. independent variable

_____ 8. slope

_____ 9. pie chart

_____ 10. minimum

_____ 11. origin

_____ 12. positive relationship

_____ 13. 45° line

_____ 14. negative relationship

_____ 15. maximum

_____ 16. dependent variable

A. The upright line in a coordinate system that shows the values of the dependent variable; the vertical axis.

B. The horizontal line in a coordinate system that shows the values of the independent variable; the horizontal axis.

C. The intersection of the vertical and horizontal axes of a coordinate system, at which the values of both the x-variable and the y-variable are zero.

D. The variable, usually plotted on the horizontal axis, that affects or influences the other variable.

E. The variable, usually plotted on the vertical axis, that is affected or influenced by the other variable.

F. The values of x and y that define the location of a point in a coordinate system.

G. A graph that plots actual pairs of values of two variables to determine whether there appears to be any consistent relationship between them.

H. A relationship between two variables in which an increase in one is associated with an increase in the other and a decrease in one is associated with a decrease in the other.

I. A relationship between two variables in which an increase in the value of one is associated with a decrease in the value of the other.

J. The ratio of the change in the dependent variable (y) to the change in the independent variable (x).

K. A straight line just touching a curve (nonlinear graphic relationship) at a single point. The slope of the line is equal to the slope of the curve at that point.

L. The point on a graph at which the y-variable, or dependent variable, reaches its highest value.

M. The point on the graph at which the y-variable, or dependent variable, reaches its lowest value.

N. A line in the first quadrant, passing through the origin, with a slope of +1, which divides the quadrant in half. If the scales on the axes are the same, the value of the x-variable is equal to the value of the y-variable along this line.

O. A graphic representation in the shape of a pie that expresses actual economic data as parts of a whole. The sizes of the slices of the pie correspond to the percentage shares of the components.

P. A graphic representation that expresses data using columns of different heights.

TESTING YOURSELF

In the next three sections, you will answer questions and work problems that are based on information in the text. Master all of the terms before you begin these sections. Work each section without referring to your notes or the text, and then check your answers.

Part I: True or False

Mark each statement as true or false. Whenever you mark a statement as false, jot down a sentence stating why it is false. Statements 11–14 are based on material in the Appendix.

_____ 1. The study of economics is concerned with how people react to changing income and prices.

_____ 2. The level of employment in the economy is a macroeconomic issue.

_____ 3. Microeconomics is concerned with the interactions of producers and consumers in individual markets.

_____ 4. Opportunity cost is always measured in monetary terms.

_____ 5. When some of a society's resources are unemployed, the society is operating at a point inside the production possibilities curve.

_____ 6. The typical production possibilities curve has a bowed-out shape because of increasing opportunity costs.

_____ 7. When the Vietnam War began, the United States was operating at a point inside its production possibilities curve.

_____ 8. The question, "What will happen to the price of corn in a year when there is both a flood and a fall in the price of fertilizer?" observes the *ceteris paribus* assumption.

_____ 9. An economics teacher tells her class that all transfer payments to veterans should be eliminated. This is an example of a positive economic statement.

_____ 10. The self-interest assumption holds that all people are selfish.

_____ 11. If for every increase in x, y increases by 2, 3, or 4 units, the graph of the equation will be a straight line.

_____ 12. If two variables are negatively (inversely) related, then one variable will increase in value as the other variable decreases.

_____ 13. The slope of a curve at a particular point is equal to the slope of the straight line tangent to that point.

_____ 14. If the numbers reported are accurate, statistical reports always give an undistorted view of reality.

Part II: Problems

Problem 3 is based on the Appendix.

1. You are given the following data for a small country that can produce either bread or tractors.

Bread	Tractors
70	0
60	2
50	4
40	6
30	8
20	10
10	12
0	14

   a. On the graph below, plot the production possibilities curve.

   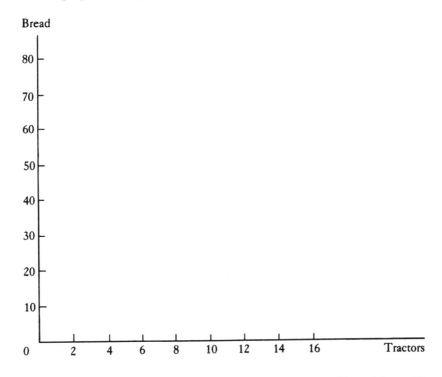

   b. What is the opportunity cost of increasing production of bread from 10 units to 20 units? From 40 units to 50 units?

Chapter 1   Economics, Economic Methods, and Economic Policy

c. What role do increasing opportunity costs play in this model?

d. On your graph, mark the point representing the production of 45 units of bread and 8 tractors. Will this economy ever produce at this point? Why or why not?

2. On the graph below, plot the sales of a typical retail store during the months of October through February. It is not necessary to use exact values; simply graph the relationship.

3. Consider each of the following relationships:

Relationship A		Relationship B		Relationship C	
x	y	x	y	x	y
1	5	10	20	100	90
2	4	12	15	125	100
3	3	14	10	150	110
4	2	16	5	175	120

a. Which of these relationships is/are positive? How can you tell?

b. What is the slope of each relationship?

c. In the graph provided below, plot relationship B.

Part III: Multiple Choice

Questions 13–15 are based on the Appendix.

_____ 1. Economics can be defined as the
   a. study of money and commerce.
   b. science of behavior modification.
   c. study of how people and institutions respond to the problems of scarcity.
   d. study of how labor and product markets are related.

_____ 2. The study of the overall price level and the levels of unemployment and output is called
   a. macroeconomics.
   b. microeconomics.
   c. decision science.
   d. global economics.

_____ 3. In microeconomics we would expect to study
   a. the effects of inflation.
   b. the tax policies of the federal government.
   c. changes in the consumer price index.
   d. the determination of the price of corn.

Use this graph to answer Questions 4–6.

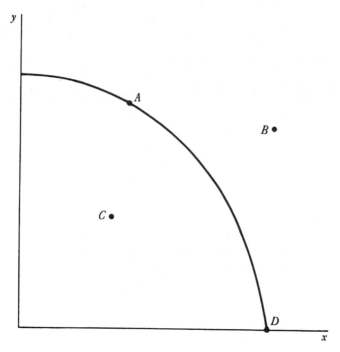

_____ 4. If the economy is producing at point C,
   a. there is considerable unemployment in the economy.
   b. the economy is operating at full employment.
   c. there is excessive production of Good x.
   d. The point is unattainable.

_____ 5. In this economy, the opportunity cost of an additional unit of y in terms of unit x will
   a. increase as more y is produced.
   b. increase as more x is produced.
   c. remain constant at all levels of production.
   d. increase at a low level of production of y and then become constant.

_____ 6. If the economy is operating at full employment and producing some of both Good x and Good y, it is at point
   a. A.
   b. B.
   c. C.
   d. D.

_____ 7. When an individual makes decisions based on a comparison of costs and benefits, economists say that this individual is acting
   a. selfishly.
   b. out of self-interest.
   c. uneconomically.
   d. in a way that will minimize the general welfare.

_____ 8. Economists tend to think of the basic decision-making unit as the
   a. government.
   b. firm.
   c. individual.
   d. institution (bank, church, etc.).

_____ 9. Economists prefer market solutions to economic problems because market solutions are
   a. fairer.
   b. more efficient.
   c. faster.
   d. easier to understand.

_____ 10. Economic models are used
   a. because economists don't really understand the way markets work.
   b. because they explain all of the economy at one specific time.
   c. to predict behavior under specific circumstances.
   d. to give accurate and explicit forecasts of the future.

_____ 11. Employment is a macroeconomic issue
   a. because everyone is likely to be unemployed at some time.
   b. because unemployed workers represent lost potential output.
   c. because unemployment benefits are spent on consumer goods.
   d. because employment takes place in labor markets.

_____ 12. Economist Milton Friedman maintains that the best test of the usefulness of a theory is
   a. the strength of its assumptions.
   b. if it makes accurate predictions.
   c. its logical correctness.
   d. if it demonstrates market behavior.

_____ 13. If for every increase of 5 units in the x-variable, the y-variable increases by 10 units, a graph of the equation
   a. has a slope of 1/2.
   b. has a slope of 2.
   c. has no slope.
   d. would show a negative slope, reach a minimum, and then become positive.

_____ 14. If for every increase of 10 units in the x-variable, the y-variable decreases by 15 units, a graph of the equation
   a. has a slope of 0.666.
   b. has a negative slope.
   c. is a straight line.
   d. is a straight line with a negative slope.

____ 15. A straight line that cuts through the origin and divides Quadrant 1 into two equal sections
    a. is called the 45° line.
    b. has a slope of +1.
    c. measures equal values of both the *x*- and *y*-variables.
    d. All of the above.

CHECKING OUT

Now that you have finished studying this chapter, you should be able to:

1. Define economics, and discuss how it is related to other social sciences.

2. Recognize the value of studying economics.

3. Explain the relationship between scarcity and choice, and the role of opportunity costs.

4. Use the production possibilities model to identify unemployment of resources and to explain the concept of economic growth.

5. Recognize the difference between theories, hypotheses, and models.

6. List the elements of the economic approach to policy analysis.

7. Understand and develop the steps followed in policy analysis.

ANSWERS

Trying Out the Terms

Part I

1. B	5. K	9. F	13. A	17. P
2. O	6. Q	10. R	14. N	18. I
3. L	7. J	11. C	15. D	
4. M	8. G	12. E	16. H	

Part II

1. F	5. B	9. O	13. N
2. A	6. P	10. M	14. I
3. G	7. D	11. C	15. L
4. K	8. J	12. H	16. E

Testing Yourself

Part I: True or False

1. false. Economics is concerned with how people make choices when resources are scarce.
2. true
3. true
4. false. Opportunity cost is the value of the next-best alternatives given up in order to enjoy a particular activity or service. It may or may not be stated in monetary terms.
5. true
6. true
7. false. There was very little unemployment. The economy was on its production possibilities curve.
8. false. The *ceteris paribus* assumption means that we are assuming only one thing will change: either the weather or the price of fertilizer.
9. false. This is a normative statement.
10. false. The self-interest assumption holds that individuals make decisions by comparing costs and benefits and then doing what is best for themselves.
11. false. When the graph of an equation is a straight line, y always responds with the same change. For example, for every change in x, y increases by 2.
12. true
13. true
14. false. The way in which accurate numbers are reported (scale, use of averages, etc.) can easily distort reality.

Part II: Problems

1. a.

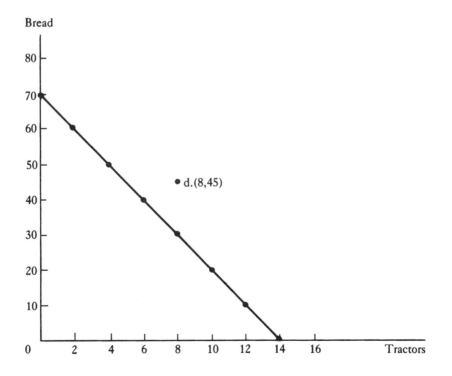

Chapter 1   Economics, Economic Methods, and Economic Policy

b. The opportunity cost of increasing bread production from 10 units to 20 units is 2 tractors. The opportunity cost of increasing bread production from 40 units to 50 units is also 2 tractors.

c. In this case, costs are not increasing. The opportunity cost of 1 unit of bread is always 1/5 of a tractor. In other words, the opportunity cost of 1 tractor is always 5 units of bread.

d. This economy will never be able to produce 45 units of bread and 8 tractors, because that combination is beyond the production possibilities curve.

2. We would expect sales to increase during the fall months, peak in December, fall off dramatically in January, and then level off in February.

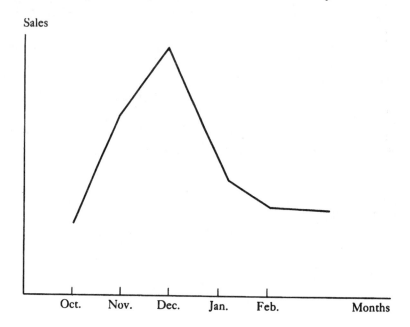

3. a. Relationship C is positive. The two variables change in the same direction; when x increases, so does y. The other relationships are negative.

   b. Relationship A: slope = –1/1 = –1
      Relationship B: slope = –5/2 = –2.5
      Relationship C: slope = 10/25 = 0.4

c.

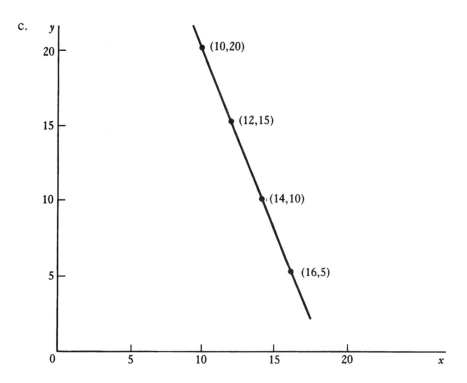

Part III: Multiple Choice

1. c
2. a
3. d
4. a
5. a
6. a
7. b
8. c
9. b
10. c
11. b
12. b
13. b
14. d
15. d

Name _____

CHAPTER 1 EXERCISES

1. List and describe, in one sentence each, the five steps for using economic methods in policy analysis.

   a.

   b.

   c.

   d.

   e.

2. You are given this information about a country's ability to produce toys and typewriters.

Toys	Typewriters	Opportunity Cost of 5 Additional Typewriters
75	0	
68	5	_____
58	10	_____
44	15	_____
25	20	_____
0	25	_____

a. Fill in the opportunity cost of 5 additional typewriters in terms of toys.

b. Plot the production possibilities curve on the graph below.

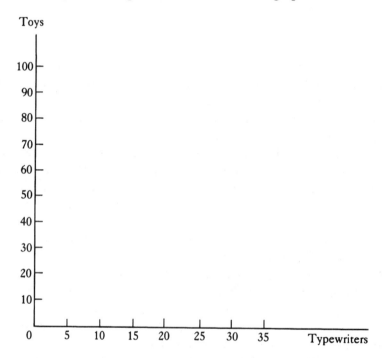

c. Suppose that this country experiences 10 years of peace, prosperity, and economic growth. At the end of those 10 years, it can produce more of all goods. Draw a new production possibilities curve on your graph. Label it *Good Times*.

d. Now suppose that this country has 10 years of war, famine, and disaster. At the end of those 10 years, it has fewer productive resources than it did 10 years earlier. Draw this production possibilities curve and label it *Bad Times*.

CHAPTER 2

MARKETS, GOVERNMENTS, AND NATIONS: THE ORGANIZATION OF ECONOMIC ACTIVITY

CHECKING IN

From Chapter 1, you learned that scarcity is the inescapable economic problem. Regardless of their levels of wealth and types of economic organization, all economies must face and attempt to solve this problem. Because resources are limited, economies must decide how they are to be used by answering three basic questions: *What* will be produced? *How* shall it be produced? *Who* gets a share of what is produced? All of these are questions about how an economy decides to use its resources. *Productive resources* can be divided into four general groups: labor (which receives the payment of wages), land (which receives the payment of rent), capital (which receives the payment of interest), and enterprise (which receives profit).

Although all economies must answer the three basic questions, different economies go about doing so in different ways. The three general ways are tradition, command, and the market. Most countries use a combination of these methods, with one predominating. The majority of Western industrial nations, including the United States, use a mixed economy that relies heavily on the market but allows some government intervention in certain areas. A simple but useful model of the idealized market economy is the circular flow model. We will use this model throughout the rest of the course.

A mixed economy depends both on the market and on the government to answer the basic economic questions. This is because the market either does not perform or does not perform very well some necessary functions. For markets to function at all, we must have clearly defined and protected property rights. There are some goods that markets simply do not provide or provide in the wrong amounts. Markets do answer the question of who is to receive production, but they sometimes answer this question in very uneven ways. Governments often make adjustments in this distribution. Governments also attempt to stabilize the economy.

Whenever government produces a public good or participates in activities that affect private decisions about production and consumption, it is affecting the allocation of resources. Some other ways in which government affects allocation are through taxes, subsidies, and regulation. Government can directly change the market distribution of income by redistributing it through taxes and transfer payments. However, any other action of government (allocation or stabilization, for example) will also have an effect on the distribution of income. The newest function of government is stabilization. Government uses its ability to tax, spend, and regulate to attempt to bring about full employment, stable prices, and real economic growth.

One way individuals and nations alleviate the problem of scarcity is by specializing in producing goods with low opportunity costs and trading for goods with higher opportunity costs. This principle is known as comparative advantage. International trade in goods, services, and resources benefits both trading partners. Although some workers and firms in a nation may experience losses because of foreign competition, the gains for the nation as a whole will usually exceed such losses.

TRYING OUT THE TERMS

Match each of the following terms with its definition, and then check your answers. If you are having trouble, go back to the text and find the definition there.

Part I

_____ 1. resources   _____ 9. circular flow model

_____ 2. positive externalities   _____ 10. land

_____ 3. enterprise   _____ 11. command economy

_____ 4. resource market   _____ 12. human capital

_____ 5. capital   _____ 13. allocation

_____ 6. property rights   _____ 14. product market

_____ 7. market   _____ 15. market economy

_____ 8. labor   _____ 16. mixed economy

A. Set of markets in which owners of productive resources sell these to producers.

B. The inputs of land, labor, capital, and enterprise that a firm uses to produce outputs.

C. A place where buyers and sellers meet to exchange goods, services, and productive resources.

D. An economy in which the three basic questions are answered through the market, by relying on self-interested behavior and incentives.

E. An economy in which the three basic questions are answered partly by market forces and partly through government.

F. The physical and mental exertion that human beings put into production activities.

G. Natural resources that can be used as inputs to production.

H. Any activities by government or its agents that affect the distribution of resources and the combination of goods and services produced.

I. The durable inputs into the production process created by people; machines, tools, and buildings are examples.

J. A visual representation of the relationships between the resource market (in which income is obtained) and the product market (in which income is used to purchase goods and services).

K. An economy in which the three basic questions are answered through central planning and control (also called a planned economy).

L. The input to the production process that involves organizing, innovation, and risk taking.

M. The investment made to improve the quality of people's labor skills through education, training, health care, and so on.

N. Spillover benefits to third parties (free riders) that result from production or consumption of certain goods.

O. Set of markets in which goods and services produced by firms are sold.

P. The legal rights to a specific piece of property, including the rights to own, buy, sell, or use in specific ways. Markets can exist and exchanges can occur only if individuals have property rights to goods, services, and productive resources.

Part II

_____ 1. negative externalities
_____ 2. public goods
_____ 3. free riders
_____ 4. investment
_____ 5. profit
_____ 6. rent
_____ 7. specialization
_____ 8. redistribution
_____ 9. wages
_____ 10. public bads
_____ 11. traditional economy
_____ 12. principle of comparative advantage
_____ 13. interest
_____ 14. stabilization

A. Negative external effects of production or consumption that impact a large number of individuals—for example, acid rain.

B. Goods that are nonrival in consumption and not subject to exclusion.

C. The return to enterprise, one of the productive resources of production; profit is whatever remains after all other resources have been paid.

D. The idea that output will be maximized if people specialize in producing those goods or services for which their opportunity costs are lowest and engage in exchange to obtain other things they want.

E. Actions by government that transfer income from one group to another.

F. The return to land, one of the productive resources.

G. Limiting production activities to one or a few goods and services that one produces best in order to exchange for other goods.

H. An economy in which the three basic questions are answered by custom, or how things have been done in the past.

I. People or business firms who consume collective goods without contributing to the cost of their production.

J. Harmful spillovers to third parties that result from production or consumption of certain goods.

K. The return to labor, one of the productive resources.

L. The return to capital, one of the productive resources.

M. Purchase of real tangible assets, such as machines, factories, or inventories, that are used to produce goods and services.

N. Actions by the government to reduce changes in output, employment, and prices.

TESTING YOURSELF

In the next three sections, you will answer questions and work problems that are based on information in the text. Master all of the terms before you begin these sections. Work each section without referring to your notes or the text, and then check your answers.

Part I: True or False

Mark each statement as true or false. Whenever you mark a statement as false, jot down a sentence stating why it is false.

_____ 1. People are forced to make economic choices only when their wants are greater than their resources.

_____ 2. The salary of a college professor represents wages, the payment to labor, as well as interest, the payment to investment.

_____ 3. The productive resources include land, labor, capital, and enterprise.

_____ 4. Common stocks are a good example of economic capital.

_____ 5. If a farmer leases a farm and all of the equipment on the farm, her payment to the owner of the farm is considered as both a payment to land (rent) and a payment to capital (interest).

_____ 6. The basic economic questions are what, how, and when.

_____ 7. In a traditional economy, distribution of economic resources is determined primarily by an individual's contribution to society.

_____ 8. A command economy answers the basic economic questions through central planning and control.

_____ 9. A market economy depends on a combination of tradition, planning, and incentives to answer the basic economic questions.

_____ 10. Property rights must be clearly established for a market economy to function.

_____ 11. A mixed economy may have elements of traditional and planned economies, but a traditional economy never incorporates elements of the market.

_____ 12. The circular flow model illustrates the relationship between product markets and resource markets.

_____ 13. When specialization and trade are taking place, people become more dependent on one another.

_____ 14. Specialization can increase the variety of goods produced, but it cannot increase total production.

_____ 15. Although economists frequently disagree, they generally agree that a country benefits from free trade policies.

Part II: Problems

1. Classify each of the following ways of answering the basic economic questions (market, command, or tradition).

    a. The New York Stock Exchange

    b. Gun registration

    c. Going to Fort Lauderdale every year for spring break

    d. Going to Padre Island for spring break because it is cheaper

    e. Cuban students spending spring break harvesting sugar cane as part of the privilege of attending college

    f. Football scholarships at major universities

2. Classify each of the following government actions as being primarily allocation, stabilization, or redistribution.

    a. Raising taxes to control inflation

    b. Cutting out food stamps as a form of welfare payment

    c. Buying a new airplane for the vice president

    d. Holding the annual Easter Egg Roll on the White House lawn

    e. Reinstituting the GI Bill to pay college tuition for veterans

  f. Bailing out the savings and loan industry

3. Bob and Pat work at a service station. Bob can change 6 tires or do 6 oil changes in an hour. Pat can change 8 tires or do 4 oil changes in an hour. On Saturday morning at 8:00, they are told that they can leave as soon as they have changed 40 tires and done 30 oil changes. Neither can leave until both have finished working.

  a. If Bob and Pat split the work, each doing half of the tire changes and half of the oil changes, when will they leave?

  b. If Bob and Pat specialize, using the principle of comparative advantage, when will they leave?

Part III: Multiple Choice

_____ 1. The productive resources include
  a. land, labor, and services.
  b. enterprise and goods.
  c. labor, goods, and services.
  d. enterprise, capital, and labor.

_____ 2. Which is *not* one of the basic economic questions?
  a. For whom?
  b. What?
  c. How much?
  d. How?

_____ 3. Which of the following would be defined by an economist as embodying enterprise?
  a. A doctor
  b. A professor
  c. The owner of a dry-cleaning business
  d. A coal miner

_____ 4. A planned economy answers the basic economic questions
  a. in the same way economies did in the past.
  b. through a central board or commission.
  c. by relying on the market system and incentives.
  d. by a combination of government regulation and markets.

5. Sylvia's parents are both doctors, but she decides to study accounting because she thinks it offers better career opportunities. This is an example of what kind of economic decision making?
   a. Command
   b. Rebellion
   c. Market
   d. Anti-tradition

6. The economies of the United States and Canada are generally thought of as
   a. market economies.
   b. free-trade economies.
   c. mixed economies.
   d. planned economies.

7. In the simplified pure market economy described by the two-sector circular flow model, the participants are
   a. domestic and foreign countries.
   b. households and government.
   c. commercial institutions and government institutions.
   d. households and firms.

8. In the pure market economy described by the two-sector circular flow model,
   a. the flow of income to households is equal to the flow of payments to firms.
   b. the flow of income to households is less than the flow of payments to firms.
   c. households are permitted to save, but firms are not.
   d. total production that is not sold becomes investment.

9. The redistributive function of government is most likely to be answering the economic question of
   a. for whom?
   b. what?
   c. how?
   d. both how and what?

10. Which of the following is not an economic function of the government?
    a. Redistribution
    b. Optimization
    c. Stablization
    d. Allocation

11. A public library provides an example of
    a. provision of a nearly public good.
    b. public provision of a private good.
    c. the redistributive function of government.
    d. the stabilization function of government.

_____ 12. If Ralph Elliott, after refusing to contribute to the neighborhood park fund, spends every Saturday picnicking in the park, we could call him a
   a. tax avoider.
   b. public consumer.
   c. free rider.
   d. cheater.

_____ 13. The stabilization function of government has as a goal
   a. consumer protection.
   b. market equilibrium.
   c. national defense.
   d. stable prices.

_____ 14. Who is generally regarded as the founder of modern economics?
   a. Milton Friedman
   b. Francois Quesnay
   c. Benjamin Franklin
   d. Adam Smith

_____ 15. The transfer of government assets and/or activities to the private sector is called
   a. pro-market implementation.
   b. deficit financing.
   c. privatization.
   d. private sector initiative.

TAKING ANOTHER LOOK

I

We think of the United States as depending strongly on the market to answer the basic economic questions. However, some market decisions are viewed unfavorably. For example, who will get limited experimental medical care? Usually we rely on medical institutions to funnel the care evenly to those who will benefit the most, but often there are more eligible patients than there is treatment.

Lately, some hospitals have developed what they refer to as *patient-funded research.* They offer scarce experimental treatments to those patients who are willing to pay for them. Some people view this practice as unfair and perhaps unethical. Others (generally, the patients receiving the treatment) say that it is simply the market at work and that they have as much right to purchase medical treatment that they can afford as they do to purchase an expensive car or a mansion.

II

Could you open an accounting practice in your extra bedroom or a barber shop in your garage? In most cities, you would run into trouble with the zoning commission. *Zoning* is government regulation of land use in a municipality. Most commercial activity is prohibited in residential areas. The only large city in the United States that does not have zoning is Houston, Texas. In Houston, land can be purchased anywhere and put to any use the new owner wishes. In some residential areas, there are deed restrictions that limit land use to single-family residences, but the city does not enforce these restrictions; it is up to the other owners to make sure that they are observed. Visitors can easily tell if they are in Houston or one of its zoned suburbs. In the suburbs, even the busy streets are residential, and commercial activity tends to be concentrated in shopping centers and along major thoroughfares. As soon as visitors enter Houston, they find liquor stores, dry cleaners, video shops, and hardware stores scattered along the streets among the homes.

CHECKING OUT

Now that you have finished studying this chapter, you should be able to:

1. List the three basic economic questions that must be addressed by every economic system.

2. Analyze how traditional, command, and market economies answer the three basic economic questions.

3. Identify the productive resources and use a circular flow model to show the relationships between firms and households in product markets and in resource markets in a market economy.

4. Explain and give examples of the basic economic functions of government.

5. Evaluate the benefits of specialization and exchange based on comparative advantage.

ANSWERS

Trying Out the Terms

Part I

1. B	5. I	9. J	13. H
2. N	6. P	10. G	14. O
3. L	7. C	11. K	15. D
4. A	8. F	12. M	16. E

Part II

1. J	5. C	9. K	13. L
2. B	6. F	10. A	14. N
3. I	7. G	11. H	
4. M	8. E	12. D	

Testing Yourself

Part I: True or False

1. false. All people are forced to economize because resources are limited and have many possible uses.

2. false. The entire salary is considered a wage; however, because the professor chose to invest in human capital, his wage may be higher than if he had not gone to college.
3. true
4. false. In economics, capital refers to *real* goods, such as factories, tractors, and machines.
5. true
6. false. They are what, how, and for whom?
7. false. In a traditional economy, distribution is generally determined by a person's position in the hierarchy.
8. true
9. false. A market economy relies entirely on incentives and the self-interested behavior of individuals to answer the economic questions.
10. true
11. false. Even the most traditional economies will exhibit some market behavior.
12. true
13. true
14. false. Specialization can increase total output using the same amount of resources.
15. true

Part II: Problems

1. a. market
   b. command
   c. tradition
   d. market
   e. command
   f. market

2. a. stabilization
   b. redistribution
   c. allocation
   d. allocation (with some redistribution of fun to the kids)
   e. redistribution
   f. redistribution

3. a. They will leave at 2:15. Bob will finish his work in 5.83 hours. It will take him 2.5 hours to do the oil changes (15/6) and 3.33 hours to change the tires (20/6). However, he can't leave until Pat finishes. Pat will take 6.25 hours: 3.75 hours to do the oil changes (15/4) and 2.5 hours to change the tires (20/8).
   b. They will leave at 1:00. Bob will do all the oil changes in 5 hours (30/6), and Pat will change all the tires in 5 hours (40/8).

Part III: Multiple Choice

1. d
2. c
3. c
4. b
5. c
6. c
7. d
8. a
9. a
10. b
11. a
12. c
13. d
14. d
15. c

Name _____

CHAPTER 2 EXERCISES

_____ 1. The most basic economic function of government is
   a. providing public goods.
   b. providing public education.
   c. defining and enforcing property rights.
   d. defining and enforcing contract law.

_____ 2. Which is *not* an example of a transfer payment?
   a. The salary of a public school teacher
   b. The payment of an agricultural subsidy to a dairy farmer
   c. An unemployment check
   d. A Medicare payment

_____ 3. Which function of government affects the answer to the question of what goods to produce?
   a. Stabilization
   b. Redistribution
   c. Allocation
   d. Fiscal federalism

_____ 4. Without government intervention, a market economy will provide
   a. too many public goods.
   b. too few private goods.
   c. too many public bads.
   d. the proper amount of all goods.

_____ 5. Which government function is usually executed by state and local governments?
   a. Stabilization
   b. Redistribution
   c. Allocation
   d. All three are carried out at the state and local levels.

6. Identify each of the following as belonging in the factor market or the product market, and state by whom it is supplied or demanded.

	Market	Supplier	Demander
Land	_____	_____	_____
Goods	_____	_____	_____
Enterprise	_____	_____	_____
Labor	_____	_____	_____
Services	_____	_____	_____
Capital	_____	_____	_____

Chapter 2   Markets, Governments, and Nations: The Organization of Economic Activity

7. Fill in the two-sector circular flow model below.

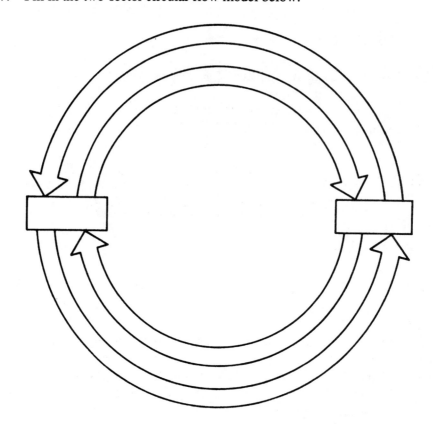

CHAPTER 3

SUPPLY AND DEMAND: THE BASICS OF ECONOMIC ANALYSIS

CHECKING IN

A mixed economy depends on the market to solve many economic problems. This chapter explains the workings of the most basic model of economics: supply and demand, the forces that move markets. This model is one of the most powerful and useful economic tools. Supply and demand are concepts that explain the behavior of market participants during a specified time period. In order to understand the interactions of supply and demand, we must look first at each separately.

Demand is the desire and ability to purchase certain quantities at various prices during a particular time period. In the product market, demand depends on many things: the current price of the good or service, the size of the group demanding the good, the tastes of the group demanding the good, the income and wealth of that group, the prices of related goods and services, and expectations concerning the future. Usually demand is analyzed by holding all but one of these determinants constant (*ceteris paribus*) and then examining how changes in one determinant can affect demand.

The law of demand states that, *ceteris paribus,* the quantity demanded of a good or service is negatively related to its price. This relationship can be illustrated for specific cases through demand schedules and demand curves. When price changes, the quantity demanded changes in the opposite direction and there is movement along the demand schedule or demand curve.

A change in one of the *ceteris paribus* conditions affecting demand will cause a *change in demand,* resulting in a whole new demand curve or schedule. For example, an increase in income will cause demand for some goods (normal goods) to increase and demand for other goods (inferior goods) to decrease. If two goods are complementary, when the price of one goes up, demand for the other will decrease. If two goods are substitutes for each other, when the price of one goes up, demand for the other will increase.

Supply refers to what firms are willing and able to offer for sale over a period of time at various prices. Supply, like demand, depends on a number of variables: the current price of the good or service, the prices of the factors of production, the level of technology, the price of other goods that could be produced, the number of suppliers, and expectations. The (not quite) law of supply states that the quantity supplied of a good or service is usually a positive function of price, *ceteris paribus*. Just as with demand, this relationship can be illustrated through supply schedules and supply curves. When price changes, the quantity supplied changes in the same direction and there is movement along the supply schedule or supply curve.

A change in one of the *ceteris paribus* conditions affecting supply will cause a *change in supply*, resulting in a new supply schedule or curve. If technology improves, we would expect to see an increase in supply at every possible price. Likewise, a decrease in the cost of resources would cause supply to increase; an increase in the cost of resources would cause supply to decrease.

Market price and quantity are determined by the interaction of supply and demand. The market is said to be in equilibrium when the quantity supplied is equal to the quantity demanded. The price and quantity at which quantity supplied equals quantity demanded are the equilibrium price and the equilibrium quantity. The equilibrium price is also called the *market-clearing price*. If the quantity supplied is greater than the quantity demanded, a surplus is present. This surplus places downward pressure on the market price, which will fall until it reaches the market-clearing level. When the quantity demanded is greater than the quantity supplied, a shortage exists. This shortage places upward pressure on the market price, which will rise until it reaches the market-clearing level. Price and quantity are endogenous variables of the supply and demand model. Variables that are determined outside of the model but that influence it, such as taste and expectations, are exogenous variables.

Marginal analysis is used with the supply and demand model, as well as with other economic models. It focuses on decisions about the next unit purchased or sold, rather than on aggregate decisions.

Because prices change in response to changes in demand, they perform important functions by informing, directing, and motivating consumers and producers. Markets maximize individual freedom by allowing individuals to pursue their own self-interest. Markets also provide for the efficient allocation of resources, as they answer the basic economic questions.

Although markets are efficient and useful, they are not without shortcomings. Organizing, negotiating, and searching for market opportunities all take time and cause both suppliers and demanders to incur transactions costs. When transactions costs exist, different people often pay different prices for the same product. Market transactions can also affect those who are neither suppliers nor demanders (oil spills on supplies of public drinking water, for example); in such cases, the allocation of resources is inefficient.

Some will argue that a market economy is unstable and that markets do not function well if they are not highly competitive. Often, market shortcomings lead to circumvention of the market; the solutions to economic problems are then provided by the government. Government intervention does not mean that the problems of allocation are avoided; it means only that they are solved by means other than the market.

TRYING OUT THE TERMS

Match each of the following terms with its definition, and then check your answers. If you are having trouble, go back to the text and find the definition there.

Part I

_____ 1. endogenous variables
_____ 2. expectations
_____ 3. marginal analysis
_____ 4. complementary goods
_____ 5. demand
_____ 6. exogenous variables
_____ 7. inferior good
_____ 8. decrease in demand
_____ 9. decrease in supply
_____ 10. law of demand
_____ 11. increase in demand
_____ 12. demand schedule
_____ 13. demand curve

A. Goods that are jointly consumed. The consumption of one enhances the consumption of the other.

B. A shift in the demand curve indicating that at every price, consumers demand a smaller amount than before.

C. A shift in the supply curve indicating that at every price, a smaller quantity will be offered for sale than before.

D. The desire and ability to consume certain quantities of a good at various prices over a certain period of time.

E. A graph representing a demand schedule and showing the quantity demanded at various prices in a certain time period.

F. Variables that are explained or determined within a model.

G. Variables that are determined outside a model and affect endogenous variables.

H. A table that shows quantities demanded at various prices during a specific time period.

I. Feelings that individuals have about future conditions.

J. A shift in the demand curve indicating that at every price, a larger quantity will be offered for sale than before.

K. A good for which demand decreases as income increases.

L. The quantity demanded of a good or service is negatively related to its price, *ceteris paribus*.

M. A technique for analyzing problems by examining the results of small changes.

Part II

_____ 1. secondary effects
_____ 2. market supply curve
_____ 3. normal good
_____ 4. substitute goods
_____ 5. comparative statics
_____ 6. supply curve
_____ 7. (not quite) law of supply
_____ 8. market equilibrium
_____ 9. supply
_____ 10. transaction costs
_____ 11. market-clearing price
_____ 12. primary effect
_____ 13. supply schedule
_____ 14. increase in supply
_____ 15. market demand curve

A. The equilibrium price, which clears the market because there are no frustrated consumers or suppliers.

B. The sum of all of the individual demand curves; it shows what quantities will be demanded by all consumers in a specific time frame in a certain market at various prices.

C. A point at which quantity demanded by consumers is equal to quantity supplied by producers. The price at which this occurs is the equilibrium price, or market-clearing price.

D. The sum of all of the individual supply curves; it shows what quantities will be supplied by all firms at various prices during a specific time period.

E. The quantity supplied of a good or service is usually a positive function of price, _ceteris paribus_.

F. The dominant or immediate effect of a change in an economic variable.

G. Effects indirectly related to the immediate effect, often smaller and felt after some time.

H. Goods that can be interchanged. The consumption of one replaces the consumption of the other.

I. The quantity of a good offered for sale at various prices during a certain time period.

J. A graph representing a supply schedule and showing the quantities supplied at various prices in a certain time period.

K. A table that shows quantities offered for sale at various prices over a particular time period.

L. A good for which demand increases as income increases.

M. A technique of comparing two equilibrium positions to determine the changing relationships between variables.

N. A shift in the supply curve indicating that at every price, a larger quantity will be offered for sale than before.

O. Costs associated with gathering information about markets (prices and quantities supplied) for consuming or producing.

TESTING YOURSELF

In the next three sections, you will answer questions and work problems that are based on information in the text. Master all of the terms before you begin these sections. Work each section without referring to your notes or the text, and then check your answers.

Part I: True or False

Mark each statement as true or false. Whenever you mark a statement as false, jot down a sentence stating why it is false.

_____ 1. A demand curve has a positive slope.

_____ 2. If income increases, the quantity demanded will increase.

_____ 3. If people expect the price of automobiles to increase drastically next year, it is likely that the demand curve for this year's automobiles will shift to the right.

_____ 4. Assume that the demand curve for soft drinks is downward sloping. If the price of a case of soft drinks falls from $7 to $6, we would expect the quantity demanded of soft drinks to increase.

_____ 5. An increase in price would cause the supply curve to shift to the right.

_____ 6. If an earthquake destroys most of the steel mills in a country, then the supply curve of steel will shift to the left.

_____ 7. Market supply can be found by adding together all of the individual supply schedules.

_____ 8. The quantity demanded is always equal to the quantity supplied.

_____ 9. If the quantity demanded exceeds the quantity supplied, we would expect the price to increase.

_____ 10. The equilibrium price is the market-clearing price.

_____ 11. If the quantity supplied exceeds the quantity demanded, prices will rise.

_____ 12. If supply of a product decreases and demand is unchanged, we would expect equilibrium price to rise and equilibrium quantity to fall.

_____ 13. If supply of a product decreases at the same time the demand for the product increases, both equilibrium price and equilibrium quantity will increase. (Hint: draw a graph.)

_____ 14. If airports charged higher fees at popular times, airport congestion would be relieved.

_____ 15. Prices of automobiles made in the United States are currently higher than they would be if imports were restricted.

Part II: Problems

1. Consider the following information about the market for cable TV hook-ups.

Schedule A		Schedule B	
Price (P)	Hook-ups per Month (Q)	Price (P)	Hook-ups per Month (Q)
$50	95	$50	50
45	90	45	60
40	85	40	70
35	80	35	80
30	75	30	90
25	70	25	100
20	65	20	110
15	60	15	120

   a. Which schedule represents the demand schedule? How did you make this determination?

   b. Plot the two schedules on the following graph. Label each one, and mark the equilibrium or market-clearing price and quantity.

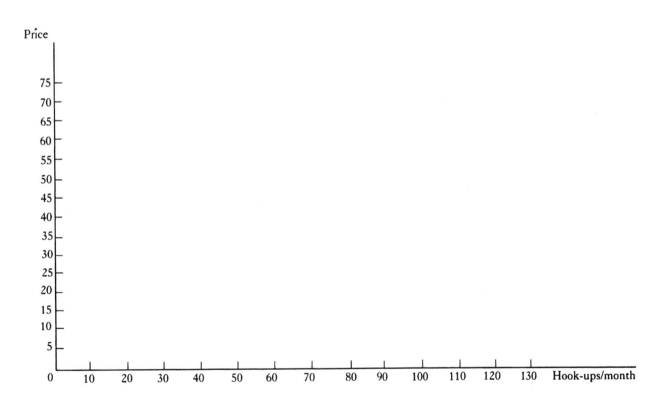

Chapter 3 Supply and Demand: The Basics of Economic Analysis

c. What conditions will prevail in the market if the price is $25? What would you expect to happen?

d. What conditions will prevail in the market if the price is $45? What would you expect to happen?

2. Consider the market shown in the graph below. The original supply and demand curves are labeled S_0 and D_0.

   a. For the original supply and demand curves (S_0 and D_0), what are the equilibrium price and quantity?

   b. If demand increases from D_0 to D_1 while supply is unchanged, what will be the resulting equilibrium price and quantity?

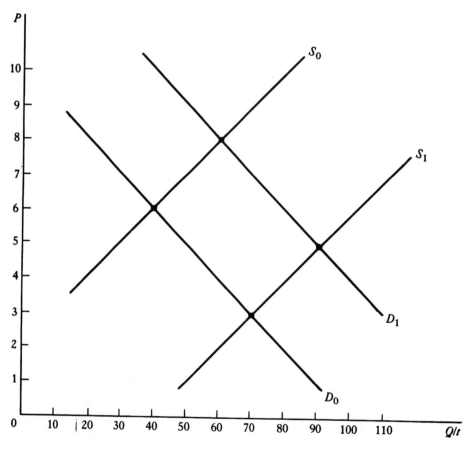

c. If supply increases from S_0 to S_1 while demand remains at D_0, what will be the resulting equilibrium price and quantity?

d. If supply and demand increase to S_1 and D_1 respectively, what will be the resulting equilibrium price and quantity?

In Problems 3 and 4, identify the effects listed as primary (P) or secondary (S).

3. Consumers decide to buy American-made cars rather than imported cars.

    _____ a. Sales of American cars increase.

    _____ b. Wages of U.S. auto workers increase.

    _____ c. Consumption of TV sets in Japan decreases.

    _____ d. The prices of American cars increase.

4. The price of hay falls dramatically.

    _____ a. Beef prices fall.

    _____ b. Farmers buy more hay to feed to cattle.

    _____ c. Sales of feed corn fall.

    _____ d. People eat less chicken.

Part III: Multiple Choice

_____ 1. Demand relates the various amounts that consumers are willing to buy over a specified time period
   a. at various prices.
   b. as their incomes change.
   c. as their tastes change.
   d. when prices increase.

_____ 2. The law of demand states that, *ceteris paribus*,
   a. as price increases, the quantity demanded increases.
   b. as price increases, the quantity demanded decreases.
   c. as price decreases, demand decreases.
   d. demand responds to changes in supply but not to changes in prices.

3. A demand curve
   a. slopes upward.
   b. is a graph of the demand schedule.
   c. shifts in response to shifts in the supply curve.
   d. holds price constant and allows income to vary.

4. Price per unit is measured along a demand curve. What is the other variable measured along a demand curve?
   a. Income over a period of time
   b. Tastes over a period of time
   c. Expectations over a period of time
   d. Quantity demanded over a period of time

5. Which of the following would cause an increase in the quantity demanded of Rich Kid sweatshirts?
   a. An increase in the under 10 population
   b. An increase in the price of Super Baby sweatshirts
   c. A decrease in the price of Rich Kid sweatshirts
   d. A decrease in the supply of Rich Kid sweatshirts

6. If caviar is a normal good, a decrease in income will
   a. cause the price of caviar to increase.
   b. shift the demand curve for caviar to the left.
   c. shift the demand curve for caviar to the right.
   d. increase the production of caviar.

7. A rightward shift of an entire demand curve could be the result of an increase in
   a. income, if the good is inferior.
   b. the quantity demanded.
   c. the price of a complement.
   d. the price of a substitute.

8. Which of the following will cause a change in supply?
   a. An increase in the cost of production
   b. An increase in the price of the product
   c. An increase in the number of demanders in the market
   d. A change in consumers' tastes

9. There is an increase in the demand for aspirin at the same time that workers in the aspirin industry receive a substantial pay increase. We would expect equilibrium
   a. price and quantity to increase.
   b. price to decrease and quantity to increase.
   c. price to increase and quantity to increase, decrease, or stay the same.
   d. price to be uncertain and quantity to decrease.

_____ 10. If supply remains unchanged, an increase in demand will be followed by _____ equilibrium price and _____ equilibrium quantity.
   a. higher; higher
   b. higher; lower
   c. lower; higher
   d. unchanged; higher

_____ 11. Which of the following is *not* a function of price in the market system?
   a. Informing
   b. Motivating
   c. Producing
   d. Directing

_____ 12. The directing function of prices ensures that
   a. consumers and business participate in proper markets.
   b. production will increase for goods with relatively more intense demands.
   c. prices move in the right direction.
   d. consumers know how to get correct market information.

_____ 13. When the goods most desired by society are produced, we have
   a. basic allocation.
   b. income inequity.
   c. technical optimization.
   d. efficiency.

_____ 14. Which of the following is *not* a drawback of the market system?
   a. The presence of negative external costs
   b. Economic instability
   c. Allocation by pricing
   d. Uneven distribution of income

_____ 15. The fact that different people often pay different prices for the same good may be due to the presence of
   a. transactions costs.
   b. market direction.
   c. market allocation.
   d. consumer disinterest.

TAKING ANOTHER LOOK

One recent Christmas, the owner of a holiday decorations store in Nebraska had a real supply and demand problem. Too many people wanted to come in and see the lavish Christmas displays; long lines formed and kept serious shoppers from making their purchases. The owner applied a market solution to her problem by charging everyone $1 to come in and look around. The lines quickly got shorter. She refunded the dollar to anyone who made a purchase. Was this the spirit of Christmas at work, or had she simply found a way to charge noncustomers for looking around?

CHECKING OUT

Now that you have finished studying this chapter, you should be able to:

1. Define demand and list the factors influencing demand. Show how changes in the *ceteris paribus* conditions affect demand.

2. Define supply, and list the factors influencing supply. Show how changes in the *ceteris paribus* conditions affect supply.

3. Explain how market equilibrium is reached and what disequilibrium and equilibrium mean.

4. Use the supply and demand model to illustrate comparative statics, endogenous and exogenous variables, and marginal analysis.

5. Evaluate the functions of prices in a free market and assess how interference with the market distorts its allocative mechanism.

ANSWERS

Trying Out the Terms

Part I

1. F
2. I
3. M
4. A
5. D
6. G
7. K
8. B
9. C
10. L
11. J
12. H
13. E

Part II

1. G
2. D
3. L
4. H
5. M
6. J
7. E
8. C
9. I
10. O
11. A
12. F
13. K
14. N
15. B

Testing Yourself

Part I: True or False

1. false. A demand curve has a negative slope. This illustrates the law of demand, which states that as price declines, the quantity demanded will increase.
2. false. This will cause a change in demand (a shift of the demand curve).
3. true
4. true
5. false. It would cause a movement along and up the supply curve. This is a change in the quantity supplied.
6. true
7. true

8. false. This is true only when the market is in equilibrium; however, the amount bought is always equal to the amount sold.
9. true
10. true
11. false. Prices will fall.
12. true
13. false. The equilibrium price will increase, but the effect on quantity is uncertain.
14. true
15. false. The presence of foreign-made automobiles increases the available supply and therefore causes prices to be lower.

Part II: Problems

1. a. The demand curve is shown by schedule B. As the price decreases, the quantity demanded increases.

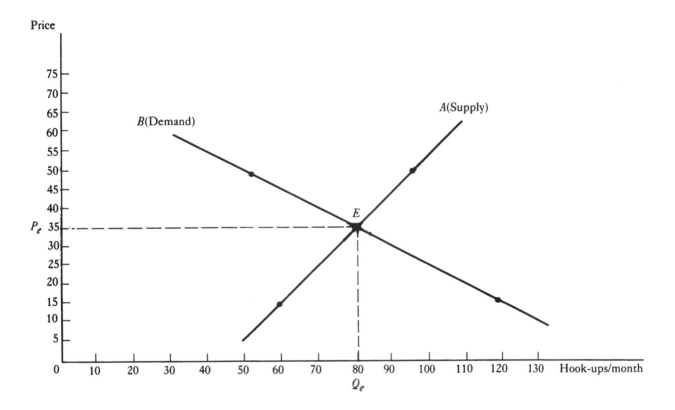

   c. At $25, there is a shortage of 30 units. The quantity demanded is greater than the quantity supplied. The price will rise until the market clears at the equilibrium price of $35 and the equilibrium quantity of 80.
   d. At $45, there is a surplus of 30 units. The quantity supplied is greater than the quantity demanded. The price will fall until the market clears at the equilibrium price of $35 and the equilibrium quantity of 80.

2. a. $6, 40
   b. $8, 60
   c. $3, 70
   d. $5, 90

3. a. Primary
   b. Secondary
   c. Secondary
   d. Primary

4. a. Secondary
   b. Primary
   c. Secondary
   d. Secondary

Part III: Multiple Choice

1. a
2. b
3. b
4. d
5. c
6. b
7. d
8. a
9. c
10. a
11. c
12. b
13. d
14. c
15. a

CHAPTER 3 EXERCISES

1. Listed below are the *ceteris paribus* factors for supply and demand. Indicate what each factor affects by writing "supply," "demand," or "both" in the space provided.

    a. tastes   _____

    b. technology   _____

    c. number of consumers   _____

    d. price of factors of production _____

    e. expectations   _____

    f. price of other goods   _____

    g. income and/or wealth   _____

    h. number of producers   _____

2. The markets shown on the next page are in equilibrium. A change affecting each of these markets is listed below. Draw either a new supply curve or a new demand curve on each graph to show the effect of the specified change on equilibrium.

    a. There is a drought in North Carolina, and rosebush suppliers lose most of their stock.

    b. The leading home magazine indicates that the "in" flower to grow this year is the rose.

    c. The price of beef falls.

    d. An enormous snowstorm blankets the entire country, as far south as Miami.

    e. The snowstorm that hit the South killed all of this year's cotton crop.

    f. An announcement is made that the 2000 Republican National Convention will be held in Omaha.

Chapter 3   Supply and Demand: The Basics of Economic Analysis

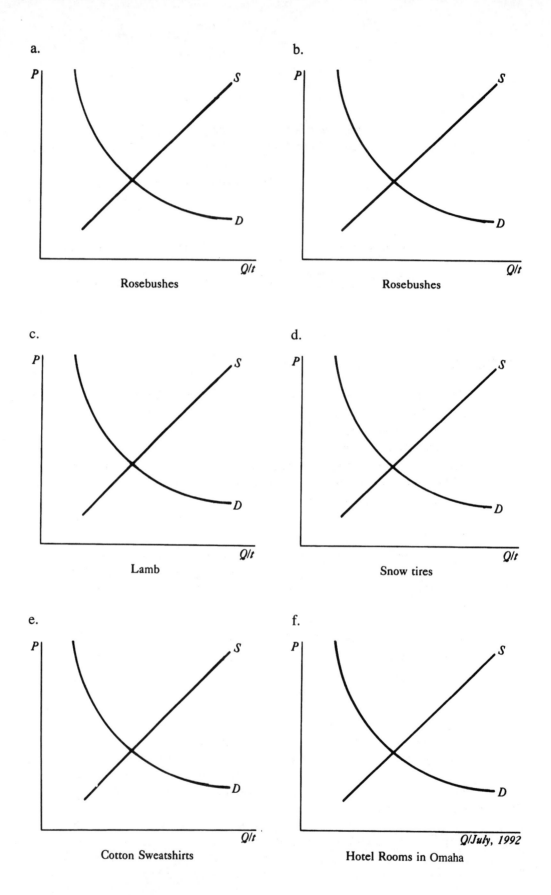

CHAPTER 4

UNEMPLOYMENT, INFLATION, AND ECONOMIC FLUCTUATIONS

CHECKING IN

This chapter begins your study of macroeconomics. There are three major macroeconomic goals: full employment, price stability, and economic growth. This chapter concentrates on employment and prices.

Full employment means that most adults who want to work are employed (about 94 or 95 percent). When there is substantial and/or sustained unemployment, not only do those without a job suffer, but the economy is also hurt by lower output and less growth. There are several types of unemployment: frictional, structural, and cyclical. Macroeconomists are primarily concerned with alleviating cyclical unemployment, although government-induced structural unemployment is also a macroeconomic problem.

Unemployment is measured as the percentage of the labor force not employed but actively seeking work. The unemployment rate can be affected by many variables, such as the percentage of the adults who want to work and government policies toward those without jobs.

Price stability is the absence of a rising or falling price level. Relative prices tend to shift in response to market signals; this is not a matter of macroeconomic concern. Problems occur when all prices (the price level) change. The Consumer Price Index (CPI) measures changes in the average price level. Inflation, a sustained general rise in the price level, can impose costs on society, particularly when it is unanticipated.

The level of output in the economy is neither static nor growing at a constant rate; it fluctuates. These fluctuations, along with those in employment and price level, are the basis of the business cycle. The most profound downturn in the business cycle in U.S. history was the Great Depression of the 1930s.

TRYING OUT THE TERMS

Match each of the following terms with its definition, and then check your answers. If you are having trouble, go back to the text and find the definition there.

_____ 1. peak   _____ 12. depression
_____ 2. stabilization policy   _____ 13. labor force participation rate
_____ 3. structural unemployment   _____ 14. Consumer Price Index (CPI)
_____ 4. productivity   _____ 15. real income
_____ 5. frictional unemployment   _____ 16. GDP deflator
_____ 6. unemployment rate   _____ 17. inflation
_____ 7. trough   _____ 18. business cycle
_____ 8. full employment   _____ 19. recession
_____ 9. cyclical unemployment   _____ 20. stagflation
_____ 10. labor force   _____ 21. price index
_____ 11. Producer Price Index   _____ 22. expansion

A. The level of employment at which approximately 94 to 95 percent of those who want to work are employed.

B. Unemployment caused by workers temporarily between jobs or new entrants to the labor force.

C. Unemployment caused by a mismatch of the skills or location of unemployed workers and the skills required or locations of available jobs.

D. Unemployment caused by fluctuations in the level of total output, or GDP.

E. Measures year-to-year changes in productivity per worker hour.

F. The percentage of the labor force that want to work but do not currently have jobs.

G. Those who are working or actively seeking work.

H. The fraction of the population over 16 years of age who are employed or actively seeking work.

I. A rise in the general, or average, level of prices.

J. A measure of changes in price levels from year to year.

K. A measure of the year-to-year increase in the price level based on the cost of a representative market basket of consumer goods.

L. A current-weights index used to correct for price changes in the GDP.

M. A group of three indexes for raw materials, semi-finished goods, and finished goods that shows what is happening to prices paid by producers and wholesalers.

N. Government actions designed to dampen fluctuations in output, employment, and prices.

O. Fluctuations in economic activity measured by the ups and downs in real output, employment, and prices.

P. The highest output level in a business cycle: the upper turning point.

Q. A decline in real output for two or more successive quarters.

R. The lower turning point in a business cycle.

S. A very severe recession.

T. An economic condition of slow growth, high unemployment, and inflation.

U. Income measured in terms of the goods and services it will buy.

V. A period of growth in real output following a recession.

TESTING YOURSELF

In the next three sections, you will answer questions and work problems that are based on this chapter in the text. Master all of the terms before you begin these sections. Work each section without referring to your notes or the text, and then check your answers.

Part I: True or False

Mark each statement as true or false. Whenever you mark a statement as false, jot down a sentence stating why it is false.

_____ 1. The three primary economic goals of the government are full employment, price stability, and economic stability.

_____ 2. An economy is at full employment when all people who want to work have a job.

_____ 3. If more unskilled workers enter the labor force, we would expect unemployment to rise.

_____ 4. Frictional unemployment is the most difficult form of unemployment to combat.

_____ 5. When economists change the definition of full employment, it is usually to reflect a long-term change in cyclical unemployment.

_____ 6. A program teaching unemployed defense workers to become accountants combats structural unemployment.

_____ 7. Macroeconomic policies to combat cyclical unemployment include increasing demand for final products.

_____ 8. Although unemployment is costly to the individuals involved, it does not hurt the economy as a whole.

_____ 9. When Dave resigns from his job as assistant district attorney to be a full-time dad, the labor force participation rate declines.

_____ 10. After the youngest child starts to school, Dave begins to look for a new job; he won't be counted in the labor force until he accepts a position.

_____ 11. During a period of inflation, it would be better to own a mortgage company than to own the Hope Diamond.

_____ 12. Because of revisions in the federal income tax laws during the last 15 years, the government gains less from inflation than in the past.

_____ 13. A recession occurs whenever there is a decline in real output for two or more successive quarters.

_____ 14. Stagflation occurs when growth is slow or absent while prices are rising.

_____ 15. The economic suffering of the Great Depression was assuaged by economic programs put in place by the federal government.

Part II: Problem

1. a. Complete the table below. Has this economy experienced inflation or real growth?

Item	Quantity	Year 1 Price	Year 1 Total	Year 2 Price	Year 2 Total
Bread	75	$0.75	_____	$1.25	_____
Movies	20	4.00	_____	7.00	_____
Tennis	10	5.00	_____	3.00	_____
Medicine	2	9.00	_____	15.00	_____
Computer games	8	15.00	_____	10.00	_____

b. Assuming the quantities do not change, what is the value of the market basket for each year?

c. If Year 1 is the base year, what is the price index for Year 2?

Part III: Multiple Choice

_____ 1. Unemployment statistics from the 1960s through the present indicate that
   a. unemployment was much lower in the 1980s than in the 1960s.
   b. there has been a gradual rise in the level of unemployment.
   c. the highest unemployment in the period occurred during the 1970s.
   d. unemployment has been rather constant at about 5 percent.

_____ 2. When the jobs available in a market don't fit the skills of those looking for work, we have _____ unemployment.
   a. frictional
   b. embedded
   c. structural
   d. cyclical

_____ 3. We would expect to see a high level of cyclical unemployment in
   a. the heavy (manufacturing) industry.
   b. the service industry.
   c. the government.
   d. the retail industry.

_____ 4. When the government "subsidizes" unemployment
   a. people are able to get jobs faster.
   b. it benefits the service industries more than manufacturing.
   c. the number of available jobs decreases.
   d. the unemployment rate is likely to rise.

_____ 5. Unemployment is a macroeconomic issue when
   a. it is mostly frictional.
   b. it is entirely structural.
   c. it is sustained for more than two quarters.
   d. it is cyclical or structural caused by major shifts in government spending.

_____ 6. When productivity increases
   a. firms hire fewer workers since they can do more work.
   b. wages will rise but employment may fall.
   c. wages are not affected by changes in productivity.
   d. wages and employment will rise together.

_____ 7. Which of the following would *not* be considered a part of the labor force?
   a. A steel worker who was laid off his last job
   b. A steel worker who was laid off his last job and isn't looking for a job
   c. A student who works part time
   d. A member of the U.S. Navy

_____ 8. Which of the following is most likely to gain during inflationary times?
   a. A savings and loan association
   b. A person who owns a lot of government bonds
   c. A retired person living on a pension
   d. A person who owes a lot on her mortgage

_____ 9. Governments try to restrain inflation because it
   a. moves in the same direction as unemployment.
   b. rewards savers and penalizes investors.
   c. causes unintended redistribution of income and wealth.
   d. usually results in falling government revenues.

_____ 10. Which of the following is *not* a problem with inflation?
   a. Lower savings and investment
   b. Confused market signals
   c. Increased government spending
   d. Costs associated with adjustments

_____ 11. The government may attempt to smooth out irregularities in output, employment, and prices by
   a. administering prices.
   b. subsidizing unemployment.
   c. setting unemployment limits.
   d. implementing stabilization policy.

_____ 12. The phrase *business cycle* refers to the pattern of fluctuations in
   a. the stock market.
   b. employment.
   c. unemployment.
   d. output, employment, and the price level.

_____ 13. The Kondratieff cycle (long wave) has been attributed to
   a. excessive government intervention in the economy.
   b. the development of entirely new industries.
   c. over response to the economic policies of other countries.
   d. extended periods of unemployment.

_____ 14. The Great Depression ended when
   a. Franklin Roosevelt was elected president.
   b. the Federal Reserve System took control of the money supply.
   c. the Social Security system was established.
   d. World War II began.

_____ 15. The leading indicator series is helpful in predicting
   a. which job markets are likely to improve.
   b. the price level of the stock market.
   c. ups and downs in the business cycle.
   d. the general price level.

TAKING ANOTHER LOOK

I

Policy makers, particularly those who have to run for reelection, must sometimes walk a narrow path. Consider this dilemma.

Frankie has been on welfare for three years. She doesn't look for work because she feels that she probably gets more from the various transfer programs than she could earn. This may be okay for Frankie, but it is very expensive for the taxpayers who have to continue paying the taxes that fund Frankie's benefits. Can a policy be designed that would give long-term welfare recipients an incentive to get off welfare and go to work?

One suggestion has been to tie the benefits to job search. People would not receive payments unless they were actively seeking work. (This might be preceded by a period of job training.) Some of these folks would find jobs and get off welfare.

Sound good? What would happen to the unemployment rate when these welfare recipients entered the labor force?

What would you remember about an official's term of office—fewer people on the welfare roles or a higher unemployment rate?

II

We always like to remember the good old days. One favorite memory is of gas prices before the first oil supply crisis more than 20 years ago, in 1973. A gallon of gas cost about 40 cents then; now it sells for more than dollar. A casual observer might suggest that the increased price is the result of restricted supplies or a government policy to restrict consumption.

But closer examination reveals that gas prices really haven't gone up at all. In fact, in 1993 the **real** cost of gasoline was less than in 1973. By using the Consumer Price Index to restate the 1973 price to 1993 dollars, we find that a gallon of gas cost $1.25 then compared to an average of $1.12 in 1993. The highest price for gas was in 1981, when a gallon cost $2.28 in 1993 dollars.

Although there have been calls for an "energy policy" for twenty years, the lower real price indicates that one has never been seriously implemented. Another indication of this is the level of imported oil. In **1973,** we imported about 37 percent of our oil; by **1993,** the figure had grown to almost 45 percent.

CHECKING OUT

Now that you have finished studying this chapter, you should be able to:

1. Define full employment and the various kinds of unemployment, and explain why unemployment is an important policy concern.

2. Explain how unemployment is measured.

3. Define inflation and identify those who gain and lose from inflation, and explain why inflation is an important policy concern.

4. Compute a price index, and use it to adjust dollar values for inflation.

5. Explore the relationship between unemployment, inflation, and the business cycle.

ANSWERS

Trying Out the Terms

1. P
2. N
3. C
4. E
5. B
6. F
7. R
8. A
9. D
10. G
11. M
12. S
13. H
14. K
15. U
16. L
17. I
18. O
19. Q
20. T
21. J
22. V

Testing Yourself

Part I: True or False

1. false. The economic goals are full employment, price stability, and economic growth.
2. false. Full employment occurs when there is a "normal" amount of unemployment in the system, currently about 5 to 6 percent.
3. true
4. false. Frictional unemployment naturally occurs as part of the labor market process.
5. false. Generally, it is to reflect a shift in structural unemployment.
6. true
7. true
8. false. The economy loses the potential production of the unemployed workers.
9. true
10. false. As soon as he begins to look, he is back in the labor force; he will be counted as unemployed until he accepts a position.
11. false. During a period of inflation, creditors are losers; owners of real assets are winners.
12. true
13. true
14. true
15. false. While a few federal programs operated, people out of work relied mainly on assistance from state and local government and private sources.

Part II: Problems

1. a.

Item	Quantity	Year 1 Price	Year 1 Total	Year 2 Price	Year 2 Total
Bread	75	$0.75	$56.25	$1.25	$93.75
Movies	20	4.00	80.00	7.00	140.00
Tennis	10	5.00	50.00	3.00	30.00
Medicine	2	9.00	18.00	15.00	30.00
Computer games	8	15.00	120.00	10.00	80.00

a. This economy has experienced both inflation and real economic growth.
b. The value of the market basket for Year 1 is $324.25. The value of the market basket for Year 2 is $373.75.
c. The price index for Year 2 is $373.75/$324.25 = 1.15. You may think this figure is too low, but remember that the computer games represent a big part of the basket; the big drop in that price offsets the other rising prices.

Part III: Multiple Choice

1. b
2. c
3. a
4. d
5. d
6. d
7. b
8. d
9. c
10. c
11. d
12. d
13. b
14. d
15. c

Name _____

CHAPTER 4 EXERCISES

_____ 1. Suppose you anticipate an inflation rate of 12 percent next year. Fred comes to you and asks to borrow $250 for one year. He offers to pay 6 percent to compensate you for your costs, your risk of not being repaid, and your not being able to spend the money for a year. You should
   a. turn Fred down.
   b. accept, if Fred will pay 12 percent.
   c. accept, if Fred will pay 18 percent.
   d. accept Fred's offer to pay 6 percent.

_____ 2. Which of the following is an indication of an inflationary period?
   a. As more accountants graduate from college, their starting wages decline.
   b. When a new hospital opens in Evans, Iowa, the nurses at the existing hospital get a raise.
   c. The Marshalls notice that not only is their food bill for the year higher than last year's, but their rent is also higher.
   d. There is a wheat crop failure, and the price of bread doubles.

_____ 3. Which of the following is *not* a cost of inflation?
   a. Loss of tax revenues by the government
   b. Unintended redistribution of income and wealth among individuals
   c. Confused market signals
   d. Lower levels of saving and investment

_____ 4. When analyzing a business cycle, we should expect
   a. successive peaks at higher levels of output each time and successive troughs at lower levels.
   b. successive peaks to reach the previous level of output, while troughs may be higher or lower.
   c. successive troughs to be lower than previous troughs, while peaks may be higher or lower.
   d. successive peaks and troughs to be higher each time.

_____ 5. A good measure of economic fluctuations is the movement of
   a. the price level.
   b. the unemployment rate.
   c. wholesale prices.
   d. the labor force participation rate.

_____ 6. In the expansionary phase of the business cycle, we would expect to see
   a. output rise.
   b. unemployment fall.
   c. productivity fall.
   d. output rise and unemployment fall.

_____ 7. The Great Depression of the 1930s
   a. began in Germany and spread to the United States.
   b. occurred only in the United States.
   c. was a world event.
   d. was more severe in Europe than in the United States and Canada.

_____ 8. An index is useful for measuring
   a. absolute values.
   b. differences between two groups.
   c. year-to-year changes.
   d. both differences between groups and year-to-year changes.

CHAPTER 5

THE MEASURE OF OUTPUT, INCOME, AND ECONOMIC GROWTH

CHECKING IN

The government keeps track of the macroeconomy in a number of ways. Chapter 4 discussed the unemployment rate and price indexes. Chapter 5 introduces several other macroeconomic variables and explains exactly what they measure.

The chapter begins by returning to the most elementary macroeconomic model, the circular flow model, presented in Chapter 2, which diagrams the entire economy. This model represents the aggregate level of economic activity. By adding the credit market, government, and the foreign market, we gain a very realistic picture of the interrelationships in the economy.

Economic activity can be described by stocks, which are existing quantities, and by flows, which measure quantities over time. A balance sheet measures stocks, whereas an income statement measures flows.

The national income accounts measure the flows of expenditure and income in an economy. They allow us to insert numbers into the circular flow model. The basic national income account is gross domestic product (GDP), the final output of an economy over a given time period. It can be measured by adding total expenditures on goods and services or by adding all the income earned in the production of those services. Both methods yield the same amount. Other national income account measures are national income (NI), net national product (NNP), personal income (PI), and disposable income.

The national income accounts are the best measures we have for studying the economy. They are used both to measure economic well-being and to make comparisons with other times and other countries. However, they are not totally satisfactory. Problems include omission of nonmarket and illegal transactions and leisure and failure to correct for economic bads. Some other measures have been developed, such as the Measure of Economic Welfare (MEW), but to date we rely most heavily on the standard measures.

Movements in the price level are recorded by price indexes. The price index used to measure the national income account, the GDP deflator, uses the current out mix as the "basket" of goods and services. Real economic growth is distinguished from growth due to the effects of inflation by applying the GDP deflator.

Economic growth of about 4 percent a year is generally considered attainable; however, there are costs associated with real growth that must be considered.

TRYING OUT THE TERMS

Match each of the following terms with its definition, and then check your answers. If you are having trouble, go back to the text and find the definition there.

Part I

_____ 1. balance sheet   _____ 8. injections
_____ 2. leakages   _____ 9. saving
_____ 3. exports   _____ 10. imports
_____ 4. stock variable   _____ 11. income statement
_____ 5. economic growth   _____ 12. flow variable
_____ 6. credit market   _____ 13. investment
_____ 7. balance of goods and services   _____ 14. net worth

A. An increase in the level of real per capita output.

B. The part of an income flow not spent on purchases of goods and services.

C. Business purchases of some real, tangible asset, such as a machine, a factory, or a stock of inventories.

D. The aggregate market consisting of financial institutions that channel household savings to business firms that want to invest.

E. Flows out of the circular flow that occur when factor income is not spent directly on purchases from domestic firms, but goes to savings, taxes, and imports.

F. Spending added to the circular flow that is not paid for out of resource income, such as business investment, government expenditures, and/or exports.

G. Purchases of goods and services from foreign sellers.

H. Goods and services sold to foreign buyers.

I. The difference between the value of exports and the value of imports for a country in any given year.

J. Measures the total flow of revenues to an economic unit, such as a household, individual, or firm, over a particular period of time.

K. A statement of assets owned, liabilities owned, and the difference between them at a particular point in time.

L. The difference between assets and liabilities for a person or firm at a point in time.

M. A variable that is defined over a period of time.

N. A variable that is defined at a point in time.

Part II

_____ 1. national income (NI)   _____ 10. gross private domestic investment

_____ 2. final goods   _____ 11. fixed investment

_____ 3. transfer payments   _____ 12. intermediate goods

_____ 4. business inventories   _____ 13. disposable income

_____ 5. consumption expenditures   _____ 14. capital consumption allowance

_____ 6. personal income   _____ 15. consumer durables

_____ 7. consumer nondurables   _____ 16. net national product (NNP)

_____ 8. Gross Domestic Product (GDP)   _____ 17. net private domestic investment

_____ 9. consumer services

A. The total market value of all final products produced by a country's residents in a given year.

B. Goods that do not have to be further processed or resold before final sale.

C. Goods sold to be further processed into final goods.

D. Stocks of goods held by businesses from which it can make sales to meet demand.

E. Sales to the household sector.

F. Goods that last, on average, a substantial length of time.

G. Goods that last, on average, only a short period of time.

H. That part of consumption composed of nontangible activities.

I. Business sector purchases of final output in the GDP.

J. The part of investment that does not add to inventories; consists of business plant and equipment and residential construction.

K. Income payments to individuals who do not have to provide any goods or services in exchange.

L. Equal to GDP less capital consumption allowance and adjustments (depreciation).

M. Income earned by resources; consists of wages, rent, interest, profit, and proprietors' net income.

N. The national income accountants' estimate of the amount of the nation's capital stock used up in production during the current year.

O. Gross private domestic investment less capital consumption allowances and adjustments (depreciation).

P. Equals NI after the subtraction of corporate profits taxes, undistributed corporate profits, Social Security contributions, and the addition of net transfer payments.

Q. Income received by households and available to spend or save; equals PI less personal taxes.

TESTING YOURSELF

In the next three sections, you will answer questions and work problems that are based on information in the text. Master all of the terms before you begin these sections. Work each section without referring to your notes or the text, and then check your answers.

Part I: True or False

Mark each statement as true or false. Whenever you mark a statement as false, jot down a sentence stating why it is false.

_____ 1. The two markets analyzed in the basic circular flow model are the product market and the goods market.

_____ 2. Income that is earned but not spent is a leakage from the income stream.

_____ 3. When leakages are greater than injections, the income stream will grow.

_____ 4. In the circular flow model, when the government spends more than it receives in taxes, it must borrow directly from the households.

_____ 5. The grain stored in an elevator in Hereford, Texas, at a particular time represents a stock variable.

_____ 6. The gross domestic product account is the nation's balance sheet.

_____ 7. Gross domestic product includes the market value of goods at all stages of production.

_____ 8. The largest buying sector in GDP is households (consumption).

_____ 9. New residential housing is a good example of a consumer durable.

_____ 10. The purchase of stocks and bonds is recorded in the investment sector of GDP.

_____ 11. National income is the sum of the earnings of the factors of production.

_____ 12. Disposable income includes only earned income.

_____ 13. In the national income accounts, leakages are equal to injections.

_____ 14. National income account statistics are adjusted to include leisure activities and services produced at home.

_____ 15. Improved technology provides the sole source of real economic growth.

_____ 16. Economic growth guarantees that living standards are improving.

_____ 17. The trend rate of growth in the United States since 1950 has been between 4 and 5 percent.

Part II: Problems

1. Use the table to find the amount in the specified account.

Consumption expenditures	$500
Net transfer payments	70
Personal taxes	100
Exports	60
Capital consumption allowances	20
Government purchases of goods and services	250
Net private domestic investment	70
Undistributed corporate profit	65
Corporate income taxes	40
Imports	60
Indirect business taxes	32

   a. GDP

   b. NNP

   c. NI

d. PI

e. disposable income

f. personal savings

2. a. Complete the following table.

Year	Nominal GDP	Price Index	Real GDP
1	$2,000	80	_____
2	2,100	95	_____
3	2,750	100	_____
4	3,275	130	_____
5	4,500	150	_____

b. Describe the behavior of prices and economic growth in this economy.

Part III: Multiple Choice

____ 1. If the average person in an economy has more goods and services this year than last year, the economy has experienced
  a. an increase in real total output.
  b. an increase real output per capita.
  c. an increase in non-price-adjusted output.
  d. equilibrium.

____ 2. The transfer of funds from savers to investors takes place in the
  a. product market.
  b. goods market.
  c. business market.
  d. credit market.

3. Which of the following are leakages from the circular flow of income?
   a. Savings, taxes, imports
   b. Savings, government borrowing, exports
   c. Exports, investment, saving
   d. Investment, saving, taxes

4. In the circular flow models, the government
   a. is absent.
   b. causes leakages but not injections.
   c. causes injections but not leakages.
   d. causes both leakages and injections.

5. An account of the revenues going to an economic unit over time is called
   a. a balance sheet.
   b. a profit statement.
   c. an income statement.
   d. a cash account.

6. A firm reduces the value of production equipment as it is used. This is called
   a. capital accounting.
   b. depreciation.
   c. stock accounting.
   d. inventory accounting.

7. If USX sells sheet metal to General Motors, the metal will be counted in the national income accounts as
   a. a producer good.
   b. a business investment.
   c. a temporary investment.
   d. nothing, since the sheet metal is an intermediate good.

8. Which of the following is *not* part of net private domestic investment?
   a. Housing
   b. Plant and equipment
   c. Capital consumption allowance
   d. Inventory changes

9. Planned inventory changes are counted as investment; unplanned changes are
   a. also counted as investment.
   b. carried forward into the next year.
   c. counted as future consumption.
   d. ignored.

10. The government component of GDP includes government expenditures on
    a. goods, services, and taxes.
    b. goods, services, and transfers.
    c. goods and services.
    d. goods only.

_____ 11. National income is equal to
   a. the earnings of all factors of production.
   b. GDP less NNP.
   c. GDP less depreciation.
   d. GDP less indirect business taxes.

_____ 12. Income received by households is called
   a. national income.
   b. personal income.
   c. household income.
   d. final income.

_____ 13. If $C = 500$, $I = 200$, $G = 150$, and $X - M = -5$, what is GDP?
   a. 850
   b. 855
   c. 845
   d. GDP cannot be determined.

_____ 14. If nominal GDP increased in the same year that real GDP fell, we could conclude that
   a. the unemployment rate had also fallen.
   b. there had been inflation.
   c. prices had fallen.
   d. a mistake had been made, since real GDP and nominal GDP must change in the same direction.

_____ 15. Which of the following is a result of slow economic growth?
   a. Decreasing tax revenues
   b. Decreasing tax rates
   c. Increasing employment
   d. Increasing political stability

TAKING ANOTHER LOOK

After sixty years, there is still much discussion and even disagreement about the true causes of the Great Depression. There is less controversy over the point that marks its beginning: the stock market crash on October 29, 1929. It was no surprise, then, that following the stunning fall of the stock market on October 19, 1987, there was much speculation about whether another depression would occur. Some felt there would be another depression; others disagreed. Many of the gloomy forecasts were based on the belief that consumers, feeling poorer, would spend less of their incomes, and businesses, anticipating lower sales, would cut back on investment. This would be a double whammy to the circular flow: leakages would increase and injections would fall, a sure route to lower real output. It didn't happen.

CHECKING OUT

Now that you have finished studying this chapter, you should be able to:

1. Expand the circular flow model as a basis for developing the GDP accounts.

2. Become familiar with income statements and balance sheets and the relationship between income statement flows and balance sheet stocks and the national income accounts.

3. Explain how gross domestic product (GDP), net domestic product (NNP), domestic income (NI), and personal income (PI) are computed.

4. Learn how to compute real GDP and rates of growth of real GDP, and to evaluate the costs and benefits of economic growth.

ANSWERS

Trying Out the Terms

Part 1

1. K
2. E
3. H
4. N
5. A
6. D
7. I
8. F
9. B
10. G
11. J
12. M
13. C
14. L

Part 2

1. M
2. B
3. K
4. D
5. E
6. P
7. G
8. A
9. H
10. I
11. J
12. C
13. Q
14. N
15. F
16. L
17. O

Testing Yourself

Part I: True or False

1. false. The two markets are the resource market and the product market.
2. true
3. false. When leakages are greater than injections, the income stream will shrink.
4. false. In the circular flow model, the government will borrow in the credit market when it spends more than it receives in taxes.
5. true
6. false. It's the nation's income statement.
7. false. GDP includes only final goods.
8. true
9. false. New residential housing is counted as investment.
10. false. Purchase of stocks and bonds is not counted in GDP.

11. true
12. false. Disposable income includes all income that goes to households, including unearned transfer payments, less personal income taxes.
13. true
14. false. These are not included in GDP.
15. false. An increase in the quantity or quality of inputs can also cause real economic growth.
16. false. There are costs, such as pollution and litter, that are associated with economic growth.
17. false. The trend rate of growth in the United States since 1950 has been about 3.6 percent.

Part II: Problems

1. Gross private domestic investment equals net private domestic investment plus capital consumption allowances; therefore, I = $70 + $20 = $90.
   a. GDP = $500 + $90 + $250 + ($60 − $60) = $840
   b. NNP = $840 − $20 = $820
   c. NI = $820 − $32 = $788
   d. PI = $788 − $65 − $40 + F$70 = $753
   e. disposable income = $753 − $100 = $653
   f. personal saving = $653 − $500 = $153

2. a.

Year	Nominal GDP	Price Index	Real GDP
1	$2,000	80	$2,000/0.80 = $2,500
2	2,100	95	$2,100/0.95 = $2,210.50
3	2,750	100	$2,750/1.00 = $2,750
4	3,275	130	$3,275/1.30 = $2,519.20
5	4,500	150	$4,500/1.50 = $3,000

   b. The economy has experienced both inflation and economic growth.

Part III: Multiple Choice

1. b
2. d
3. a
4. d
5. c
6. b
7. d
8. c
9. a
10. c
11. a
12. b
13. c
14. b
15. a

Chapter 5   The Measure of Output, Income, and Economic Growth

Name _____

CHAPTER 5 EXERCISES

Use the following table to answer Questions 1–4.

Account	Billions of Dollars
Net private domestic investment	$85
Wages and supplements	350
Corporate profit tax	30
Corporate saving	10
Indirect business tax	25
Rental income of persons	45
Corporate profits	63
Personal income tax	40
Net exports of goods and services	20
Capital consumption allowances	10
Government purchases of goods and services	240
Net interest	54
Proprietors' income	60

1. What is NI?

2. What is NNP?

3. What is GDP?

4. What is *C*?

Chapter 5   The Measure of Output, Income, and Economic Growth

5. a. The circular flow diagram shown below illustrates the product, factor, and credit markets. Households are allowed to save and businesses to invest. Correctly label this diagram.

b. This circular flow diagram also includes the government and the foreign sectors. Correctly label each flow.

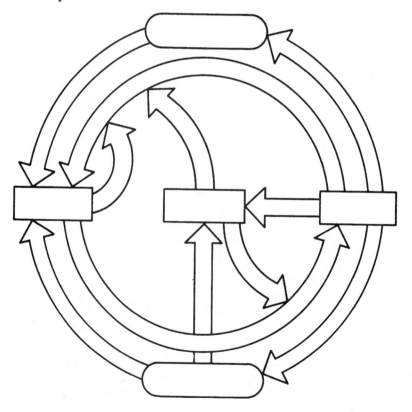

CHAPTER 6

AGGREGATE DEMAND AND AGGREGATE SUPPLY

CHECKING IN

Just as a simple market transaction can be analyzed using the supply and demand model, the behavior of the entire economy can be analyzed using the model of aggregate supply and aggregate demand. This model is more controversial than the microeconomic supply and demand model. In this chapter, you will learn about the aggregate supply and demand model and some of the major theories that explain and define it. This model comes directly from the circular flow model presented in the last two chapters.

The aggregate demand curve shows the amounts of total real output that all buyers will purchase at various price levels. This curve slopes downward from the left to the right. A higher price level is associated with less demand for real output. Aggregate demand will shift if there is a change in consumption, investment, government spending, net exports, or the money supply.

The aggregate supply curve shows the amounts of total real output (NI) that the economy will produce at various price levels. Economists disagree about the shape of this curve. It may be vertical, horizontal, upward sloping, or a combination of these three. The shape of this curve may vary between the short run and the long run.

The aggregate demand curve and the aggregate supply curve intersect at the equilibrium levels of price and output. A shift of either curve results in a new equilibrium. The addition of the aggregate production function provides a view of the employment level in relation to aggregate supply and aggregate demand.

In the last hundred years, there have been many theories of how the macroeconomy operates. In the nineteenth century, the classical economists believed in a self-correcting economy. These philosophical descendants of Adam Smith felt that any disturbances in the economy would naturally work themselves out, and the economy would return to full employment and output without government intervention. Classical economists were mostly concerned with the price level and the money supply. Another nineteenth-century group, the business cycle theorists, focused its attention on the prolonged periods of falling output and unemployment that seemed to occur with predictable regularity. Although they did not share the classical economists' belief that the economy would naturally return to full employment, they did hold the same *laissez-faire* attitude toward government involvement.

The Great Depression of the 1930s, with its extended period of unemployment, triggered the Keynesian revolution. Building on the work of the business cycle theorists and emphasizing the role of aggregate demand, John Maynard Keynes developed a model of the economy with a horizontal aggregate supply curve. In this setting, unemployment can persist because there is no automatic tendency to return to full employment unless, as Keynes advocated, the government intervenes by using fiscal or monetary policy.

Although Keynesian economics became widely accepted in the decades following the Great Depression, it has not been without critics who continue to embrace the basic tenets of classical theory. Keynesian ideas continue to be popular, particularly in periods of recession.

TRYING OUT THE TERMS

Match each of the following terms with its definition, and then check your answers. If you are having trouble, go back to the text and find the definition there.

_____ 1. Keynesians

_____ 2. aggregate supply curve (AS)

_____ 3. full-employment level of output

_____ 4. classical school

_____ 5. aggregate demand curve (AD)

_____ 6. aggregate production function

A. A graph showing the amounts of total real output that all buyers in an economy wish to purchase at various price levels.

B. A graph showing the amounts of total real output that all producers in an economy will offer for sale at various price levels.

C. The level of real output associated with full use of all resources, especially labor.

D. A graph showing the relationship between total real output and the number of workers employed.

E. A group of economists in the eighteenth and nineteenth centuries who believed that the economy automatically tended toward the full employment level of output.

F. Twentieth-century economists who share the views of Keynes that there could be persistent unemployment and low levels of production that could be corrected only with government intervention.

TESTING YOURSELF

In the next three sections, you will answer questions and work problems that are based on information in the text. Master all of the terms before you begin these sections. Work each section without referring to your notes or the text, and then check your answers.

Part I: True or False

Mark each statement as true or false. Whenever you mark a statement as false, jot down a sentence stating why it is false.

_____ 1. The aggregate demand curve demonstrates the quantity of real output that will be purchased at various price levels.

_____ 2. If real output stays the same while prices are going up, nominal income will increase.

_____ 3. When there is inflation we would observe an increase in both imports and exports.

_____ 4. National income (NI) at factor cost represents one point on an aggregate supply curve.

_____ 5. Along a classical aggregate supply curve changes in prices have no effect on real output.

_____ 6 In the composite aggregate supply model, the long run is defined as more than one year.

_____ 7. If producers charge prices that are higher than consumers are willing to pay for a particular level of output (Y), then more will be sold than will be purchased.

_____ 8. An increase in aggregate demand will cause an increase in output, but the price level will be unchanged.

_____ 9. An increase in the money supply may cause the aggregate demand curve to shift to the right.

_____ 10. The aggregate supply curve is fixed and does not shift regardless of its shape (vertical, horizontal, or sloping upward).

_____ 11. The aggregate production function shows the relationship between real output and employment.

_____ 12. If an economy is at less than full employment, then a shift to the right of either the *AS* or the *AD* may bring the economy to a higher level of both output and employment.

_____ 13. Classical economists usually focus on long run results.

_____ 14. Classical economists believe that the economy is basically unstable without government intervention.

_____ 15. Keynes was concerned with both unemployment and inflation.

Part II: Problems

1. On the following graphs, draw
   a. an upward sloping aggregate supply curve.
   b. a classical aggregate supply curve.
   c. a Keynesian aggregate supply curve.

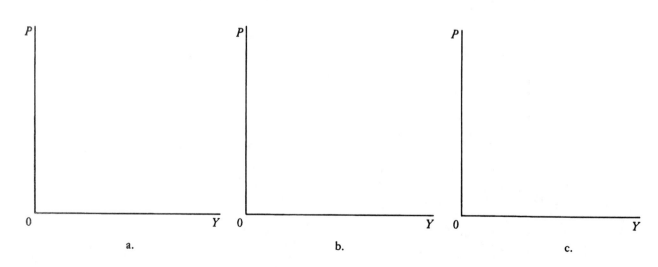

2. To each of the graphs in Problem 1, add a downward sloping aggregate demand curve. Label the equilibrium levels of price and output. Now suppose aggregate demand increases; on each graph, show the new demand curve and indicate the new equilibrium levels of price and output. Indicate the direction of changes in price (P) and output (Y) below.

	P	Y
a.		
b.		
c.		

3. a. In the following graph, the lower portion shows an aggregate production function. In the upper graph, draw in an AS and an AD that are consistent with an equilibrium output of N_1. AS should be upward sloping.

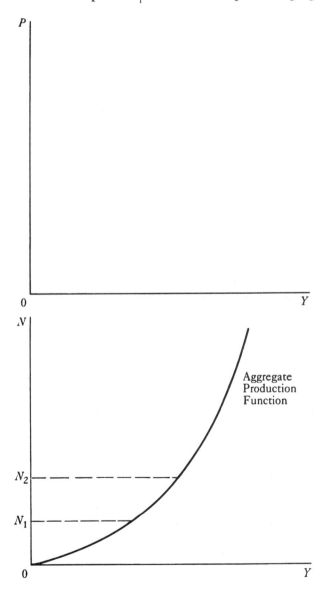

Chapter 6 Aggregate Demand and Aggregate Supply

b. Now suppose we determine that the level of full employment is N_2. Can that level of employment be reached by a shift of the AS curve? Illustrate your answer on your graph.

Part III: Multiple Choice

_____ 1. A point on the aggregate demand curve represents a combination of
   a. GDP and NI.
   b. factor income and factor prices.
   c. the price level and real output.
   d. the price level and nominal output.

_____ 2. The typical aggregate demand curve
   a. has a positive slope in the short run and is vertical in the long run.
   b. is horizontal.
   c. is downward sloping.
   d. has no slope in either the short run or the long run.

_____ 3. If an aggregate demand curve is downward sloping, a higher price level will reduce consumption because
   a. household financial assets lose value.
   b. consumers are paying less of their income as taxes.
   c. consumers substitute imported goods for domestic ones.
   d. interest rates have fallen.

_____ 4. Which of the following is a reason the aggregate supply curve might be upward sloping?
   a. There is unemployment in the economy.
   b. Wages rise as production increases.
   c. There are more consumers in the market.
   d. The trade balance changes.

_____ 5. A horizontal aggregate supply curve would indicate that
   a. there are unemployed resources.
   b. the price level is indeterminate.
   c. the economy is operating on its production possibilities frontier.
   d. the classical model is being used.

_____ 6. When the aggregate demand curve shifts to the right,
   a. price increases and output falls.
   b. price falls and output falls.
   c. price increases and output increases.
   d. price and output movements cannot be predicted without a definite shape for the aggregate supply curve.

_____ 7. If the number of employed workers in an economy increases,
   a. the price level must also increase.
   b. the level of output should also increase.
   c. the aggregate demand curve will shift to the left.
   d. the production function shifts to the right.

_____ 8. Changes in government spending may be affected by
   a. changes in the interest rate.
   b. shifts in the aggregate supply curve.
   c. the price level.
   d. expectations of the voters.

_____ 9. The Mississippi River flooding of 1993 may have
   a. shifted the aggregate demand curve to the left.
   b. caused the aggregate supply curve to become more nearly horizontal.
   c. shifted the aggregate supply curve to the left.
   d. not affected either the aggregate supply curve or the aggregate demand curve.

_____ 10. A government wishing to implement a policy that would shift the aggregate supply curve to the right might
   a. increase the corporate tax rate.
   b. lower interest rates.
   c. give consumers a one-time tax rebate.
   d. increase government spending on goods and services.

_____ 11. The belief that the economy naturally tends to full employment is held by
   a. classical economists.
   b. historical economists.
   c. Keynesians.
   d. business cycle theorists.

_____ 12. Business cycle theorists were chiefly concerned with
   a. conditions of overemployment.
   b. fluctuations in the money supply.
   c. recurring high levels of unemployment.
   d. the level of stock prices.

_____ 13. The main characteristic distinguishing Keynes's theory from classical theory was his
   a. concern about inflation.
   b. willingness to sacrifice *laissez-faire* policies.
   c. focus on the long run.
   d. dependence on market forces.

_____ 14. Modern economists who follow the Keynesian tradition feel
   a. markets are highly responsive.
   b. there is no longer a role for government in the economy.
   c. shifting the aggregate demand curve cannot affect unemployment.
   d. the aggregate supply curve is relatively flat.

_____ 15. Using the aggregate supply and aggregate demand model we can explain the falling output and declining inflation in the United Kingdom as
   a. shift of the aggregate demand curve to the left.
   b. a simultaneous shift of the aggregate demand curve and the aggregate supply curve to the right.
   c. a shift in the aggregate production function.
   d. a steepening of the aggregate supply curve.

TAKING ANOTHER LOOK

Remember Hurricane Andrew? The television news anchor said, "Please don't send food, furniture, or clothing—what we really need is money. You can send your check to **Hurricane Andrew Fund,** care of...." What do you think happened to those dollars we were happy to send?

The text points out that even a great disaster like Hurricane Andrew has only a small effect on the national economy. We usually think of the effect, whatever the size, as a shift to the left of the aggregate supply curve. Productive resources are destroyed, workplaces are shut down, people are unemployed for long periods.

This is all true. But there is also an aggregate demand effect. As South Florida began to rebuild, demand for building materials ballooned. All of those dollars we sent and an enormous quantity of insurance payments found themselves in the cash registers of hardware stores and lumber yards. Volunteers flooded the area, filling up the hotels and eating in restaurants. Florida's sales tax revenues skyrocketed during late 1992 and 1993 as a result of Andrew.

What would happen to prices when these two shifts occur at the same time? And what is the long-run effect? If people wisely invested our dollars in productive activities, eventually the aggregate supply curve, too, would shift back to the right.

CHECKING OUT

Now that you have finished studying this chapter, you should be able to:

1. Define aggregate demand and explain why the aggregate demand curve has a negative slope.

2. Discuss the alternative possible slopes of the aggregate supply curve.

3. Identify the factors that can shift aggregate demand or aggregate supply.

4. Explain the relationship between equilibrium output, employment, and unemployment.

5. Relate the aggregate supply and aggregate demand curves to the two major alternative approaches to macroeconomic policy.

ANSWERS

Trying Out the Terms

1. F
2. B
3. C
4. E
5. A
6. D

Testing Yourself

Part I: True or False

1. true
2. true
3. false. Exports would fall, they are more expensive to foreigners while imports would increase, they are relatively cheaper than domestic substitutes.
4. true
5. true
6. false. The definition of long run is not clear and often is a matter of dispute.
7. false. The quantity sold and the quantity bought are always equal.
8. false. The effect of a change in aggregate demand will depend on the shape of the aggregate supply curve. Output may increase (horizontal or upward-sloping *AS*) or stay the same (vertical *AS*). Prices may stay the same (horizontal *AS*) or increase (upward-sloping or vertical *AS*).
9. true
10. false. The aggregate supply curve does shift; for example an earthquake would cause a shift to the left, the introduction of a new, more efficient technology would cause a shift to the right.
11. true
12. true
13. true
14. false. Classical economists believe that the economy is basically stable.
15. true

Part II: Problems

1.

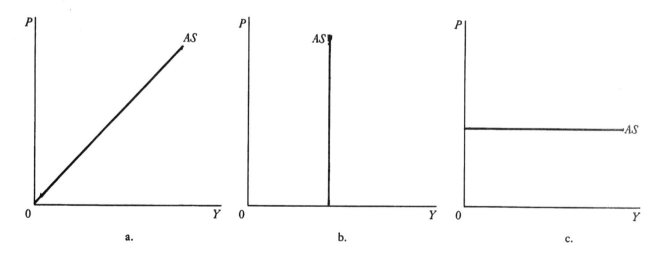

Chapter 6   Aggregate Demand and Aggregate Supply   83

2.

a.

b.

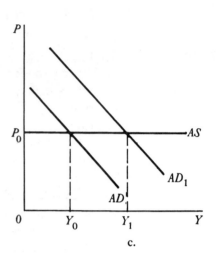
c.

	P	Y
a.	increased	increased
b.	increased	unchanged
c.	unchanged	increased

3. a.

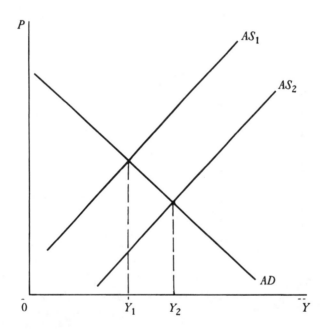

84   Chapter 6   Aggregate Demand and Aggregate Supply

b.

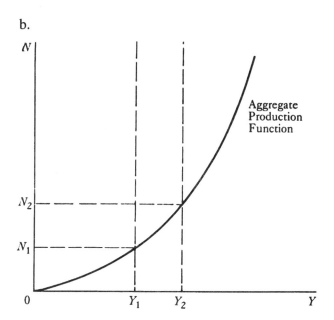

Part III: Multiple Choice

1. c
2. c
3. c
4. b
5. a
6. d
7. b
8. a
9. c
10. b
11. a
12. c
13. b
14. d
15. a

Name _____

CHAPTER 6 EXERCISES

Mark each statement as true or false. Whenever you mark a sentence as false, jot down a sentence stating why it is false.

_____ 1. Just as the aggregate demand curve is downward sloping, with much the same shape as a demand curve for a single market, the aggregate supply curve is always upward sloping.

_____ 2. In the basic macroeconomic model, Y represents real output and $P \times Y$ represents nominal output.

_____ 3. An increase in aggregate supply will cause an increase both in output and in prices.

_____ 4. A composite aggregate supply curve has three distinct regions: a horizontal region, an upward-sloping region, and a vertical region.

_____ 5. Most economists agree about the shape of the short-run aggregate supply curve, but disagree about the shape of the long-run aggregate supply curve.

_____ 6. Before the 1930s, classical economists believed that the economy tended toward natural levels of output, prices, and employment.

_____ 7. The classical school of economics dates back to Adam Smith's *The Wealth of Nations*.

_____ 8. One reason the classical economists felt the economy was self-correcting is that prior to the 1930s there were no extended periods of unemployment.

_____ 9. Contemporary followers of the classical school feel that government fiscal and monetary policy is effective only if the public does not understand it.

_____ 10. Although business cycle theorists did not agree with classical economists about the relative importance of unemployment and inflation, they did agree that the economy is naturally self-correcting.

_____ 11. Keynesian economic theory was developed as a response to the monetary crisis in 1907.

_____ 12. Keynes's argument for government intervention maintained that the private components of aggregate demand might not be sufficient to return the economy to full employment.

_____ 13. A conservative politician might attempt to solve the problems of unemployment and inflation by devising policies that will create incentives in the private sector.

_____ 14. Most of the recent growth in China has been in the northern regions where there is a strong government economic program.

CHAPTER 7

CLASSICAL MACROECONOMICS AND THE KEYNESIAN CHALLENGE

CHECKING IN

This chapter continues the discussion of classical and Keynesian economics of the previous chapter. Classical economists felt the economy always tended to a full-employment level of output and markets were self-correcting. The aggregate supply curve was vertical; output was fixed. A change in aggregate demand would influence only the price level. This effect was due to Say's law, which stated that the process of production creates enough income to purchase all of the output. All three markets (credit, factor, and product) were believed to be self-correcting. In the classical model, planned saving would always be equal to planned investment, since the changing interest rate resolved any discrepancies between them. Prices were determined by the interaction of the supply of and demand for money, as stated in the quantity theory of money.

Keynes's theory, which criticized the classical model, was based in part on the work of the business cycle theorists. They believed that insufficient consumption and unstable investment caused fluctuations in output and employment. Keynes found fault with three elements of classical macroeconomics: Say's law, the quantity theory of money, and self-regulating markets. He believed that saving and investment were not determined solely by the interest rate. He also maintained that prices and wages would not necessarily fall in order to bring markets back to full employment and that the demand for money was not as easily predicted as in the quantity theory. Keynes called for government to attempt to increase aggregate demand during periods of high unemployment.

TRYING OUT THE TERMS

Match each of the following terms with its definition, and then check your answers. If you are having trouble, go back to the text and find the definition there.

_____   1. asset demand for money   _____   5. macroeconomic equilibrium

_____   2. quantity theory of money   _____   6. transactions demand for money

_____   3. Keynesian revolution   _____   7. self-regulating markets

_____   4. equation of exchange

A. The level of output at which there is no tendency to change. The amount that buyers wish to buy is exactly equal to what is being produced.

B. Markets that quickly resolve problems of shortage and surplus through price changes, quantity adjustments, or a combination of the two.

C. The theory that changes in the price level will be proportional to changes in the money supply.

D. An identity based on the quantity theory of money that states that the money supply times the velocity of money is equal to the price level times the level of real output.

E. The change in macroeconomic theory and policy that occurred when Keynes's ideas displaced the classical theory of how output and employment are determined.

F. Demand for money to hold in order to protect the value of one's assets against changes in interest rates; it is negatively related to the interest rate.

G. Demand for money in order to make purchases and carry out other day-to-day market activities; it is positively related to income.

TESTING YOURSELF

In the next two sections, you will answer questions that are based on information in the text. Master all of the terms before you begin these sections. Work each section without referring to your notes or the text, and then check your answers.

Part I: True or False

Mark each statement as true or false. Whenever you mark a statement as false, jot down a sentence stating why it is false.

_____   1. In a macroeconomic equilibrium, both planned savings and investment and actual savings and investment must be equal.

_____ 2. In the classical model, if savings are greater than investment, the interest rate will rise.

_____ 3. In the classical model, savings are the source of loanable funds.

_____ 4. The credit market is self-regulating in the classical model, but the labor market is not.

_____ 5. After the inflow of treasure from the New World reached Europe, output increased dramatically, while prices fell in response to the increase in supply.

_____ 6. The quantity theory is better at explaining the short run than the long run.

_____ 7. The term k, developed by Marshall, indicates how much of income households want to hold in the form of money.

_____ 8. If $k = 0.25$ and $M = \$200$, then GDP = $\$2,000$.

_____ 9. Under the quantity theory, if the money supply doubles, prices will also increase, but not as much.

_____ 10. Business cycle theorists felt that when consumers did not buy up all production, the rest would be purchased by investors.

_____ 11. Keynes felt that people save for many reasons other than the desire to receive interest.

_____ 12. Keynes felt that the desire for profit was the driving motive behind investment.

_____ 13. The Keynesian model agrees with the classical model in holding that the demand for money is independent of the interest rate.

_____ 14. If the demand for money responds to changes in the interest rate, then velocity is not constant.

_____ 15. Keynesian theory holds that if consumers and investors do not buy all output, then the government should increase spending or lower taxes.

Part II: Problems

1. Labor force = 250 million   Employed workers = 225 million
   Full employment = 95%   Full employment GDP = $1,900 billion

   a. What is the current unemployment rate?

   b. What is current GDP?

   c. What prediction would a classical economist make about this situation?

2. a. $M = k \times \text{GDP}$; $M = 500$; $k = 0.2$

   What is GDP?

   What are some of the combinations of P and Y that might make up GDP?

   If Y is fixed at 1,250, what is P?

   b. Suppose M remains at 500 but k increases to 0.25. What will happen to GDP?

   If Y remains fixed at 1,250, what will happen to P?

   What might cause k to rise?

Part II: Multiple Choice

_____ 1. Which of the following is *not* a foundation of classical macroeconomics?
   a. Say's Law
   b. Keynes's revolution
   c. self-regulating markets
   d. quantity theory of money

_____ 2. Classical economists believed that the level of real output was determined by the
   a. level of employment.
   b. price level.
   c. interest rate.
   d. government.

3. Classical economists felt that
   a. saving is unrelated to the interest rate.
   b. investment is a leakage in the circular flow.
   c. output does not vary with the price level.
   d. production generates output but not income.

4. A flaw in the reasoning of Say's law is that
   a. investment is independent of the interest rate.
   b. households do not always spend all of their incomes.
   c. leakages need not equal injections in equilibrium.
   d. producers increase production if inventories increase.

5. In the classical model, savings and investment are equalized by the
   a. labor market.
   b. product market.
   c. credit market.
   d. government.

6. In the classical model, the supply of loanable funds is
   a. provided through saving by households.
   b. positively related to the interest rate.
   c. perfectly inelastic.
   d. provided through saving by households and positively related to the interest rate.

7. Suppose there is a surplus of goods and firms collectively cut their output. A classical economist would predict that
   a. the price level would increase.
   b. unemployment would increase and competition among workers for fewer jobs would drive wages down.
   c. the interest rate would increase.
   d. wages and prices would become flexible upward but inflexible downward.

8. The demand for money is
   a. the amount of wealth people want to hold as money.
   b. the amount of money the government determines should be issued.
   c. the amount of assets that banks are willing to loan.
   d. positively related to the interest rate.

9. People who have more money than they want to keep will
   a. have to hold it anyway, since the government determines the money supply.
   b. spend more on other assets like bonds.
   c. spend more on consumer goods.
   d. spend more either on bonds and other financial assets or on consumer goods.

_____ 10. The business cycle theorists felt that all output might not be consumed (the underconsumptionist argument) because
   a. workers were extraordinarily thrifty and would save out of subsistence incomes.
   b. the government would tax away disposable income.
   c. a few wealthy consumers would do most of the saving and leave more output than workers could afford to purchase.
   d. too much money would be spent on imports.

_____ 11. Which of the following is *not* a motive identified by Keynes for individuals' saving?
   a. Protection against unforeseen events
   b. Increasing the standard of living
   c. Unavailability of consumer goods
   d. Speculation

_____ 12. Keynes felt that
   a. the quantity theory did a good job of explaining the short-run behavior of the economy.
   b. the velocity of money was not stable in the short run.
   c. the quantity of money people wanted to hold would be constant across the business cycle.
   d. velocity was likely to increase during a recession or depression.

_____ 13. Keynes pointed out that one reason product markets might not be self-regulating was that
   a. interest rates have a strong influence on saving.
   b. households may choose to save rather than spend.
   c. business firms may choose to cut output rather than prices.
   d. labor markets may insist on pay increases.

_____ 14. Keynes felt that consumer spending primarily depended on
   a. the interest rate.
   b. income.
   c. wealth.
   d. expectations.

_____ 15. Russia's high inflation rate during 1992 can be explained by
   a. gold sales to the western states.
   b. a large increase in the supply of rubles.
   c. a fall in real output.
   d. both a fall in real output and an increase in the supply of rubles.

TAKING ANOTHER LOOK

It's easy to imagine runaway inflation in a lesser developed country or a country recovering from war. But could such a thing ever happen in the United States? We like to think not.

In 1977, Benjamin Stein, whom you may recognize as a television actor and writer, and his father, Herbert Stein, an important economic analyst and presidential adviser for many years, wrote a novel, *On the Brink*, that describes what might happen to the United States if the printing presses ran wild. The story is about the energy crisis in the 1970s and 1980s, so we have the security of hindsight to reassure that it didn't really happen.

It's a fascinating tale and will give you some insights into not only the disaster of hyperinflation but also how government economic policy is made. Herbert Stein has been behind those closed doors, and economic theory is not the only thing discussed in there. This book is probably in your library. Or check out the used paperback stores.

CHECKING OUT

Now that you have finished studying this chapter, you should be able to:

1. State Say's Law and explain why this law led classical economists to conclude that periods of overproduction or high unemployment would be temporary and self-correcting.

2. Describe the roles of the self-regulating product, resource, and credit markets in ensuring that the economy will tend toward the full-employment level of output.

3. State the quantity theory of money and use it to explain how increases in the money supply lead to proportional increases in the price level.

4. Identify and explain the Keynesian criticisms of the classical model.

5. List the basic ideas behind the Keynesian alternative to the classical model.

ANSWERS

Trying Out the Terms

1. F
2. C
3. E
4. D
5. A
6. G
7. B

Testing Yourself

Part 1: True of False

1. true
2. false. In the classical model, if savings are greater than investment, the interest rate will fall.
3. true
4. false. In the classical model, the credit market, the product market, and the labor market are all self-regulating.
5. false. Prices rose after the inflow of New World treasure into Europe.
6. false. The quantity theory explains long-run events.
7. true
8. false. $M = k \times P \times Y$; $200 = 0.25 \text{GDP}$; $\text{GDP} = \$800$.

9. false. Under the quantity theory of money, if the money supply doubles, so will prices.
10. false. Business cycle theorists knew that there would be underconsumption, or periods when all output would not be bought.
11. true
12. true
13. false. The Keynesian model holds that the demand for money is strongly influenced by the interest rate.
14. true
15. true

Part II: Problems

1. a. $225/250 = 0.9$; $1 - 0.9 = 0.1$. Unemployment = 10%
   b. $90/95 = 0.95$ (current employment as a percentage of full employment) $0.95 \times 1,900 = 1,805$
   c. There is excess aggregate supply. Wages will fall, prices will fall, at lower prices, greater quantities will be demand, output will increase, employment will rise, there will be a return to macroeconomic equilibrium.
2. a. $500/0.2 = 2,500$

P	Y
1	2500.00
2	1250.00
3	833.33
4	625.00
5	500.00

   b. $500/0.25 = 2,000$
   $2,000/1,250 = 1.6$

   People may be nervous about the future and want to hold more of their assets as money, the interest rate may have fallen.

Part II: Multiple Choice

1. b
2. a
3. c
4. b
5. c
6. d
7. b
8. a
9. d
10. c
11. c
12. b
13. c
14. b
15. d

Name _____

CHAPTER 7 EXERCISES

_____ 1. According to the quantity theory, a doubling of the money supply leads in the long run to
   a. a doubling of real income and no change in the price level.
   b. a doubling of real income and an increase in the price level.
   c. a decrease in the price level and no change in real income.
   d. no change in either real income or the price level.
   e. a doubling of the price level and no change in real income.

_____ 2. According to the quantity theory of money, if the money supply is $200 billion and GDP is $900 billion, k is
   a. 200.
   b. 0.222.
   c. 0.055.
   d. 4.50.
   e. 1.8.

_____ 3. According to the quantity theory of money, if the money supply is $300 billion and k is 0.333, GDP is about
   a. $100 billion.
   b. $300 billion.
   c. $900 billion.
   d. $1,000 billion.
   e. $90 billion.

_____ 4. According to the quantity theory of money, if output is 500 units, k is 0.25, and the money supply is $3,000, the price level (average price per unit of output) is
   a. $0.67.
   b. $60.
   c. $6.
   d. $24.
   e. $3,750.

_____ 5. According to the quantity theory of money, if $Y = 400$ units, $M_s = \$800$, and $k = 0.25$, then P is
   a. $4,000.
   b. $8.
   c. $16.
   d. $64.
   e. $10.

_____ 6. Business cycle theorists felt that
   a. if consumer demand were stable, there would be no need for new investment.
   b. if government and consumption spending do not buy all of the output, the surplus must go into investment.
   c. investment spending is changeable and unpredictable.
   d. All of the above

_____ 7. Keynes felt that investment
   a. would take place only when interest rates were low.
   b. was affected by factors other than the interest rate.
   c. had an insignificant effect on the economy.
   d. could not be exceeded by planned saving.

_____ 8. In the Keynesian model,
   a. output is determined by demand in the product market.
   b. output is determined by the equilibrium in the labor market.
   c. the aggregate supply curve is vertical in the long run.
   d. output cannot be increased unless prices also increase.

_____ 9. During the Great Depression,
   a. investment decreased and consumption spending increased.
   b. both investment and consumption spending decreased.
   c. investment was constant.
   d. investment increased and consumption decreased dramatically.

_____ 10. Keynes felt that the cure for the Great Depression was
   a. to reduce the money supply.
   b. to do nothing but wait for self-adjustment in the markets.
   c. for the government to cut taxes and increase spending to shift the aggregate demand curve.
   d. to enforce wage and price controls selectively.

CHAPTER 8

THE KEYNESIAN MODEL

CHECKING IN

This chapter develops material you have seen before rather than introducing something completely new. The theory of John Maynard Keynes, introduced in the preceding chapter, can be expressed in a formal model. This chapter presents it geometrically. An Appendix offers the algebraic form. The model develops logically from the circular flow model.

The Keynesian model illustrates that it is possible for the economy to reach an equilibrium level of national income and output while there is a high level of unemployment. Equilibrium national income and aggregate expenditure (output) are jointly determined in this model.

The Keynesian consumption function provides the basis of the model. Keynes felt that, although the level of consumption depends on many influences, the primary determinant of consumption is disposable income. As disposable income increases, so does consumption. Investment, government spending, and net exports are added to consumption to obtain the aggregate expenditure (*AE*) function. This function tells us the level of *planned* expenditures for any given level of output. Equilibrium occurs when planned expenditures are exactly equal to actual output. Geometrically, this is at the point on the graph where the *AE* curve crosses the 45° line, which shows all possible points of equilibrium. This equilibrium may or may not occur at the full-employment level.

If the economy is operating at a nonequilibrium level of national income and output, businesses will experience unintended inventory changes; these may be increases (when aggregate expenditure is less than output) or decreases (when aggregate expenditure is greater than output). Businesses respond to these unintended changes by decreasing or increasing output, thereby moving the economy toward equilibrium.

Any change in one of the components of aggregate expenditure that is not related to changes in income will shift the *AE* curve. Such a change in expenditure will change equilibrium national income and output in the same direction, but because of the multiplier effect, the change in income and output will be greater than the change in expenditure. As income is created, some of it is saved, but some is spent; this increased spending also adds to national income. Shifts in the *AE* curve for any reason *other than a change in the price level* will shift the aggregate demand curve.

Remember that the aggregate demand curve shows the relationship between planned spending and price level.

TRYING OUT THE TERMS

Match each of the following terms with its definition, and then check your answers. If you are having trouble, go back to the text and find the definition there.

_____ 1. expenditure multiplier

_____ 2. consumption function

_____ 3. marginal propensity to save (*MPS*)

_____ 4. aggregate expenditure (*AE*)

_____ 5. dissaving

_____ 6. marginal propensity to consume (*MPC*)

A. Total planned spending for an economy's total output.

B. Any equation, table, or graph that shows the relationship between income received by consumers and the amount they plan to spend on currently produced final output.

C. The fraction of any change in income that is consumed.

D. The fraction of any change in income that is saved.

E. Consuming by drawing on accumulated stocks (inventories) or financial assets.

F. Measures the impact of a given initial change in total expenditures on equilibrium national income; equal to $1/(1 - MPC)$.

TESTING YOURSELF

In the next three sections, you will answer questions and work problems that are based on information in the text. Master all of the terms before you begin these sections. Work each section without referring to your notes or the text, and then check your answers.

Part I: True or False

Mark each statement as true or false. Whenever you mark a statement as false, jot down a sentence stating why it is false.

_____ 1. The aggregate expenditure curve shows the relationship between the total amount of spending $[C + I + G + (X - M)]$ and the level of income.

_____ 2. The consumption function relates consumption to national income.

_____ 3. The marginal propensity to consume refers to the portion of any increase in income that is spent on consumption goods.

_____ 4. If MPC is equal to 0.6, MPS is also equal to 0.6.

_____ 5. Consumption is affected by influences other than income.

_____ 6. If most people anticipate inflation next year and consume more while saving less, there will be a movement up along the consumption function.

_____ 7. In the two-sector model, if $C + I$ is greater than Y, there will be an increase in inventory, and Y will fall.

_____ 8. Over time, investment expenditures are more stable than consumption expenditures.

_____ 9. The introduction of "just-in-time" production negated the role of inventories in the two-sector model.

_____ 10. In the two-sector model, the equilibrium level of Y is reached when leakages are equal to injections.

_____ 11. If government spending increases while nothing else changes, there will be an increase in Y equal to the increase in government spending.

_____ 12. If $MPC = 0.8$, the expenditure multiplier is 5.

_____ 13. The formula for the expenditure multiplier is $1/(1 - MPS)$.

_____ 14. If $MPC = 0.5$ and net exports increase by $200, Y will increase by $400.

_____ 15. An increase in planned saving at all levels of income will stimulate investment and cause Y to increase.

Part II: Problems

1. a. Complete the following table.

National Income (Disposable Income) $Y = Y_d$	Change in Disposable Income ΔY_d	Planned Consumption Spending C	Change in Consumption Spending ΔC	Planned Saving S	Change in Saving ΔS
$ 000	$_____	$120	$_____	$_____	$_____
300	_____	390	_____	_____	_____
600	_____	_____	_____	_____	_____
900	_____	_____	_____	_____	_____
1,200	_____	_____	_____	_____	_____
1,500	_____	_____	_____	_____	_____
1,800	_____	_____	_____	_____	_____
2,100	_____	_____	_____	_____	_____

104   Chapter 8   The Keynesian Model

b. What is the *MPC*? the *MPS*? the multiplier? C_0?

c. What is the consumption function equation?

d. If C_0 increases to $150, at what level of Y_d will $C = Y_d$?

e. In the graph below, plot the consumption function for the table and draw the 45° line. Mark the point where $C = Y_d$.

Chapter 8 The Keynesian Model

2. Consider the following graph.

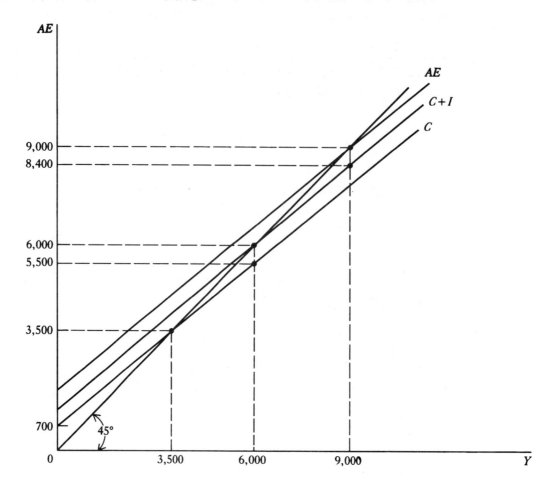

a. What is equilibrium Y?

b. What is the MPC?

c. What is the multiplier?

d. If investment increases to $800, what will be the new equilibrium Y?

3. Suppose $MPC = 0.6$. Fill in the following table to show the multiplier effect of a $500 increase in spending.

Round	Change in AE	Change in Y
1	$500 (initial expenditure)	$500
2	_____	_____
3	_____	_____
4	_____	_____
5	_____	_____
6	_____	_____
All following rounds	_____	_____
Total	_____	_____

Part III: Multiple Choice

1. In Keynesian analysis, the aggregate supply curve is
    a. upward sloping.
    b. vertical.
    c. horizontal.
    d. nonexistent.

2. According to Keynesian logic, aggregate supply
    a. determines aggregate demand.
    b. is determined by the aggregate production function.
    c. adjusts to aggregate demand.
    d. is independent of aggregate demand.

3. Suppose that income increases from $10,000 to $15,000 and saving increases from $1,800 to $3,300. What is the value of the MPC?
    a. 0.7
    b. 0.5
    c. 0.3
    d. Impossible to determine

4. If people think there is going to be a war and begin to spend more on consumer durables, then at every level of income
    a. the consumption function will shift down.
    b. the saving function will shift up.
    c. both the consumption function and the saving function will shift down.
    d. the consumption function will shift up and the saving function will shift down.

To complete Exercises 5–7, use the following equation, based on a Keynesian consumption function:

$$C = \$700 + 0.6Y_d$$

_____ 5. If Y_d is $2,000, then C is
   a. $2,000.
   b. $1,900.
   c. $1,500.
   d. $1,200.

_____ 6. What is the value of the *MPC*?
   a. 0.1
   b. 0.4
   c. 0.6
   d. Cannot be determined

_____ 7. What is the value of the *MPS*?
   a. 1.00
   b. 0.75
   c. 0.6
   d. 0.4

_____ 8. According to Keynes, the most important determinant of investment demand is
   a. the interest rate.
   b. the level of output.
   c. the level of expected profits.
   d. government policy.

_____ 9. A two-sector Keynesian model will be at equilibrium income when
   a. consumption is equal to planned investment.
   b. saving is equal to consumption.
   c. consumption is equal to disposable income.
   d. saving is equal to planned investment.

_____ 10. The larger the *MPC*,
   a. the smaller the multiplier.
   b. the larger the *MPS*.
   c. the smaller Y.
   d. the larger the multiplier.

To complete Exercises 11–13, use the following information for a hypothetical economy:

$$C = \$200 + 0.9\,Y_d \quad I = \$100 \quad G = \$150 \quad (X - M) = \$50 \quad T = \$100$$

_____ 11. What is the value of the *MPS*?
   a. 0.1
   b. 0.9
   c. 200
   d. Impossible to determine

_____ 12. If national income and output are $2,500, what is the level of consumption?
   a. $2,500
   b. $2,360
   c. $2,235
   d. Impossible to determine

_____ 13. In this economy, we would expect to see
   a. a decrease in inventories, followed by an increase in output.
   b. an increase in inventories, followed by a decrease in output.
   c. inventories and output remain constant.
   d. inventories at zero level.

_____ 14. If *MPC* = 0.6, what is the multiplier?
   a. 6
   b. 4
   c. 2.5
   d. 1

_____ 15. If *MPC* = 0.5 and investment spending increases by $100, national income will increase by
   a. $50.
   b. $100.
   c. $200.
   d. $500.

TAKING ANOTHER LOOK

It is no surprise to find a *Wall Street Journal* article stating that personal finance revolves around the family situation (10 September 1993). Anyone who has lived in a family knows that. The Keynesian consumption function is an aggregate function combining the spending habits of all of the families in the country, so that personal peculiarities should wash out. But a large demographic change could affect the aggregate consumption function.

When all of the baby boomers (individuals born between 1945 and 1960) began to mature, what happened? Young people tended to spend more of their income than people in established families as they paid for education, bought houses, and filled them up with furniture and babies; the sudden increase in young people in the market caused the consumption function to shift up.

Can you think of a situation where demographic changes might cause a change in the marginal propensities to consume and save? If people marry later and if, when they do marry, they choose not to have children, then the need to save for large homes and college educations goes down and individuals may spend more out of every change in income. You could tell another story. If families have fewer children, they may feel they need to save more for retirement since they won't have children to help them out in their declining years.

CHECKING OUT

Now that you have finished studying this chapter, you should be able to:

1. Explain the relationship between consumption and investment spending as sources of demand, and between national income and demand, as a factor in determining the level of income and output.

2. Describe the central elements of the two-sector aggregate expenditure function, the consumption function and investment demand, and how this model determines the equilibrium level of income and output.

3. Expand the aggregate expenditure function to incorporate the government and foreign sectors and determine equilibrium in a two-sector model.

4. Use the multiplier to calculate the change in the equilibrium national income that results from a given change in planned spending.

5. Explain the relationship between the Keynesian aggregate expenditure function and the aggregate demand curve.

ANSWERS

Trying Out the Terms

1. F
2. B
3. D
4. A
5. E
6. C

Testing Yourself

Part I: True or False

1. true
2. false. The consumption function links consumption to disposable income.
3. true
4. false. *MPS* is 0.4 when *MPC* is 0.6 (*MPC* + *MPS* = 1).
5. true
6. false. The consumption function curve *shifts* upward (not a movement along the curve) if consumption increases for a reason not related to the level of income.
7. false. In the two-sector model, if $C + I$ is greater than Y, inventories will decrease and Y (output) will increase.
8. false. Consumption is much more stable over time than investment.
9. false. This technique reduces the size of inventories, but it does not diminish the sensitivity of the model to changes in inventories.
10. true
11. false. If government spending increases and all other things stay the same, Y will increase by some multiple of the increase in government spending.

12. true
13. false. The expenditure multiplier formula is 1/(1 – MPC).
14. true
15. false. If savings at all levels of income increase, the level of output should fall.

Part II: Problems

1. a.

National Income (Disposable Income) $Y = Y_d$	Change in Disposable Income ΔY_d	Planned Consumption Spending C	Change in Consumption Spending ΔC	Planned Saving S	Change in Saving ΔS
$ 000	$ ___	$ 120	$ ___	$–120	$ ___
300	300	390	270	–90	30
600	300	660	270	–60	30
900	300	930	270	–30	30
1,200	300	1,200	270	0	30
1,500	300	1,470	270	30	30
1,800	300	1,740	270	60	30
2,100	300	2,010	270	90	30

b. $MPC = 0.9$; $MPS = 0.1$; multiplier = 10; $C_0 = \$120$.
c. $C = \$120 + 0.9Y_d$
d. $1,500
e.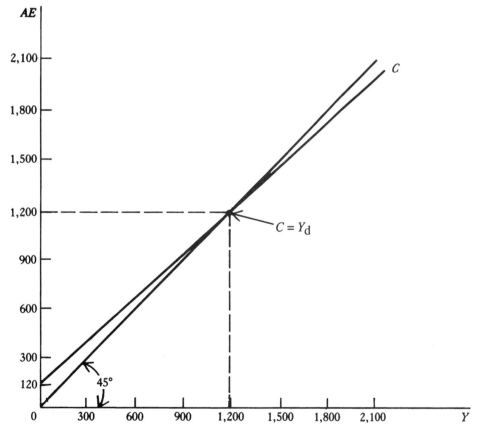

Chapter 8   *The Keynesian Model*   111

2. a. $9,000
    b. 0.8
    c. 5
    d. $10,500
3.

Round	Change in *AE*	Change in *Y*
1	$500.00	$500.00
2	300.00	300.00
3	180.00	180.00
4	108.00	108.00
5	64.80	64.80
6	38.88	38.88
All following rounds	58.32	58.32
Total	$1,250.00	$1,250.00

Part III: Multiple Choice

1. c
2. c
3. a
4. d
5. b
6. c
7. d
8. c
9. d
10. d
11. a
12. b
13. a
14. c
15. c

CHAPTER 8 EXERCISES

1. a. Complete the following table. Underline the line showing the equilibrium level of Y. In the last column, note whether AE is less than, equal to, or greater than Y.

Y	T	Y_d	C	I	G	X – M	AE		
$2,000	$400	$1,600	$1,600	$800	$900	$200	$____	AE____	Y
3,000	400	2,600	2,350	800	900	200	____	AE____	Y
4,000	400	____	____	800	900	200	____	AE____	Y
5,000	400	____	____	800	900	200	____	AE____	Y
6,000	400	____	____	800	900	200	____	AE____	Y
7,000	400	____	____	800	900	200	____	AE____	Y
8,000	400	____	____	800	900	200	____	AE____	Y
9,000	400	____	____	800	900	200	____	AE____	Y
10,000	400	____	____	800	900	200	____	AE____	Y

b. What is the *MPC*? the multiplier?

c. If the government imposes a tariff on imported automobiles, causing (X – M) to increase by $250, what will be the effect on equilibrium Y?

d. If Y increases by $2,000 as a result of an increase in G, how big was the increase in G?

e. On the graph on the following page, plot AE and draw the 45° line. Mark the equilibrium point.

Chapter 8   The Keynesian Model   113

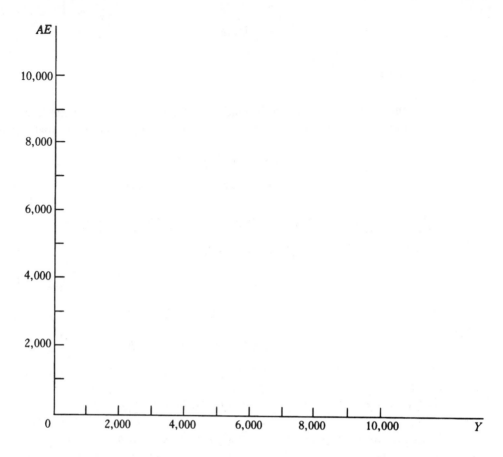

2. Suppose MPC = 0.9. Fill in the following table to show the multiplier effect of a $500 increase in spending.

Round	Change in AE	Change in Y
1	$500 (initial expenditure)	$500
2	_____	_____
3	_____	_____
4	_____	_____
5	_____	_____
6	_____	_____
All following rounds	_____	_____
Total	_____	_____

Compare your results to those of Exercise 3 in the Testing Yourself section. Notice that the larger the MPC, the greater the multiplier and, therefore, the larger the increase in Y resulting from an increase in AE.

CHAPTER 9

TAXES, GOVERNMENT SPENDING, AND FISCAL POLICY

CHECKING IN

The Keynesian model developed in the preceding chapter explains the way an economy adjusts to changes in planned aggregate expenditure. This chapter explains how Keynesian fiscal policy can be used to move the economy toward full employment.

Keynesian fiscal policy is based on three assumptions. First, equilibrium output may occur at high rates of unemployment or inflation. Second, changes in private or foreign-sector spending may move the economy to an equilibrium that, in the view of society, is not acceptable. Third, changes in spending or taxation by the government sector are most likely to move the economy toward an acceptable equilibrium.

Just after World War II, the U.S. Congress passed the Employment Act of 1946. It declared that the federal government is responsible for achieving and maintaining full employment, stable prices, and steady growth. This act embraces the concept of Keynesian fiscal policy.

When there is a decline in planned private expenditures (spending by households, businesses, and foreigners), output and employment can fall. This creates a recessionary gap, which is the difference between aggregate planned expenditure and the output that could be supplied if the economy were at full employment. The government can implement fiscal policy to close this gap. The government can increase government spending, increase transfer payments, decrease taxes, or undertake some combination of these three. These actions increase aggregate expenditure and, through the multiplier effect, the level of output.

Some fiscal policies do not require direct action from Congress and the president because they were established by previous legislation. These policies are known as automatic stabilizers. They include the progressive income tax and unemployment insurance. Other policies, called discretionary fiscal policies, require direct legislation. The Kennedy tax cut, the Ford rebate, and the Reagan tax cut are examples of such policies. Unfortunately, discretionary fiscal policy is subject to many lags before it can fully affect the economy.

Fiscal policy has both supporters and critics. Its supporters maintain that it can reduce or eliminate the ills of unemployment and inflation. Its critics hold that it causes both the public sector and the national debt to grow at unacceptable rates.

TRYING OUT THE TERMS

Match each of the following terms with its definition, and then check your answers. If you are having trouble, go back to the text and find the definition there.

_____ 1. proportional tax   _____ 9. impact lag

_____ 2. implementation lag   _____ 10. progressive tax

_____ 3. recessionary gap   _____ 11. contractionary fiscal policy

_____ 4. political business cycle _____ 12. permanent income hypothesis

_____ 5. automatic stabilizers   _____ 13. public choice economics

_____ 6. regressive tax   _____ 14. recognition lag

_____ 7. fiscal policy   _____ 15. income gap

_____ 8. expansionary fiscal policy _____ 16. discretionary fiscal policy

A. The use of government spending and taxes to try to influence the levels of output, employment, and prices.

B. The difference between aggregate expenditure and the full-employment level of output.

C. The difference between the equilibrium level of output and the full-employment level of output: equal to the recessionary gap times the multiplier.

D. Cutting taxes, raising transfer payments, or increasing government purchases to try to increase the level of income and employment.

E. Changes in tax collections and transfer payments that are automatically triggered by changes in national income and tend to reduce changes in output and employment.

F. A tax that takes a smaller share (percentage) of income as income rises.

G. A tax that takes the same share (percentage) of income from all taxpayers.

H. A tax that takes a larger share (percentage) of income as income rises.

I. Deliberate changes in tax rates, transfer programs, or government purchases designed to change the equilibrium level of national income.

J. Raising taxes, lowering transfer payments, or reducing government purchases in an attempt to reduce the equilibrium level of output to one that is attainable with available resources.

K. The view that consumption does not depend on current income alone, but on past income and expected future income as well.

L. A branch of economic theory that attempts to integrate economics and politics by examining the motives and rewards facing individuals in the public sector.

M. The length of time it takes to determine that an economic problem exists.

N. The time it takes after a problem is recognized to choose and enact a fiscal policy in response.

O. The time that elapses between implementation of a fiscal policy and its full effect on economic activity.

P. A business cycle that results from the use of fiscal (or monetary) policy to influence the outcome of elections.

TESTING YOURSELF

In the next three sections, you will answer questions and work problems that are based on information in the text. Master all of the terms before you begin these sections. Work each section without referring to your notes or the text, and then check your answers.

Part I: True or False

Mark each statement as true or false. Whenever you mark a statment as false, jot down a sentence stating why it is false.

_____ 1. When the government uses taxation or spending policy to affect the level of national income, it is engaging in fiscal policy.

_____ 2. The Keynesian argument for fiscal policy maintains that the economy is basically stable.

_____ 3. Keynesian fiscal policy can be effective when there is inadequate demand but not when there is excess demand.

_____ 4. If Y falls, we would expect transfer payments to increase.

_____ 5. If *AE* is less than *Y**, a recessionary gap exists.

_____ 6. Suppose there was a recessionary gap. An appropriate Keynesian fiscal policy would be to raise taxes.

_____ 7. If $MPC = 0.75$, $Y = \$1,500$, and $Y^* = \$1,900$, government spending must increase by $400 to close the recessionary gap.

_____ 8. If $MPC = 0.9$ and taxes are increased by $100, *Y* will fall by $900.

_____ 9. The effects of a $100 billion decrease in taxes will be exactly the same as those of an increase in government spending of the same amount.

_____ 10. The progressive income tax is a discretionary stabilizer.

_____ 11. The lag between the passage of a policy law and its effect on the economy is known as the implementation lag.

_____ 12. The Employment Act of 1946 made the U.S. government responsible for achieving and maintaining full employment, steady growth, and stable prices.

_____ 13. The Investment Tax Credit was passed as an incentive for businesses to increase investment expenditures.

_____ 14. After the Reagan tax cut, the unemployment rate decreased.

_____ 15. After the Ford tax rebate, the unemployment rate decreased.

Part II: Problems

1. $C = \$500 + 0.75Y_d$; $T = \$400$; $G = \$300$; $I = \$300$; $X - M = \$100$.

   a. Fill in the equilibrium values of

   Y _____ Y_d _____ C _____ S _____

   b. Suppose government spending increases by $100. Fill in the new equilibrium values of

   Y _____ Y_d _____ C _____ S _____

   c. Suppose instead of an increase in government spending, there is a $100 decrease in taxes. Fill in the new equilibrium values of

   Y _____ Y_d _____ C _____ S _____

   d. If $Y^* = \$4,200$, by how much would government spending have to rise from the equilibrium in (a) to bring the economy to full employment?

2. Consider these four families and their income taxes. Calculate the tax rate that each family is paying. Is the tax in this country regressive, proportional, or progressive?

	Income	Tax	Tax Rate
Anderson	$23,000	$2,760	_____
Jones	55,000	4,400	_____
Cooper	79,000	4,740	_____
Riley	100,000	5,000	_____

   The tax is _____, because _____
   _____.

Chapter 9   Taxes, Government Spending, and Fiscal Policy

3. Suppose the tax changes to a proportional tax of 7 percent. Show the amount each family will pay in taxes.

Anderson _____

Cooper   _____

Jones   _____

Riley   _____

Part III: Multiple Choice

_____ 1. If an economy is at equilibrium at the full-employment income, Y^*, the appropriate fiscal policy would be to
   a. increase taxes and decrease government spending.
   b. increase taxes and leave government spending alone.
   c. leave taxes alone and increase transfer payments.
   d. do nothing.

_____ 2. Keynes believed that
   a. aggregate expenditure was basically stable.
   b. government manipulation of aggregate expenditure might be necessary to bring an economy to full employment.
   c. changes in consumption and investment were as predictable as changes in government spending in shifting the aggregate expenditure curve.
   d. tariffs were an effective tool of fiscal policy.

_____ 3. When aggregate planned expenditure is less than full-employment aggregate output, there is
   a. a recessionary gap.
   b. overemployment.
   c. an inventory drawdown.
   d. a balanced budget.

_____ 4. Adherents of Keynesian fiscal policy believe that
   a. tax cuts will have a stronger effect on aggregate expenditure than will changes in government spending.
   b. fiscal policy is less effective in recessionary periods than in inflationary periods.
   c. the economy will tend to reach a full-employment equilibrium if there is an annually balanced budget.
   d. tax increases are appropriate fiscal policy in some circumstances.

_____ 5. Which of the following is a method of affecting the level of net exports?
   a. Tariffs
   b. Quotas
   c. Currency adjustments
   d. All three options will affect net exports

6. If the equilibrium level of national income is greater than the level required to ensure full employment at stable prices, we would expect
    a. an increase in government spending.
    b. an increase in the unemployment rate.
    c. a decrease in transfer payments.
    d. a budget deficit.

7. Automatic stabilizers
    a. affect investment but not consumption.
    b. are ineffective in a recession.
    c. are stronger when the income tax is progressive.
    d. act more slowly than discretionary fiscal policy.

To complete Exercises 8–10, use the following information:

$Y = \$3{,}000 \qquad Y^* = \$3{,}900 \qquad MPC = 0.9$

8. This economy is experiencing
    a. high inflation.
    b. high unemployment.
    c. a recessionary gap.
    d. both a recessionary gap and high unemployment.

9. If the government wishes to use government spending to bring the economy to Y^*, it should
    a. increase government spending by $90.
    b. decrease government spending by $90.
    c. increase government spending by $900.
    d. increase government spending by $100.

10. If the government wishes to use taxation to bring the economy to Y^*, it should
    a. increase taxes by $90.
    b. decrease taxes by $90.
    c. decrease taxes by $100.
    d. leave taxes unchanged.

11. According to Keynesian theory, which of the following policies would be most contractionary?
    a. A $60 increase in government spending
    b. A $60 decrease in government spending
    c. A $60 increase in both taxes and government spending
    d. A $60 decrease in taxes

12. Which of the following is the largest source of funds for the federal government?
    a. Property taxes
    b. Borrowing
    c. Grants-in-aid
    d. Personal income tax

_____ 13. The time lapse that occurs after an economic problem is recognized while appropriate action is formulated and moved through legislative channels is called
   a. a recognition lag.
   b. an implementation lag.
   c. a policy lag.
   d. an impact lag.

_____ 14. After the Kennedy tax cut in 1964,
   a. the unemployment rate fell and the economic growth rate increased.
   b. the inflation rate increased and unemployment was unchanged.
   c. the rate of economic growth was unchanged but unemployment fell.
   d. there was a budget surplus.

_____ 15. Expansionary fiscal policy
   a. affects only output; prices are unchanged.
   b. can cause prices to increase if the aggregate demand curve intersects the aggregate supply curve in its horizontal region.
   c. can cause prices to increase if the aggregate demand curve intersects the aggregate supply curve in its vertical region.
   d. is always inflationary.

TAKING ANOTHER LOOK

The text discusses the tax rebate enacted during the Ford administration. The purpose of the rebate was to increase AE, which would only happen if households spent the unexpected increase in income. President Ford made a comment that surprised some economists. When questioned about how he intended to use the tax rebate, he announced plans to support the government by purchasing a savings bond. If every family had done that, there would have been no expansionary effect. Other economists weren't surprised; President Ford's reaction was consistent with the permanent income hypothesis. Families are much more likely to save a one-time increase in income than they are one that is permanent.

CHECKING OUT

Now that you have finished studying this chapter, you should be able to:

1. Summarize the Keynesian argument for active fiscal policy as the only way to assure full employment with stable prices.

2. Describe the use of an appropriate fiscal policy to promote growth and full employment through both demand and supply effects.

3. Distinguish between automatic stabilizers and discretionary fiscal policy, and give examples of each.

4. Describe experience with discretionary fiscal policy in the United States since 1960.

5. Critically analyze the arguments for and against active fiscal policy.

ANSWERS

Trying Out the Terms

1. G
2. N
3. B
4. P
5. E
6. F
7. A
8. D
9. O
10. H
11. J
12. K
13. L
14. M
15. C
16. I

Testing Yourself

Part I: True or False

1. true
2. false. Keynesian theory maintains that the economy is *not* basically stable.
3. false. Keynesian policy can work, in theory, to cure both inadequate demand and excess demand.
4. true
5. true
6. false. The appropriate policy with a recessionary gap is to lower taxes or increase government spending.
7. false. If $MPC = 0.75$, the multiplier is 4. Government spending should increase by $100 to increase Y by $400.
8. true
9. false. The tax multiplier is smaller than the government multiplier.
10. false. The progressive income tax is an automatic stabilizer.
11. false. The lag between the passage of a policy law and its effect on the economy is known as the impact lag.
12. true
13. true
14. true
15. true

Part II: Problems

1. a. $Y = \$3,600$; $Y_d = \$3,200$; $C = \$2,900$; $S = \$300$
   b. $Y = \$4,000$; $Y_d = \$3,600$; $C = \$3,200$; $S = \$400$
   c. $Y = \$3,900$; $Y_d = \$3,600$ (3,900 − $300); $C = \$3,200$; $S = \$400$
   d. $150
2. Anderson, 12 percent; Jones, 8 percent; Cooper, 6 percent; Riley, 5 percent. The tax is regressive because the percentage of income paid in taxes decreases as the level of income increases.
3. Anderson, $1,610; Jones, $3,850; Cooper, $5,530; Riley, $7,000

Part III: Multiple Choice

1. d
2. b
3. a
4. d
5. d
6. c
7. c
8. d
9. a
10. c
11. b
12. d
13. b
14. a
15. c

Name _____

CHAPTER 9 EXERCISES

1. Consider the economy shown in the following graph.

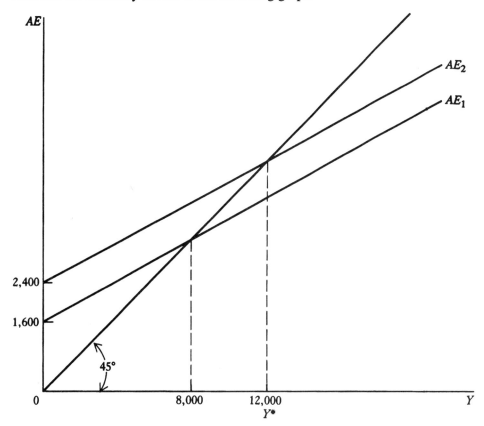

a. If this economy is operating at AE_1, is it at full employment? If not, does it have a recessionary gap or an inflationary gap?

b. What is the government multiplier?

c. How much would taxes have to be changed in order to bring the economy to a full-employment equilibrium?

Chapter 9   Taxes, Government Spending, and Fiscal Policy

2. What is the significance of each of the following?

   a. Full Employment Act of 1946

   b. Kennedy tax cut

3. a. Explain how fiscal policy differs from routine government expenditures and tax collections.

   b. Why is the tax multiplier smaller than the government expenditure multiplier?

CHAPTER 10

BUDGET DEFICITS AND THE NATIONAL DEBT

CHECKING IN

For the past two decades, the macroeconomic spotlight has been on the budget deficit and the national debt. This chapter takes a close look at these important issues.

It is important to distinguish between the deficit and the debt. The deficit is the budget shortfall in any particular year. The debt is the accumulated value of these deficits. Fiscal policy leads to a larger national debt when deficits exceed surpluses. The national debt has grown in the years since World War II. However, until the 1980s, the size of the debt as a percentage of GDP fell. During the 1980s, this trend reversed.

There is much controversy over whether the deficit is a problem and, if it is, how to solve this problem. One difficulty lies in measuring what portion of the deficit is due to discretionary fiscal policy and what portion is due to the automatic stabilizers coming into play during a recession. Various ideas about the budget include the annually balanced budget, the cyclically balanced budget, and the full-employment budget. The full-employment balanced budget would set the tax rates and government transfer programs in such a way that when the economy operates at full employment, the budget is balanced. In times of recession, the automatic stabilizers would cause a deficit to occur.

Those who believe that the deficit does matter and is indeed a problem argue that an uncontrolled deficit leads to an undesirably large public sector; that government borrowing to finance the deficit drives up the interest rate and crowds private investment out of the market; that the accumulating deficits place an onerous burden on future generations; and that because a great deal of this debt is owned by foreigners, there would be a loss of assets should it be repaid. Those who view the deficit with less alarm maintain that rational people know about the debt and reduce their spending in anticipation of repaying the debt some day (the Ricardian Equivalence); they also argue that when the deficit is viewed in real inflation-adjusted terms, it appears a much smaller problem; finally, they point out that the surpluses run by state and local governments to some extent offset the federal deficit.

TRYING OUT THE TERMS

Match each of the following terms with its definition, and then check your answers. If you are having trouble, go back to the text and find the definition there.

_____ 1. structural deficit

_____ 2. crowding out

_____ 3. national debt

_____ 4. cyclical deficit

_____ 5. real deficit

_____ 6. deficit

_____ 7. potential output

A. The difference between the federal government's revenues and expenditures in a given year (the fiscal year), when the government spends more than it collects in taxes.

B. The total of all past budget deficits minus all past surpluses, or the net amount owed to bond holders by the federal government.

C. The part of a deficit that would persist even if the economy were at the full-employment level of output.

D. The part of a deficit that is due to a downturn in economic activity.

E. The output an economy could produce if all of its resources were fully employed.

F. The negative effect on borrowing for private investment due to competition from the federal government in the credit market.

G. A measure of the federal budget deficit as the change in the real (inflation-adjusted) value of the national debt from one year to the next.

TESTING YOURSELF

In the next three sections, you will answer questions and work problems that are based on information in the text. Master all of the terms before you begin these sections. Work each section without referring to your notes or the text, and then check your answers.

Part I: True or False

Mark each statement as true or false. Whenever you mark a statement as false, jot down a sentence stating why it is false.

_____ 1. Before the Reagan administration, the United States always had a balanced budget.

_____ 2. As a percentage of GDP, the national debt has fallen in the years since 1980.

_____ 3. During a recession, it is not unusual for the budget to be in deficit.

_____ 4. During the 1980s, interest rates were high in nominal terms, but low in real terms.

_____ 5. The Gramm-Rudman-Hollings Act originally called for a balanced budget by 1990.

_____ 6. If the budget were balanced annually, there would be no role for fiscal policy.

_____ 7. The full-employment balanced budget allows us to measure the direction of fiscal policy.

_____ 8. The presence of a structural deficit indicates that there are unemployed resources in the economy.

_____ 9. The presence of the Social Security Trust Fund makes the deficit appear smaller.

_____ 10. If the government is borrowing in the credit markets, it may outbid private firms and cause investment to fall.

_____ 11. Interest rates provide the link between the budget deficit and the trade deficit.

_____ 12. The national debt will have to be repaid at some time. The cost of the debt will be paid by people alive at that time.

_____ 13. Although the nominal deficit grew during the 1980s, the real deficit did not.

_____ 14. In the 1980s, most states had budget deficits.

_____ 15. States are able to conduct fiscal policy on a regional level.

Part II: Problem

1. Suppose that $G = \$200$, taxes $= -\$50 + 0.25Y$, and transfer payments $= \$230 - 0.15Y$. Fill in the table. At what level of Y will the budget be balanced?

Y	G	Transfers	Tax	Surplus (Deficit)
$1,000	$200	_____	_____	_____
1,100	200	_____	_____	_____
1,200	200	_____	_____	_____
1,300	200	_____	_____	_____
1,400	200	_____	_____	_____

Part III: Multiple Choice

_____ 1. The national debt is
   a. a stock concept.
   b. a flow concept.
   c. the shortfall of revenues over expenditures.
   d. the amount owed to the federal government by the states.

_____ 2. The debt that was incurred during the Revolutionary War
   a. is still owed.
   b. was repudiated by the federal government.
   c. was paid back by the mid-1830s.
   d. There was no debt associated with the Revolutionary War.

_____ 3. The national debt
   a. has, since 1945, decreased in times of peace and increased in times of war.
   b. decreased as a percentage of GDP during the 1950s and 1960s.
   c. decreased as a percentage of GDP during the 1980s.
   d. has decreased every year since 1945.

_____ 4. Keynesian policy is thought by some to create large deficits because
   a. the tax multiplier is not effective during a recession.
   b. the automatic stabilizers will contribute to a structural deficit.
   c. Keynesians believe that surpluses harm the economy regardless of the state of the business cycle.
   d. it is more difficult for politicians to carry out contractionary policy than to carry out expansionary policy.

_____ 5. The large budget deficits of the 1980s were
   a. the result of Keynesian fiscal policy.
   b. a legacy of the Vietnam War.
   c. caused by concurrent increases in spending and decreases in taxes.
   d. a result of the Gramm-Rudman-Hollings Act.

_____ 6. The recession of 1980–1982
   a. had no effect on the budget deficit during that period.
   b. had a cyclical effect on the budget deficit.
   c. was a result, not a cause, of the budget deficit.
   d. was deepened substantially by the presence of the automatic stabilizers.

_____ 7. The decrease in the size of the deficit during the late 1980s can be attributed to
   a. increasing tax revenues.
   b. spending cuts.
   c. the presence of the Social Security Trust Fund in the calculation.
   d. All three options contributed to the decreasing size.

_____ 8. Keynesian economists called for
   a. an annually balanced budget.
   b. a cyclically balanced budget.
   c. a balanced budget amendment to the Constitution.
   d. a deficit in inflationary periods and a surplus during recessions.

_____ 9. The actual deficit is a poor measure of fiscal policy because
   a. it measures both discretionary fiscal policy and the automatic stabilizers.
   b. it omits the automatic stabilizers from its measure.
   c. it overstates the inflation rate.
   d. it is unaffected by discretionary fiscal policy.

_____ 10. If, during a recession, there is a full-employment balanced budget, the actual budget
   a. will show a deficit.
   b. will show a surplus.
   c. will also be balanced.
   d. may show either a surplus or a deficit, but will not be balanced.

11. Which of the following is *not* considered a possible burden of the national debt?
    a. A larger and growing public sector
    b. The taxes that will have to be levied when it is repaid
    c. The income redistribution that will occur when it is repaid
    d. Higher interest rates

12. The burden of the national debt will fall on future generations if
    a. it is financed with long-term bonds.
    b. the proceeds of the borrowing have gone to fight wars rather that to build infrastructures.
    c. it is repaid with tax revenues.
    d. it is owed to foreigners.

13. State and local government budget surpluses
    a. totally offset the federal budget deficit in most years.
    b. have no effect on the federal budget deficit.
    c. are forecast to be smaller during the coming decade.
    d. never occur because these levels of government are required by law to have balanced budgets.

14. The balance of trade and the current accounts
    a. tend to be in surplus when the federal budget is in deficit.
    b. tend to be in deficit when the federal budget is in deficit.
    c. are unrelated to the federal budget deficit.
    d. are insensitive to movement in the interest rate.

15. Economists who are concerned about a third deficit believe that the 1980s saw too little spending in the areas of
    a. infrastructure.
    b. defense.
    c. investment in children.
    d. investment in both children and infrastructure.

TAKING ANOTHER LOOK

Expansionary fiscal policy can be quite popular, particularly with the groups receiving direct benefits. Often these groups exert a lot of pressure on their legislators to vote for bills calling for these activities, even if the overall macroeconomic effect is undesirable. They are driven by their private interests. In the fall of 1993, Newt Gingrich, the Republican minority whip in the House of Representatives commented that whatever the focus of such bills they could be considered "jobs bills." "You want to keep your job? Then vote for the bill."

CHECKING OUT

Now that you have finished studying this chapter, you should be able to:

1. Distinguish between a federal budget deficit and the national debt.
2. Explain the links between fiscal policy and the national debt, and why the national debt grew so rapidly during the 1980s.
3. Distinguish among the actual deficit, the structural deficit, and the cyclical deficit.
4. Discuss the pros and cons of running deficits and having a large national debt.
5. Explain why it is so difficult to reduce the deficit.

ANSWERS

Trying Out the Terms

1. C
2. F
3. B
4. D
5. G
6. A
7. E

Testing Yourself

Part I: True or False

1. false. In the nineteenth century the government frequently ran a surplus, and during the Civil War (as well as subsequent wars) it ran a deficit.
2. false. In most of these years it increased.
3. true
4. false. They were high in both real and nominal terms.
5. true
6. true
7. true
8. false. Structural deficits can occur at full employment.
9. true
10. true
11. true
12. false. The burden of the debt falls at the time it is created; that is when people have to give up the private goods and services in order to finance the public spending.
13. false. They both grew.
14. false. By and large, they had surpluses.
15. false. Only the national government can conduct fiscal policy.

Part II: Problem

1.

Y	G	Transfers	Tax	Surplus (Deficit)
$1,000	$200	$80	$200	$(80)
1,100	200	65	225	(40)
1,200	200	50	250	00 Balance
1,300	200	35	275	40
1,400	200	20	300	80

Part III: Multiple Choice

1. a
2. c
3. b
4. d
5. c
6. b
7. d
8. b
9. a
10. a
11. b
12. d
13. c
14. b
15. d

CHAPTER 10 EXERCISES

1. Using the following table, calculate the nominal deficit as a percentage of nominal GDP. Describe the behavior of this ratio during this period. How does it compare to its behavior during the following decade, as described in the text?

Year	Nominal GDP (in billions)	Nominal Deficit (in billions)	Deficit/GDP (%)
1972	$1,185.9	$23.4	_____
1973	1,326.4	14.9	_____
1974	1,434.2	4.6	_____
1975	1,549.2	45.1	_____
1976	1,718.0	66.4	_____

Source: Council of Economic Advisers, *Economic Report of the President* (Washington DC: U.S. Government Printing Office, 1981).

2. Using the following table, calculate the real deficit for each year. (Divide the change in debt by the GDP deflator.) Note that this table uses 1972 as a base year. What can be said about nominal deficits in the early 1970s?

Year	Change in Debt Outstanding (in billions)	GDP Deflator	Real Deficit (in billions)
1972	$27.8	1.00	_____
1973	31.1	1.06	_____
1974	17.8	1.15	_____
1975	57.9	1.26	_____
1976	87.7	1.32	_____

Source: Council of Economic Advisers, *Economic Report of the President* (Washington DC: U.S. Government Printing Office, 1981).

Chapter 10 Budget Deficits and the National Debt

CHAPTER 11

THE ROLE OF MONEY IN A MARKET ECONOMY

CHECKING IN

This chapter introduces the world of money. We are fascinated by money because it can be exchanged for things that we want. If others found our money unacceptable, it would not be so interesting. Money allows us to make purchases without resorting to the time-consuming practice of barter by serving as a medium of exchange.

In addition to expediting exchange, money serves other functions. It allows us to assign uniform values to different items serving as a value; it can also be a store of wealth.

Throughout history, items as various as shells, cattle, and rocks have been used as money. Generally, the goods we choose to use as money have certain desirable properties: scarcity, portability, durability, uniformity, divisibility, and acceptability.

Banks are closely associated with the use of money. Banking began when goldsmiths began to issue written promises for gold to people who left gold with them for safekeeping. These promises were the beginning of paper money and the ability of banks to create money.

Early in the history of the United States, money generally took the form of bank notes, which were written promises that could be exchanged for gold on demand. Today, the money supply is backed not by gold but by faith in the government, which has declared it legal tender. The money stock in the United States consists of currency in circulation, travelers' checks, and, the largest component, checkable deposits.

People want to hold money for many reasons. They need it to make routine transactions. This reason for holding money is called the *transactions demand for money;* it is positively related to real income. People also want to hold money as an asset. This reason for holding money is called the *asset demand for money;* it is negatively related to the interest rate.

Aggregate demand and, accordingly, prices and output are affected by changes in money demand and money supply.

TRYING OUT THE TERMS

Match each of the following terms with its definition, and then check your answers. If you are having trouble, go back to the text and find the definition there.

_____ 1. representative money

_____ 2. near money

_____ 3. legal tender

_____ 4. checkable deposits

_____ 5. barter

_____ 6. store of wealth

_____ 7. fiat money

_____ 8. money stock

_____ 9. M1 money supply

_____ 10. standard of value

_____ 11. full-bodied money

_____ 12. liquidity

_____ 13. token money

_____ 14. currency

_____ 15. M2 money supply

_____ 16. medium of exchange

_____ 17. money

A. Direct exchange of one good or service for another without the use of money.

B. A function of money in simplifying transactions by allowing people to exchange the goods and services they produce for money and then exchange money for other goods and services they want.

C. A function of money in providing a measuring unit in which goods can be valued and compared with each other and in providing a medium in which to write contracts for future payment.

D. A function of money in providing purchasing power in a generalized form that can be held in order to buy goods and services in the future.

E. The measure of how quickly a financial asset can be converted into the medium of exchange.

F. Any financial asset that serves as a medium of exchange, a standard of value, and a store of wealth.

G. Money that is redeemable in a commodity or commodities, such as gold.

H. Money that is not a commodity and not redeemable in commodities.

I. Money that, by law, must be accepted by private parties and governments in payment of debts and obligations.

J. Money that has a value in other uses equal to its monetary value.

K. Money whose monetary value is greater than its commodity value.

L. The amount of financial assets in existence at a particular time that perform the function of money as a medium of exchange.

M. Paper money with a specified value, issued by the government or a central bank.

N. Balances in accounts at depository institutions against which checks can be drawn.

O. Highly liquid financial assets that are very similar to those assets that are included in the money stock.

P. The total of all financial assets in the United States that function as a medium of exchange: currency, traveler's checks, demand deposits, and other checkable deposits.

Q. The total of M1 and small denomination time and savings deposits at all financial institutions, money market accounts, and a few other items.

TESTING YOURSELF

In the next two sections, you will answer questions and work problems that are based on information in the text. Master all of the terms before you begin these sections. Work each section without referring to your notes or the text, and then check your answers.

Part I: True or False

Mark each statement as true or false. Whenever you mark a statement as false, jot down a sentence stating why it is false.

_____ 1. If everyone on the Island of Where accepts coconut shells in exchange for other goods, then coconut shells are money in Where.

_____ 2. All financial assets having a value stated in dollars are considered money.

_____ 3. When money is used to avoid the need for a double coincidence of wants, it is being used in place of barter.

_____ 4. When money is used to compare the relative values of other goods, it is being used as a medium of exchange.

_____ 5. Typically, certificates of deposit are more liquid than money market accounts.

_____ 6. Liquidity refers to the ability of an asset to be converted easily and conveniently into money.

_____ 7. During a period of prolonged inflation, the value of money will increase.

_____ 8. One reason that you will accept a Federal Reserve note when you sell a textbook back to the bookstore is that you recognize it as money.

_____ 9. When your great-grandfather kept the family savings in the sugar bowl, he was using money as a standard of value.

_____ 10. In the Middle Ages when a merchant accepted a gold receipt as payment for a coat of armor, he was treating the receipt as money.

_____ 11. A Maple Leaf, a gold coin issued by the government of Canada, is an example of full-bodied money.

_____ 12. Greenbacks were Confederate currency not backed by gold.

_____ 13. If Rachel uses $500 from her checking account to make a $500 deposit in a money market fund, M1 will decrease and M2 will increase.

_____ 14. Currency represents the largest component of the M1 money supply.

_____ 15. M3 is the most liquid measure of the money stock.

_____ 16. The only reason people want to hold money is for transactions.

_____ 17. The desire to hold money to make transactions is positively related to the level of income.

_____ 18. Suppose people are holding one-fourth of GDP in the form of money. If they decide to increase their money holdings to one-third of GDP, k will increase.

_____ 19. If a sudden increase in demand for housing caused many people to expect the price of existing housing to increase, we would expect the asset demand for money to increase.

_____ 20. If velocity is constant, an increase in the money supply will cause the aggregate demand curve to shift to the right.

Part II: Multiple Choice

_____ 1. The basic requirement for a substance to serve as money is that it is
   a. durable.
   b. backed by a government.
   c. accepted by banks for deposit.
   d. accepted by both parties to an exchange.

_____ 2. Financial assets that are highly liquid
   a. usually have a higher yield than more liquid assets.
   b. can readily be exchanged for money.
   c. carry a high degree of risk.
   d. cannot be exchanged for money.

_____ 3. In an inflationary period,
   a. people are likely to hoard money.
   b. the value of money increases.
   c. people are likely to exchange money for real assets.
   d. people are unconcerned about their money holdings, since they are issued by the government.

_____ 4. A Federal Reserve note is accepted as money by most Americans because
   a. it is fully backed by gold.
   b. it is partially backed by both gold and silver.
   c. U.S. law establishes it as legal tender.
   d. it is commodity money.

_____ 5. The silver certificates issued by the United States government until 1963 were
   a. commodity money.
   b. representative money.
   c. high-yield money.
   d. fiat money.

_____ 6. In the United States, the official currency
   a. can be either Federal Reserve Notes or checkable deposits.
   b. is issued by national banks and state banks.
   c. is issued by national banks only.
   d. is issued by the central bank only.

_____ 7. A document that entitles the bearer to an amount of gold on demand at a bank is a
   a. certificate of deposit.
   b. bank note.
   c. gold certificate.
   d. Federal Reserve note.

_____ 8. During the 1980s, it became difficult to measure the size of the money supply because
   a. new types of bank accounts allowed people to write checks on interest-bearing accounts.
   b. there was an influx of foreign currencies into the banking system.
   c. the United States went off of the gold standard.
   d. inflation was constantly causing the value of money to change.

_____ 9. The M1 money supply includes
   a. small-denomination time deposits.
   b. certificates of deposit.
   c. money market accounts.
   d. checkable deposit accounts.

To complete Exercises 10–12, use the following information.

Component	Billions
Large-denomination time deposits	$541
Currency and coin	780
Demand deposits at commercial banks	1065
Repurchase agreements (long-term)	150
Money market mutual fund shares	206
Demand deposits at mutual savings banks	304
Small-denomination time and savings deposits	227
Credit union checkable deposits	45
Traveler's checks of non-bank issuers	23

_____ 10. M1 is how many billion dollars?
   a. $2,000
   b. $2,217
   c. $2,318
   d. $2,545

_____ 11. M2 is how many billion dollars greater than M1?
   a. $356
   b. $410
   c. $433
   d. $660

_____ 12. M3 is how many billion dollars?
   a. $2,112
   b. $2,545
   c. $3,086
   d. $3,341

_____ 13. Which of the following is *not* a motive for holding money?
   a. Transactions
   b. Assets
   c. Accumulation
   d. Neither transactions nor assets

____ 14. The classical quantity theory of money emphasizes the demand for money as a
   a. medium of exchange.
   b. standard of value.
   c. accounting unit.
   d. proxy for gold.

____ 15. $M_s = \$720$, $V = 4$, $Y = \$576$, $P =$ _____.
   a. 3
   b. 4
   c. 5
   d. P cannot be determined.

____ 16. $M_s = \$800$, $V =$ _____, $Y = \$600$, $P = 4$.
   a. 3
   b. 4
   c. 5
   d. V cannot be determined.

____ 17. $M_s =$ _____, $V = 8$, $Y = \$800$, $P = 7$.
   a. $300
   b. $500
   c. $700
   d. $900

____ 18. $M_s = \$3,720$, $V = 6$, $Y =$ _____, $P = 9$.
   a. $2,480
   b. $2,805
   c. $3,916
   d. Y cannot be determined.

____ 19. If the money supply increases, then
   a. prices will fall.
   b. people may decide not to hold the additional money.
   c. the increase will either be spent or be used to make loans.
   d. banks may choose to hold it in their vaults.

____ 20. A decrease in the demand for money will cause excessive money balances. This will result in
   a. a shift in the aggregate demand curve to the right; both price and real income will increase.
   b. a shift in the aggregate demand curve to the left; both price and real income will decrease.
   c. an increase in the supply of money.
   d. an increase in the level of risk associated with nonliquid assets.

TAKING ANOTHER LOOK

Some years since, Mademoiselle Zelie, a singer of the Theatre Lyriques at Paris, made a professional tour around the world, and gave a concert in the Society Islands. In exchange for an air from *Norma* and a few other songs, she was to receive a third part of the receipts. When counted, her share was found to consist of three pigs, twenty-three turkeys, forty-four chickens, five thousand cocoa-nuts, besides considerable quantities of bananas, lemons, and oranges. At Les Halles in Paris, this amount of livestock and vegetables might have brought four thousand francs, which would have been good remuneration for five songs. In the Society Islands, however, pieces of money were very scarce; and as Mademoiselle could not consume any considerable portion of the receipts herself, it became necessary in the mean time to feed the pigs and poultry with the fruit.

Stanley Jevons recounted this delightful story demonstrating the difficulties of barter in the first chapter of a famous book about money, *Money and the Mechanism of Exchange* (New York: D. Appleton and Company, 1890, 1–2), which he wrote in 1875. The book is a classic, and it discusses many of the concepts you have learned in this chapter. If you want to learn more about the history of money and banking, you should start with this book. It is probably in your school's library.

CHECKING OUT

Now that you have finished studying this chapter, you should be able to:

1. Describe the three functions of money and the properties that money should have in order to perform those functions well.

2. Discuss the role of banks in the production of money and the main components of the U.S. money supply.

3. Explain why people hold money and how they decide how much money to hold.

4. Determine equilibrium in the money market.

5. Analyze the relationship between changes in the demand for and supply of money and aggregate demand.

ANSWERS

Trying Out the Terms

1. G	5. A	9. P	13. K	17. F
2. O	6. D	10. C	14. M	
3. I	7. H	11. J	15. Q	
4. N	8. L	12. E	16. B	

Testing Yourself

Part I: True or False

1. true
2. false. *Money* refers to items that are generally accepted as means of payment.
3. true
4. false. It is being used as a standard of value.
5. false. Money market accounts are more liquid than certificates of deposit.
6. true
7. false. Inflation causes the value of money to decrease.
8. true
9. false. He was using it as a store of wealth.
10. true
11. true
12. false. Greenbacks were U.S. currency first issued during the Civil War and not redeemable in gold.
13. false. M1 will decrease, but M2 will be unchanged.
14. false. The largest component is deposits in checking accounts.
15. false. It is the least liquid measure.
16. false. Money is also demanded as an asset.
17. true
18. true
19. false. We would expect it to fall as people used money to buy houses.
20. true

Part II: Multiple Choice

1. d	5. b	9. d	13. c	17. c
2. b	6. d	10. b	14. a	18. a
3. c	7. b	11. c	15. c	19. c
4. c	8. a	12. d	16. a	20. a

Name _____

CHAPTER 11 EXERCISES

Exercises 1–10: Mark each statement as true or false. Whenever you mark a statement as false, jot down a sentence stating why it is false.

_____ 1. The function of money that avoids the problem of finding a double coincidence of wants is the unit of account function.

_____ 2. Near money is less liquid than M1.

_____ 3. If there were a sustained fall in prices, people would hoard money.

_____ 4. Liquidity is the most important criterion for determining what financial assets are a part of the money supply.

_____ 5. The velocity of money increased during the Great Depression.

_____ 6. If people wish to hold more money relative to GDP, k will increase.

_____ 7. Keynesians argue that velocity is unstable.

_____ 8. Most of the M1 money supply consists of Federal Reserve notes.

_____ 9. The demand for money is positively related to real income.

_____ 10. The demand for money is positively related to the interest rate.

_____ 11. Use the following information to calculate the levels of M1, M2, and M3.

Component	Billions
Noncommerical banks checkable deposits	$ 500
Money market mutual funds (non-institutional)	350
Term repurchase agreements at banks	275
Checkable deposits at banks	800
Overnight repurchase agreements at commercial banks plus overnight Eurodollars	545
Large-denomination time deposits ($100,000 or more) in banks and thrift institutions	625
Traveler's checks	32
Small-denomination time deposits in banks and thrift institutions	1,325
Currency	500
Savings deposits in banks and thrift institutions	725

M1 = _____

M2 = _____

M3 = _____

CHAPTER 12

BANKING AND THE FEDERAL RESERVE SYSTEM

CHECKING IN

This chapter discusses how the money supply is affected by the actions of banks and other depository institutions. When a bank makes a loan, it creates new money. When a bank calls a loan in, it shrinks the money supply. The banking system cannot expand the money supply indefinitely. In fractional reserve banking, banks have to keep a certain percentage of their deposits as reserves. The need for these reserves places an upper limit on the amount of money banks can create.

The central bank of the United States is the Federal Reserve System (the Fed). It was created in 1913 in response to a series of bank panics that occurred during the late ninteenth and early twentieth centuries. There are twelve Federal Reserve districts; each district has a Federal Reserve District Bank. The central authority of the system is the seven-member Board of Governors in Washington D.C.

In the years since the Federal Reserve System was created, its focus has changed. The original purpose of the Fed was to regulate its member banks and be a lender of last resort to them. Today, the Fed is mainly concerned with monetary policy. By implementing monetary policy, the Fed can affect interest rates, credit conditions, and the money supply. These in turn can influence output and the price level.

The Fed uses three tools to implement monetary policy: open market operations, changes in the reserve ratio, and changes in the discount rate. The Fed has a large portfolio of government bonds. By buying and selling these bonds, the Federal Open Market Committee can change the level of bank reserves. The Fed uses this tool most often in implementing monetary policy. The Fed dictates the amount of reserves that must be held by all financial institutions offering checking accounts. When the Fed raises the reserve ratio, banks and other institutions must hold more reserves; in order to get these reserves, they must call in loans, thereby shrinking the money supply. The final tool of the Fed is changing the discount rate—the interest rate charged by the Fed when it makes loans to other financial institutions.

TRYING OUT THE TERMS

Match each of the following terms with its definition, and then check your answers. If you are having trouble, go back to the text and find the definition there.

_____ 1. lender of last resort
_____ 2. discount rate
_____ 3. fractional reserve banking
_____ 4. open market operations
_____ 5. moral suasion
_____ 6. bank panics
_____ 7. excess reserves
_____ 8. Federal Reserve System (Fed)
_____ 9. Board of Governors
_____ 10. federal funds rate
_____ 11. reserves
_____ 12. deposit multiplier
_____ 13. federal funds market
_____ 14. T-accounts
_____ 15. reserve ratio
_____ 16. currency drain
_____ 17. Federal Open Market Committee (FOMC)

A. The practice of holding a fraction of money deposited as reserves and lending the rest.

B. Bank assets that can be used to pay depositors when checks are presented for payment, consisting of currency and reserve deposits at the central bank.

C. Partial balance sheets showing changes in assets and/or liabilities resulting from a transaction or group of transactions.

D. Reserves above the level required by law.

E. Fraction of deposits that banks are required to hold in reserves.

F. Ratio between the maximum increase in the money supply and a given increase in excess reserves. It equals the reciprocal of the reserve ratio.

G. An increase in currency holdings by the public that causes a dollar-for-dollar decline in bank reserves.

H. The central bank of the United States.

I. Sudden waves of fear that banks will not be able to pay off their depositors.

J. A source of funds for rescuing sound banks by lending them funds to meet temporary high demands from depositors.

K. Central governing body of the Federal Reserve System.

L. Committee that supervises the conduct of monetary policy.

M. Purchases and sales of U.S. Treasury securities on the open market by the Fed in order to affect bank reserves.

N. The interest rate the Fed charges on loans to banks.

O. The market in which banks borrow reserves from each other.

P. The interest rate charged in the federal funds market.

Q. Attempts by the Fed to convince depository institutions to do what the Fed favors.

TESTING YOURSELF

In the next three sections, you will answer questions and work problems that are based on information in the text. Master all of the terms before you begin these sections. Work each section without referring to your notes or the text, and then check your answers.

Part I: True or False

_____ 1. The principal interest-earning assets of a commercial bank are loans and government bonds.

_____ 2. Government securities are a form of reserves.

_____ 3. If the reserve ratio increases, excess reserves also increase.

_____ 4. Vault cash is an asset of a commercial bank.

_____ 5. If Rod Evans withdraws $100 in cash from his checking account, his bank's assets and liabilities both decline.

To complete exercises 6–7, use the following information: Friendly National Bank has checkable deposits of $5,000,000 and total reserves of $2,000,000. The reserve ratio is 20 percent.

_____ 6. The Friendly National Bank is fully loaned up.

_____ 7. The Friendly National Bank's required reserves are $2,000,000.

_____ 8. Banks must lend out all of their excess reserves.

_____ 9. The Federal Reserve System is the central bank of the United States.

_____ 10. All depository institutions fall under the control of the Federal Reserve System.

_____ 11. Only national banks are able to borrow from the Fed.

_____ 12. The discount rate and the federal funds rate are the same thing.

_____ 13. If the Fed sells securities on the open market, the money supply will decrease.

_____ 14. Open market operations are the Fed's most frequently used tool of monetary policy.

_____ 15. Currency withdrawals by the public will cause expansion of the money supply to be less than the possible maximum.

Part II: Problems

1. Sort the following accounts into the assets and liabilities of the Federal Reserve System, and complete the balance sheet. Be sure that your accounts balance.

Government securities	$300,902
Reserves of banks	40,825
Other assets	32,509
Federal Reserve notes	225,615
Loans to depository institutions	625
Gold certificates	10,500
Other liabilities	11,500
Treasury deposits	9,752

FEDERAL RESERVE BALANCE SHEET
(millions of dollars)

Assets		Liabilities and Net Worth	
		Total liabilities	$
		Net worth	
TOTAL ASSETS	$	TOTAL LIABILITIES AND NET WORTH	$

152 *Chapter 12 Banking and the Federal Reserve System*

2. Complete the following table. Assume that the reserve ratio is 15 percent and $15,000 is added to the bank's excess reserves.

INCREASE IN MONEY SUPPLY WITH INITIAL EXCESS RESERVES

Bank	Change in Checkable Deposits	Change in Reserves	Amount the Bank Lends
A	$ 0	$ 0	$ 15,000
B	_____	_____	_____
C	_____	_____	_____
D	_____	_____	_____
E	_____	_____	_____
F	_____	_____	_____
G	_____	_____	_____
All other	_____	_____	_____
All banks	$_____	$_____	$_____

Part III: Multiple Choice

____ 1. The largest liability for most banks is
   a. loans from the central bank.
   b. vault cash.
   c. checkable deposit accounts.
   d. certificates of deposit.

____ 2. If a bank sells a bond and uses the proceeds to make a loan, it has
   a. created a liability and an asset.
   b. exchanged one asset for another.
   c. exchanged one liability for another.
   d. decreased its net worth.

____ 3. When a bank lends money,
   a. it creates money.
   b. the money supply is unchanged.
   c. it decreases its available vault cash.
   d. it creates a liability and destroys an asset.

_____ 4. The banking system can expand the total number of loans
   a. as long as it wants to.
   b. as long as there are excess reserves in the system.
   c. only if it has the consent of the Fed.
   d. only if all banks are national banks.

_____ 5. The banking system is fully loaned up when
   a. there are no required reserves.
   b. all reserves have become required reserves.
   c. excess reserves exceed required reserves.
   d. required reserves exceed excess reserves.

_____ 6. If $rr = 0.12$, then an increase in excess reserves of $10,000 could cause the money supply to increase by as much as
   a. $10,000.
   b. $12,275.
   c. $83,333.
   d. $99,999.

_____ 7. Suppose the reserve ratio is 0.25 and total reserves in the banking system equal $200,000. What is the level of checkable deposits if the system is fully loaned up?
   a. $100,000
   b. $200,000
   c. $500,000
   d. $800,000

_____ 8. In the nineteenth century, banks
   a. could not make loans because there was no central bank.
   b. often issued bank notes that were redeemable in gold.
   c. had a 100 percent reserve requirement.
   d. were all chartered by the federal government.

_____ 9. The Federal Reserve System is modeled after the
   a. First United States Bank.
   b. World Bank.
   c. Bank of England.
   d. United States Constitution.

_____ 10. The Federal Reserve System
   a. was established by Alexander Hamilton.
   b. has twelve Federal Reserve districts.
   c. began operating in 1934.
   d. is directed by the Secretary of the Treasury.

_____ 11. When the Federal Open Market Committee buys a government security from a bank,
   a. reserves in the banking system increase.
   b. the deposit multiplier increases.
   c. the bank must call in existing loans.
   d. the money supply is unaffected, since a government security is not part of the money supply.

To complete Exercises 12–14, use the following information: The Silver National Bank of Spring Gulch, Nevada, has checkable deposits of $250,000 and total reserves of $75,000. The reserve ratio is 25 percent.

_____ 12. How much is the Silver National Bank required to hold as reserves?
   a. Nothing, since it is a national bank
   b. $25,000
   c. $50,000
   d. $62,500

_____ 13. The Silver National Bank can lend out as much as
   a. $12,500.
   b. $25,000.
   c. $50,000.
   d. $75,000.

_____ 14. In this system, the deposit multiplier is
   a. 2.5.
   b. 4.
   c. 5.
   d. impossible to determine.

_____ 15. The most frequently used tool of monetary control is
   a. moral suasion.
   b. the discount rate.
   c. open market operations.
   d. the reserve ratio.

TAKING ANOTHER LOOK

Every economy depends on a reliable supply of money. Yet, because the supply is so reliable, we rarely think much about where our money comes from. When you go to your bank to make a withdrawal, you have confidence that you will leave with currency. If the teller told you, "Not today, maybe next week," you would be justifiably angry, and so would the people you had intended to pay with that money.

In the spring of 1988, the United States government wanted to put political pressure on Panama to force a military leader from power. Panama uses U.S. currency as its national currency. The United States halted the shipment of money to Panama, which forced Panamanian banks to close. People could not get the funds they had deposited. The result was a great deal of financial distress for most of the residents of Panama. Many stores closed, people lost their jobs, and many began to barter to get what they needed.

Taking away the liquidity of an individual or a nation is certainly an effective means of influencing that individual or nation.

CHECKING OUT

Now that you have finished studying this chapter, you should be able to:

1. Explain how banks create money.

2. Analyze the role of reserves in money creation and control of the money supply.

3. Explain why a central bank is needed, and what functions the Fed performs for the banking system.

4. Describe the Fed's monetary policy tools and how they are used to influence the money supply and interest rates.

ANSWERS

Trying Out the Terms

1. J	5. Q	9. K	13. O	17. L
2. N	6. I	10. P	14. C	
3. A	7. D	11. B	15. E	
4. M	8. H	12. F	16. G	

Testing Yourself

Part I: True or False

1. true
2. false. Reserves are deposits at the central bank and vault cash.
3. false. Excess reserves would fall as some reserves were converted into required reserves.
4. true
5. true
6. false. The bank could make an additional $1,000,000 in loans.
7. false. Required reserves are $1,000,000.
8. false. Banks may choose to hold excess reserves because they want the additional liquidity or because they anticipate an increase in the interest rate.
9. true
10. true
11. false. All depository institutions enjoy this privilege.
12. false. The discount rate is the rate the Fed charges banks for loans; the federal funds rate is the market rate for borrowing between banks.
13. true
14. true
15. true

Part II: Problems

1.

FEDERAL RESERVE BALANCE SHEET
(millions of dollars)

Assets		Liabilities and Net Worth	
Government securities	$300,902	Reserves of banks	$ 40,825
Loans to depository		Federal Reserve notes	225,615
Federal institutions	625	Treasury deposits	9,752
Gold certificates	10,500	Other liabilities	11,500
Other assets	32,509		
		Total liabilities	$287,692
		Net worth	$ 56,844
TOTAL ASSETS	$344,536	TOTAL LIABILITIES AND NET WORTH	$344,536

2.

INCREASE IN MONEY SUPPLY WITH INITIAL EXCESS RESERVES

Bank	Change in Checkable Deposits	Change in Reserves	Amount the Bank Lends
A	$ 0.00	$ 0.00	$ 15,000.00
B	15,000.00	2,250.00	12,750.00
C	12,750.00	1,912.50	10,837.50
D	10,837.50	1,625.63	9,211.87
E	9,211.87	1,381.78	7,830.09
F	7,830.09	1,174.51	6,655.58
G	6,655.58	998.34	5,657.24
All others	37,714.96	5,657.24	17,057.72
All banks	$100,000.00	$15,000.00	$85,000.00

Part III: Multiple Choice

1. c
2. b
3. a
4. b
5. b
6. c
7. d
8. b
9. c
10. b
11. a
12. d
13. a
14. b
15. c

Name _____

CHAPTER 12 EXERCISES

Answer each of the following questions. You will need to do some research to find all of the answers.

1. What Federal Reserve District bank serves the town where your school is?

2. Who is the president of that bank?

3. Who is the chairman of the Board of Governors of the Federal Reserve System?

4. Which president appointed the chairman?

5. Who are the other members of the Board of Governors?

6. Identify one national bank and one state bank in the town where your school is located. If your school is in a small town, you may need to include several towns in your search.

7. What is the current federal funds rate?

Chapter 12   Banking and the Federal Reserve System

8. What is the current discount rate?

9. What is the current reserve ratio for large volumes of checkable deposits?

10. Who is the Secretary of the Treasury?

11. Suppose Bank A sells a bond to the Fed for $10,000. It immediately loans the money to a customer, who deposits the money in Bank A. Bank A then loans all of its excess reserves to an individual who deposits the loan in Bank B. This process continues, with each bank loaning out all of its excess reserves. Fill out the following table showing the effect of these changes on the banking system. In Table A, the reserve ratio is 10 percent. In Table B, the reserve ratio is 25 percent. Everything else is the same.

Table A: $rr = 0.10$

Bank	Change in Checkable Deposits	Change in Required Reserves
A	$ 10,000	$ _____
B	_____	_____
C	_____	_____
D	_____	_____
E	_____	_____
F	_____	_____
G	_____	_____
All others	_____	_____
All banks	$_____	$_____

160   Chapter 12 Banking and the Federal Reserve System

Table B: $rr = 0.25$

Bank	Change in Checkable Deposits	Change in Required Reserves
A	$ 10,000	$ _____
B	_____	_____
C	_____	_____
D	_____	_____
E	_____	_____
F	_____	_____
G	_____	_____
All others	_____	_____
All banks	$_____	$_____

CHAPTER 13

FINANCIAL MARKETS AND INTEREST RATES

CHECKING IN

The preceding chapter discussed how the Fed can affect the money supply through loans made by financial intermediaries. This chapter discusses these financial intermediaries, how they operate, and their role in the formation of aggregate demand.

The financial industry has experienced many changes since the late 1970s. Banking laws were revised to benefit banks, the Fed, and the consuming public. However, in the freer environment of the 1980s, many banks and saving and loans found themselves overextended and had to close or be sold to other institutions. The mass of banking difficulties led Congress to pass the Financial Institutions Reform, Recovery and Enforcement Act, generally known as the savings and loan bail out. This legislation attempted to provide for more stability in this industry.

The payment for the use of capital is interest. There is not just one interest rate, but a whole family of interest rates. These rates include not only the real rate of interest, the payment to capital, and the amount people are willing to pay for the right to spend now instead of later, but also differentials for such factors as risk and expectations about future prices. These expectations about inflation are reflected in the nominal rate of interest. It includes both the real rate and a premium for expected inflation. Nominal rates are set before inflation occurs. If expectations about inflation are wrong, the real rate of interest may be too high or even negative. The real rate is the nominal rate minus the expected or actual rate of inflation. The real rate is important in making investment decisions and borrowing money.

Though the focus of macroeconomics is on banks and other depository institutions, there are other important nonbank financial institutions and markets. The stock market allows firms to raise capital by selling ownership claims (shares of stock) to the public. Existing shares are also bought and sold in the stock market. Firms and governments also borrow both short-term and long-term money from the public. Short-term borrowing takes place in the money market, whereas long-term borrowing occurs in the bond market. The major participants in these nonbank markets are mutual funds, pension funds, and insurance companies (on the selling side) and businesses, households, and government (on the buying side).

Firms are the primary demanders in the financial markets, although households and governments also seek loans. Firms will consider the cost of borrowing money against the expected return from an investment project. If this return is greater than the market interest rate, they will invest in a project. As interest rates fall, more projects become feasible; therefore, the demand curve for investment is downward sloping. The investment intention of all firms will yield the investment demand schedule for the economy as a whole; this demand schedule is called the marginal efficiency of investment curve. It is through this schedule that we can see the relationship of money and aggregate demand.

When money is readily available and interest rates are low, firms are inclined to borrow more for investment. This increase in investment increases total expenditures and, through the expenditure multiplier, aggregate demand. Economists disagree on exactly how interest rates and money affect the aggregate demand curve. Their views are the subject of the next chapter.

TRYING OUT THE TERMS

Match each of the following terms with its definition, and then check your answers. If you are having trouble, go back to the text and find the definition there.

_____ 1. spread

_____ 2. yield

_____ 3. risk

_____ 4. market for loanable funds

_____ 5. real rate of interest

_____ 6. expected yield

_____ 7. stock market

_____ 8. risk premium

_____ 9. nominal rate of interest

_____ 10. marginal efficiency of investment (*MEG*) curve

_____ 11. bond market

_____ 12. stock

_____ 13. institutional investors

_____ 14. bond

_____ 15. investment demand schedule

_____ 16. capital gain

_____ 17. mutual fund

A. The difference between the average interest rate earned on bank loans and the average interest rate paid on deposits.

B. The market in which transactions between borrowers and lenders determine the interest rate and the volume of loans.

C. The difference between the interest rate charged the safest borrowers and those charged to less safe borrowers for the same length of time.

D. The rate of interest actually charged, without correction for inflation (also known as the market rate of interest).

E. The nominal rate of interest minus the expected rate of inflation.

F. The return on funds invested in an asset measured as a percentage of the price paid for the asset.

G. The rate of return on an asset that includes expected interest or dividends and the expected increase or decrease in price.

H. A measure of how much the actual yield on an asset may vary from the expected yield.

I. A financial market in which ownership claims on corporations are bought and sold.

J. An ownership claim in a corporation.

K. A market in which the debt instruments of governments and corporations are traded.

L. A debt instrument issued by a corporation or government agency with a fixed face value, annual interest payment, and maturity date.

M. An increase in the market price of an asset.

N. Large investors, including insurance companies, mutual funds, and pension funds, whose purchases and sales have a significant impact on the prices of investment assets.

O. A financial institution that pools money from many individuals in order to invest in a diversified portfolio of assets.

P. A graph that ranks possible investment projects for a firm in order of decreasing expected rate of return.

Q. A graph that represents the combined investment demand schedules for all firms in the economy, showing the volume of investment demand as a function of the expected rate of return.

TESTING YOURSELF

In the next three sections, you will answer questions and work problems that are based on information in the text. Master all of the terms before you begin these sections. Work each section without referring to your notes or the text, and then check your answers.

Part I: True or False

Mark each statement as true or false. Whenever you mark a statement as false, jot down a sentence stating why it is false.

_____ 1. Banking deregulation laws forced all banks and other financial institutions to become members of the Fed.

_____ 2. When oil prices dropped in the early 1980s, Houston banks profited by buying up abandoned houses at bargain prices.

_____ 3. A bank with a high level of reserves may still have to declare bankruptcy if its liabilities exceed its assets.

_____ 4. The interest rate is the price charged for borrowing.

_____ 5. The real interest rate tends to be higher and more volatile than the nominal interest rate.

_____ 6. If bankers are expecting inflation, they will want to lend out as much money as possible before it loses its value; the supply curve for loanable funds will shift to the right.

_____ 7. A stockholder in a profitable corporation can expect to be rewarded both by higher earnings and by capital gains.

_____ 8. Equity funds are the same as very long-term (over thirty years) debt.

_____ 9. Bonds are considered a riskier asset than stocks because they do not participate in the profits of the firm.

_____ 10. A nonbank financial intermediary acts as a perfect substitute for a commercial bank.

_____ 11. Mutual funds may invest in equities, but they cannot lend money.

_____ 12. Businesses base their borrowing decisions on a comparison of the market rate of interest and the expected return on the investment to be made with the borrowed funds.

_____ 13. If the market interest rate falls, we can anticipate an increase in both aggregate expenditure and aggregate demand.

_____ 14. Firms that invest without borrowing need not be concerned with the interest rate when making the investment decision.

_____ 15. The more open the economy, the less control its central bank can exert over the interest rate.

Part II: Problems

1. a. Find the prices of the following bonds.

Interest Payment	Yield	Price
$1,200	10%	_____
585	13%	_____
776	8%	_____

b. Find the yield on each of the following bonds.

Interest Payment	Yield	Price
$686	_____	$9,800
625	_____	12,500
1,430	_____	13,000

2. You may want to review the multiplier material in Chapter 8 before working this problem. Assume that prices do not change.

*/A Hypothetical *MEI* Schedule

Interest Rate (%)	Investment Demand (in billions)
8	$450
9	425
10	400
11	375
12	350
13	325
14	300
15	275
16	200

a. If the interest rate is initially 8 percent and then rises to 12 percent, how much will investment demand change?

b. Suppose $MPC = 0.8$ and the interest rate rises from 8 percent to 12 percent. What effect will this increase have on equilibrium national income (Y)?

c. Suppose $MPC = 0.9$, interest rate = 10 percent, $Y^* = \$5,000$ billion, and $Y = \$4,500$ billion. What will the interest rate have to be for the economy to move from Y to Y^*?

d. Suppose that $MPS = 0.25$, $Y^* = \$4,200$ billion, and $Y = \$4,300$ billion. The interest rate is 8 percent. At what new interest rate would the economy reach equilibrium at Y^*?

Part III: Multiple Choice

_____ 1. Which of the following was *not* a force underlying the banking deregulation of the 1980s?
   a. The presence of institutional investors
   b. High inflation rates
   c. The loss of member banks from the Federal Reserve System
   d. Competition with financial institutions from money market funds

_____ 2. The failure of thrift institutions during the 1980s was alleviated by
   a. issuing new equity stock in the stock markets.
   b. closing down all of the failing institutions.
   c. the development of larger, more diversified banks.
   d. selling the failing institutions to the Fed.

_____ 3. During the years of regulation, banks did not object to regulation because
   a. interest rates were high.
   b. they were protected from competition.
   c. they were protected from failure.
   d. they were protected both from failure and from competition.

_____ 4. Which of the following was *not* a factor contributing to the banking crisis?
   a. Loss of property values in Texas, Oklahoma, and Louisiana
   b. The failure of the FSLIC
   c. Growing Third World debt
   d. A high percentage of risky loans in savings and loan portfolios

_____ 5. Requiring a higher capital-to-loan ratio of lending institutions should make these institutions more cautious because
   a. they will have more money to loan.
   b. stockholders will have more to lose.
   c. their asset level will increase.
   d. All three of the above are reasons.

_____ 6. Savings and loans are weakened by a falling real estate market because
   a. they may be left with mortgages for more than the value of the underlying assets.
   b. they do not have adequate funds to meet growing demand.
   c. they are prohibited from participating in the real estate market.
   d. they are limited to making fixed-rate mortgage loans.

To complete Exercises 7–9, use the following information: Evelyn lends Sylvia $200 and charges her 8 percent interest. At the end of the year, Sylvia pays Evelyn $216.

_____ 7. If there is no inflation, what is the dollar value of the goods and services Evelyn can purchase when she is repaid?
   a. $200
   b. $208
   c. $216
   d. $233

_____ 8. If prices rise by 12 percent during the year, what is the approximate dollar value of the goods and services Evelyn can purchase when she is repaid?
   a. $216
   b. $208
   c. $200
   d. $193

_____ 9. If prices fall by 6 percent during the year, what is the dollar value of the goods and services Evelyn can purchase when she is repaid?
   a. $230
   b. $216
   c. $200
   d. $196

_____ 10. Which of the following is *not* a component of the interest rate?
   a. The inflation adjustment
   b. The capital adjustment
   c. The real rate of interest
   d. The risk premium

_____ 11. The supply of loanable funds is made up of
   a. savings.
   b. newly created money.
   c. money raised in the new equity markets.
   d. both savings and newly created money.

_____ 12. Corporations can raise new equity funds for investment by
   a. purchasing their own stock in the stock market.
   b. borrowing from their stockholders.
   c. issuing new shares of stock.
   d. selling existing shares of stock to other companies.

_____ 13. If Amy paid $833 for a bond with a face value of $1,000 and an annual income of $75, her yield on the bond is
   a. 7.5 percent.
   b. 8.33 percent.
   c. 9.0 percent.
   d. 10 percent.

_____ 14. If the interest rate fell, we would expect
   a. a movement down the *MEI* curve and increased investment.
   b. a shift to the right of the *MEI* curve and increased investment.
   c. a movement up the *MEI* curve and decreased investment.
   d. no change in investment.

_____ 15. All of the following are links between the stock market and overall economic activity *except* the
   a. presence of institutional investors in the market.
   b. presence of stocks in households' portfolios of assets.
   c. formation of expectations about the market.
   d. ability of firms to raise equity capital in the market.

TAKING ANOTHER LOOK

The banking crisis of the 1980s described in the text led to new reform legislation designed both to help the industry and to protect the public. In a similar way, in the 1930s Congress passed new laws governing both banks and the stock market. To find out more about the activities that precipitated this legislation you might check *The Embezzler* by Louis Auchincloss out of your library. This book, published in 1968, is narrated by the man who believes that his activities alone caused Congress to make its move. He's an egocentric fellow. While the book is fiction, it accurately reflects activities that make the financial shenanigans of the 1970s and 1980s look pretty tame.

CHECKING OUT

Now that you have finished studying this chapter, you should be able to:

1. Explain the problems that led to the policy decision to bail out failing banks in the late 1980s and early 1990s.

2. Identify the various kinds of interest rates, the factors that result in different rates on different financial instruments, and the relationship between bond prices and bond yields.

3. Describe the role of the stock and bond markets in transforming saving into investment.

4. Discuss the effect of interest rates on investment spending, output, and income.

ANSWERS

Trying Out the Terms

1. A	5. E	9. D	13. N	17. O
2. F	6. G	10. Q	14. L	
3. H	7. I	11. K	15. P	
4. B	8. C	12. J	16. M	

Testing Yourself

Part I: True or False

1. false. However, they did bring them more directly under the regulation of the Fed.
2. false. Houston banks were badly hurt when homes were abandoned and the mortgages held by the banks were abandoned as well.
3. true
4. true
5. false. The real interest rate is usually lower and more stable than the nominal rate. See Table 4 in the text.
6. false. They realize that they will be repaid in cheaper dollars and thus will be willing to lend only at higher interest rates; the supply curve will shift to the left.
7. true
8. false. Equity funds represent ownership in the firm and are never repaid.
9. false. Bonds are considered safer because they have a guaranteed interest payment, which must be made before owners receive any profit.
10. false. Although nonbank financial intermediaries can provide many banking services, particularly in the area of lending, they do not provide money as a medium of exchange.
11. false. They lend money when they invest in bonds or money market instruments. There are some mutual funds that specialize in these activities.
12. true
13. true
14. false. Firms must consider the interest they might receive on alternative investments. One way of looking at this is to think of the firm as lending money to itself.
15. true

Part II: Problems

1. a. $12,000, $4,500, $9,700
   b. 7 percent, 5 percent, 11 percent
2. a. It will decrease by $100 billion.
   b. Y will decrease by $500 billion (the $100 million decrease in investment times the multiplier of 5).
   c. The interest rate must fall to 8 percent. Y must increase by $500 billion. The multiplier is 10; therefore, investment must rise by $50 billion. This will require a 2 percent reduction in the interest rate.
   d. The interest rate must rise to 9 percent. The multiplier is 4. Since Y must fall by $100 billion, investment must fall by $25 billion. This fall will occur with an interest rate of 9 percent.

Part III: Multiple Choice

1. a
2. c
3. d
4. b
5. b
6. a
7. c
8. d
9. a
10. b
11. d
12. c
13. c
14. a
15. a

Name _____

CHAPTER 13 EXERCISES

1. Interest rate and inflation data for France and Switzerland are shown below.

   a. Calculate the real interest rate in each country.

   France

Year	Bond Yields	Inflation	Real Interest Rate
1981	15.79	13.4	_____
1982	15.69	11.8	_____
1983	13.63	9.6	_____
1984	12.54	7.4	_____
1985	10.94	5.8	_____
1986	8.44	2.5	_____
1987	9.43	3.3	_____

   Switzerland

Year	Bond Yields	Inflation	Real Interest Rate
1981	5.7	6.5	_____
1982	4.83	5.57	_____
1983	4.52	3.0	_____
1984	4.70	2.9	_____
1985	4.78	3.4	_____
1986	4.29	0.8	_____
1987	4.12	1.4	_____

   Source: U.S. Department of Commerce, *Statistical Abstract of the United States, 1987, 1989* (Washington DC: U.S. Government Printing Office, 1987, 1989).

   b. Why was the nominal interest rate higher in France than in Switzerland?

c. Why was the real interest rate higher in France than in Switzerland?

d. Why was the real interest rate negative in Switzerland in 1981 and 1982?

CHAPTER 14

MONETARY POLICY IN THEORY AND PRACTICE

CHECKING IN

By changing the money supply, the Fed can affect the economy. Keynesians and monetarists disagree, however, on exactly *how* these changes influence output and prices. This disagreement is the subject of this chapter.

Keynesians believe that changes in the money supply affect output and prices through the interest rate. An increase in the money supply leads to lower interest rates. Lower interest rates encourage investment. Investment increases total expenditures both directly and indirectly (through the multiplier), thereby raising the level of both prices and output. Keynesians do not see monetary policy as a very strong tool and prefer to use it as a complement to fiscal policy.

Monetarists believe that monetary policy is a very strong tool. Monetarists think that an increase in the money supply causes people to have excess cash balances. As individuals spend this excess cash, total expenditures increase, leading to a higher level of price, output, or both.

When the Fed undertakes monetary policy, it can focus on either the interest rate or the money supply. It cannot affect both simultaneously because an increasing money supply should, at least temporarily, lower interest rates.

Monetary policy has some drawbacks. Once a problem is recognized, policy can be implemented quickly, but it may take an unpredictably long time for the policy to fully affect the economy. Monetary decision makers are subjected to hard political pressures; many groups are hurt by contractionary monetary policy, and they try hard to prevent its implementation. Because of these problems, some economists, particularly monetarists, feel that the Fed should follow a rule of monetary growth. Such a rule would require the Fed to increase the money supply at a steady, predetermined rate, eliminating discretionary monetary policy.

The government usually has some ideal, or target, level of nominal GDP as a goal when it undertakes monetary policy. Although GDP is the primary target, the government must choose among a number of intermediate targets, such as the various measures of money supply and interest rates. Monetary policy does not directly affect GDP, but it is transmitted through financial markets into the real sector.

TRYING OUT THE TERMS

Match each of the following terms with its definition, and then check your answers. If you are having trouble, go back to the text and find the definition there.

_____ 1. transmission mechanism

_____ 2. monetary rule

_____ 3. free reserves

_____ 4. monetarists

_____ 5. GDP targeting

_____ 6. The Accord

_____ 7. monetary base

_____ 8. money multiplier

A. The process by which a change in the money supply is transformed into changes in demand, output, and the price level.

B. Economists who emphasize the role of money and monetary policy as the important influence on the price level and inflation.

C. The ratio of the actual money supply to the monetary base.

D. The currency in the hands of the public plus reserves held by banks.

E. A monetary policy that calls for the Fed to aim at some level of nominal GDP by influencing a number of variables that affect GDP.

F. A proposed regulation requiring the Fed to make the money supply grow at some predetermined, steady rate.

G. The 1951 agreement between the Fed and the Treasury that the Fed was no longer obliged to hold interest rates low in order to assist with the Treasury's debt financing.

H. Excess bank reserves minus loans from the Fed to member banks.

TESTING YOURSELF

In the next three sections, you will answer questions and work problems that are based on information in the text. Master all of the terms before you begin these sections. Work each section without referring to your notes or the text, and then check your answers.

Part I: True or False

Mark each statement as true or false. Whenever you mark a statement as false, jot down a sentence stating why it is false.

_____ 1. Although monetarists and Keynesian economists disagree on how monetary policy affects aggregate demand, there are areas of agreement between the two groups.

_____ 2. According to the Keynesian view, monetary policy affects real GDP through consumer spending.

_____ 3. A monetarist would say that an increase in consumption will follow an increase in cash balances.

_____ 4. To decrease the monetary base, the Fed can buy securities in the open market.

_____ 5. When the Fed sets an interest rate target, it focuses on the prime rate.

_____ 6. If the Fed wishes to keep the interest rate from rising, it must drain reserves from the banking system.

_____ 7. Changes in M1 appear to be more closely linked to changes in the monetary base than are changes in M2.

_____ 8. Keynesians believe the money demand curve slopes downward because more money is available to borrow as interest rates fall.

_____ 9. Monetarists maintain that it is possible to predict the response of households to changes in the money supply.

_____ 10. Monetarists generally believe that the best macroeconomic policy to follow is to leave the economy alone.

_____ 11. If foreigners decide to hold lots of U.S. dollars because interest rates are high in the United States, the value of the dollar will increase.

_____ 12. If the United States were to go back onto the international gold standard, discretionary monetary policy would be replaced by a monetary rule.

_____ 13. Even though the Fed kept the interest rate low during the early years of the depression, the money supply fell sharply.

_____ 14. The 1951 Accord between the Fed and the Treasury permitted the Fed to use monetary policy for stabilization efforts.

_____ 15. When he became chairman of the Federal Reserve Board, Alan Greenspan's first concern was controlling inflation.

Part II: Problems

1. M1 = $3,000 billion
   M2 = $9,000 billion
   B = $1,500 billion

   a. What is the M1 mulitiplier? _____

   b. What is the M2 multiplier? _____

2. B = $2,000 billion
   M1 multiplier = 5
   M2 multiplier = 10

   a. What is M1? _____

   b. What is M2? _____

3. M1 = $5,000 billion
   M1 mulitiplier = 4
   M2 multiplier = 8

   a. What is B? _____

   b. What is M2? _____

Part III: Multiple Choice

1. Classical economists explain how monetary policy affects aggregate demand by stressing
   a. the demand for cash.
   b. the role of interest rates.
   c. the equilibrium of money supply and money demand.
   d. both the demand for cash and the equilibrium of money supply and money demand.

2. In the Keynesian version of the transmission mechanism, monetary policy works through
   a. interest rates.
   b. consumer demand.
   c. investment demand.
   d. both interest rates and investment demand.

3. In the Keynesian model, monetary policy works by
   a. shifting *AS*.
   b. shifting *AE*.
   c. shifting *AD*.
   d. shifting both *AE* and *AD*.

4. If the Federal Reserve creates excess bank reserves, banks are likely to
   a. call in loans to cover reserves.
   b. raise interest rates.
   c. lower interest rates.
   d. raise service charges.

5. If the demand for money is highly sensitive to changes in the interest rate, a small decrease in the interest rate will cause
   a. people to buy more bonds.
   b. people to hold much more money.
   c. the money supply to fall.
   d. the aggregate supply curve to shift to the left.

6. If the expected yield on corporate bonds and other interest-bearing assets increases, the demand for money will
   a. be unaffected.
   b. increase until yields begin to fall.
   c. decrease.
   d. decrease briefly and then increase.

7. Suppose $M_s = \$9,000$, $B = \$3,000$, and m is constant. If B increases to $\$3,500$, how will M_s will change as a result?
   a. Increase by $500
   b. Increase by $1,000
   c. Increase by $1,500
   d. The result cannot be determined without knowing the value of m.

8. One obstacle the Fed faces in using a money supply target is that
   a. it cannot control the monetary base.
   b. it cannot control interest rates unless it controls the monetary base.
   c. the money multiplier is not under its control.
   d. M1 is unrelated to the monetary base.

9. Compared to fiscal policy, monetary policy has
   a. no lags.
   b. a shorter recognition lag, but a stronger implementation lag.
   c. a longer implementation lag, but no impact lag.
   d. a shorter implementation lag, but a longer impact lag.

10. When the Fed targets the interest rate
    a. it also targets the monetary base.
    b. it must make constant adjustments in the monetary base.
    c. it also targets stock prices.
    d. it loses control of the reserve requirement.

11. When monetary policy is tight, the sectors most likely to be affected are
    a. consumer durables and consumer nondurables.
    b. business investment and consumer nondurables.
    c. state and local governments.
    d. business investment, state and local governments, and consumer durables.

12. If an economy is open, then monetary policy
    a. becomes more effective.
    b. must be used along with fiscal policy.
    c. becomes less effective.
    d. is not affected in any way.

13. Although it is an independent agency, the Fed
    a. may be subject to political pressures from Congress.
    b. must follow the direction of Congress when there is a two-thirds vote.
    c. must follow the direction of the president in times of war.
    d. is often pressured by the banking industry to follow a tighter monetary policy.

14. In the early years of the Federal Reserve's existence, its primary function was to
    a. set the standards for the establishment of new banks.
    b. act as a participant in currency markets to maintain the value of the dollar relative to the English pound.
    c. set an upper limit on the size of the money supply in a fixed ratio to U.S. gold holdings.
    d. maintain the interest rate at an artificially high level.

_____ 15. In October 1979, the Fed
   a. came under the direct control of Congress.
   b. abandoned the gold standard.
   c. began to focus policy on the growth of the money supply.
   d. changed its focus from money supply to interest rates.

CHECKING OUT

Now that you have finished studying this chapter, you should be able to:

1. Explain how monetary policy works both directly and through changes in the interest rate to affect output, employment, and the price level.

2. Identify some of the difficulties in making monetary policy effective.

3. Summarize the debate over the appropriate targets for monetary policy.

4. Describe the main policy actions of the Fed over the last few decades.

ANSWERS

Trying Out the Terms

1. A   5. E
2. F   6. G
3. H   7. D
4. B   8. C

Testing Yourself

Part I: True or False

1. true
2. false. Keynesians hold that monetary policy affects aggregate demand through investment.
3. true
4. false. Buying securities increases the monetary base.
5. false. The Fed targets the federal funds rate.
6. false. It must put reserves into the system.
7. false. There appears to be a closer link between M2 and B.
8. false. As interest rates fall, people *want* to borrow more money. As interest rates rise, more money is available to borrow.
9. true
10. true
11. true
12. true
13. true
14. true
15. true

Part II: Problems

1. a. 2
   b. 6
2. a. $10,000 billion
   b. $20,000 billion
3. a. $1,250 billion
   b. $10,000 billion

Part III: Multiple Choice

1. d	5. b	9. d	13. a
2. d	6. c	10. b	14. c
3. d	7. c	11. d	15. c
4. c	8. c	12. c	

Name _____

CHAPTER 14 EXERCISES

In Exercises 1–5, mark each statement as true or false. Whenever you mark a statement as false, jot down a sentence stating why it is false.

_____ 1. Keynesians generally believe that monetary policy should be used to target the interest rate.

_____ 2. If interest rates fall, we would expect the price of bonds to fall also.

_____ 3. Monetary policy will be more effective when investment is very sensitive to the interest rate.

_____ 4. When the Fed increases bank reserves, banks are forced to make new loans.

_____ 5. The Humphrey-Hawkins Act of 1978 requires the Fed to report monetary growth targets for the year to Congress.

_____ 6. Keynes argued that investment
   a. was not very sensitive to changes in the interest rate.
   b. was completely insensitive to changes in the interest rate.
   c. was unrelated to national income (Y).
   d. affected income only when it was paid for with borrowed money.

_____ 7. An increase in the money supply is likely to lead to
   a. a fall in Y with no change in the price level.
   b. an increase in the price level with no change in Y.
   c. an increase in Y and an increase in the price level.
   d. Any of the above.

_____ 8. When the Fed targets GDP, it
   a. is engaging in fiscal policy.
   b. must choose intermediate targets since it cannot control GDP directly.
   c. may target interest rates but not the money supply.
   d. can control a recession but not inflation.

_____ 9. In 1993, Alan Greenspan announced that the Fed would emphasize
   a. M2 only.
   b. both M1 and M2.
   c. real interest rates.
   d. the flexible mortgage rate.

_____ 10. The transition to a unified Germany
   a. caused German currency to increase in value.
   b. was accompanied by large government deficits.
   c. created jobs in both former East Germany and West Germany.
   d. had little financial impact on the European Community.

CHAPTER 15

CURRENT ISSUES IN STABILIZATION POLICY

CHECKING IN

If many individuals each make decisions based on personal needs and returns, the outcome for a whole group (in this case, a country) may not be satisfactory to a majority of the group. When this happens, people expect government to improve the situation. When these problems affect the economy, the government responds by formulating and implementing macroeconomic policies.

This chapter begins by examining the disagreements between Keynesians and monetarists about appropriate macroeconomic policy. Monetarists believe that the expenditure multiplier is unstable and that long-run velocity is very stable. These conditions would make monetary policy very effective. Keynesians, of course, disagree. Historical data indicate that, over time, both the multiplier and velocity are stable, although there may be substantial short-run changes.

Even if the expenditure multiplier is stable, fiscal policy may be rendered ineffective if crowding out occurs. This situation arises when government borrowing competes with private investment in the market for loanable funds. As the interest rate rises, investment falls, offsetting the increase in government spending. Monetarists believe that no matter how the deficit is financed, fiscal policy cannot be effective. Taxing to pay for government spending reduces the impact of fiscal policy, and creating money to pay for government spending is just another form of monetary policy (expanding the money supply).

The two big problems addressed by macroeconomic policies are inflation and unemployment. The Phillips curve traces the relationship between the two. Until the 1970s, it appeared that unemployment could be lowered at the cost of higher inflation. Since the 1970s, this relationship appears to have changed. Milton Friedman suggests that a long-run Phillips curve is vertical at an output level consistent with the natural rate of unemployment.

Many issues in macroeconomics remain unresolved. The chapter concludes with a review of the differences and agreements between classical and Keynesian economists.

TRYING OUT THE TERMS

Match each of the following terms with its definition, and then check your answers. If you are having trouble, go back to the text and find the definition there.

_____ 1. auction markets   _____ 5. adaptive expectations

_____ 2. accommodating monetary policy   _____ 6. Phillips curve

_____ 3. natural rate of unemployment   _____ 7. contract markets

_____ 4. insider-outsider model

A. Monetary expansion that is undertaken to help the Treasury to finance deficits without driving interest rates up too much.

B. A graph showing the relationship between the rates of inflation and unemployment for a country over a specified period of years.

C. An explanation of labor market behavior that assumes that insiders (employed union members) will negotiate for higher wage rates for themselves at the expense of outsiders, thus worsening the inflation-unemployment trade-off.

D. The rate of unemployment that is determined by frictional and structural factors and toward which the economy tends to return.

E. Expectations about the future that are formed by economic factors on the basis of current and recent past experience and that adjust slowly to changing conditions.

F. Markets characterized by good information, many buyers and sellers, and rapid adjustment of prices to changing conditions.

G. Markets characterized by imperfect information, few buyers and sellers, long-term contracts, and sluggish price adjustments.

TESTING YOURSELF

In the next three sections, you will answer questions and work problems that are based on information in the text. Master all of the terms before you begin these sections. Work each section without referring to your notes or the text, and then check your answers.

Part I: True or False

Mark each statement as true or false. Whenever you mark a statement as false, jot down a sentence stating why it is false.

_____ 1. Thomas Schelling maintains that as a group gets larger, the individual members have less effect on aggregate outcomes.

_____ 2. Keynesians believe that velocity is basically unstable.

_____ 3. Crowding out does not occur in the Keynesian model.

_____ 4. Crowding out was made worse during the 1980s because foreigners provided funds to American markets.

_____ 5. Financing a government deficit by borrowing is more likely to lead to crowding out than is financing by selling excess government bonds to the Fed.

_____ 6. Robert Barro believes that because people have rational expectations, they will view government spending financed by borrowing as more acceptable than government spending financed by taxes.

_____ 7. The United States has endured both inflation and high unemployment during the last twenty years.

_____ 8. The Phillips curve illustrates the trade-off between monetary policy and fiscal policy.

_____ 9. The long-run Phillips curve is identical to the short-run Phillips curve.

_____ 10. The insider-outsider model indicates that widespread union bargaining will lead to higher inflation during an economic upturn.

_____ 11. Milton Friedman maintains there is never a trade off between inflation and unemployment.

_____ 12. The Keynesian focus is on short-term policy concerns.

_____ 13. When people base their expectations about the future on what happened to them in the past, they are forming rational expectations.

_____ 14. Auction markets take place when buyers and sellers are brought together in one location.

_____ 15. Different economic policies tend to benefit different economic groups.

Part II: Problem

1. Suppose the economy shown in the following graph is operating at an equilibrium output of Y^* and price level of P_1. At this level of output, the unemployment rate is 10 percent. The government attempts to reduce this unemployment rate to 7 percent by pursuing policies to increase aggregate demand.

    a. Graph the path of equilibrium prices and output if the natural rate of unemployment is 10 percent and the government remains committed to a policy aimed at 7 percent unemployment.

    b. The aggregate demand curve shifts because of the expansionary demand management policy. Why does the aggregate supply curve shift?

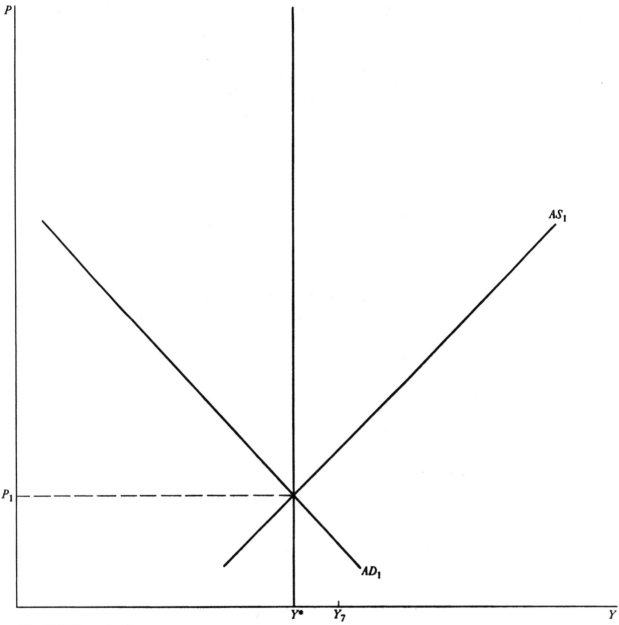

Y^* – 10% Unemployment
Y_7 – 7% Unemployment

Part III: Multiple Choice

1. Thomas Schelling maintains that
    a. people make individual choices without considering the choices of others.
    b. people consider the choices of a large group when making individual choices.
    c. when people make self-interested personal choices, their combined choices will result in the best outcome for the group.
    d. people take interdependence effects into account when making individual decisions.

2. If everyone in an economy had pessimistic expectations, it would be possible that
   a. their expectations would be offsetting and the economy would not change.
   b. increased saving and reduced consumption could actually bring on a recession.
   c. the collective action of many individuals would dampen the effects of a recession.
   d. market forces would offset the interdependencies.

3. If the sum of our collective and individual decisions leads to an unsatisfactory level of output, prices, and employment, economists may
   a. recommend that market forces be allowed to bring about a correction.
   b. call for strong government intervention with fiscal and monetary policy.
   c. recommend a small role for the government and deregulation of industries.
   d. call for some or all of these actions, depending on which school of thought is followed.

4. Monetarists feel that the MPC is not constant because
   a. the money supply is not constant.
   b. investment demand is not stable.
   c. it is affected by fiscal policy.
   d. households increase consumption when cash balances increase.

5. If we observe a complete crowding out in the loanable funds market, then the supply curve of loanable funds
   a. is upward sloping.
   b. is vertical.
   c. is horizontal.
   d. has shifted to the right.

6. Which of the following economic problems has occurred in the United States during the last twenty years?
   a. Large federal deficits
   b. High unemployment
   c. A fluctuating dollar
   d. High inflation
   e. All of the above

7. According to the original Phillips curve studies, inflation could be reduced by
   a. lowering taxes.
   b. increasing unemployment.
   c. increasing the money supply.
   d. engaging in tax incentive plans.

8. The original research underlying the Phillips curve was based on data from
   a. the United States between 1910 and 1950.
   b. Great Britain between 1861 and 1913.
   c. Australia between 1946 and 1976.
   d. Canada between 1850 and 1950.

9. The Phillips curve suggests that
   a. rising output can be accompanied by stable prices.
   b. inflation increases as the unemployment rate falls.
   c. there is a tradeoff between inflation and unemployment.
   d. fiscal policy is less inflationary than monetary policy.

10. During the 1970s, random shocks to the U.S. economy caused
    a. increases in aggregate demand and aggregate supply.
    b. increase in prices and unemployment.
    c. a shift of the Phillips curve to the right.
    d. increases in prices and unemployment, which caused the Phillips curve to shift to the right.

11. If workers expect less inflation than actually occurs,
    a. the Phillips curve will shift to the right.
    b. unemployment will fall below the natural rate.
    c. prices will fall.
    d. there will be a movement to the right along the Phillips curve.

12. During an inflationary period, a firm that does not increase prices should experience
    a. falling inventories.
    b. rising inventories.
    c. short-run profits.
    d. falling supplier prices.

13. In his analysis of the Phillips curve, Milton Friedman concludes that the long-run Phillips curve
    a. does not exist.
    b. is horizontal.
    c. is vertical.
    d. is identical to the short-run Phillips curve.

14. Regarding the manner in which the economy adjusts from one equilibrium situation to another, monetarists argue that
    a. private markets are unreliable and will not adjust at the right speed.
    b. government intervention would not lead to overall improvement and would probably be costly and inefficient.
    c. private markets are reliable and will adjust at the right speed, on average.
    d. private markets are reliable and will adjust at the right speed, on average, and government intervention would not lead to overall improvement and would probably be costly and inefficient.

15. The labor market will be in long-run equilibrium at the natural rate of unemployment when
    a. aggregate demand equals aggregate supply.
    b. the growth rate of the money supply is equal to the underlying rate of inflation.
    c. the inflation rate expected by workers and the economy's actual inflation rate are equal.
    d. the actual inflation rate is greater than what workers expect it to be.

CHECKING OUT

Now that you have finished studying this chapter, you should be able to:

1. Explain why the relative stability of velocity and the multiplier is important for the relative effectiveness of monetary and fiscal policy.

2. Discuss the impact of a policy of financing increased government spending by taxes rather than borrowing from the public or expanding the money supply.

3. Describe the shape of the Phillips curve and explain its usefulness and limitations as a way to guide or interpret demand management policy.

4. Explain why the differences between rational and adaptive expectations, and auction and contract markets, are important for the effectiveness of stabilization policy.

5. Summarize the main differences and areas of agreement between contemporary economists in the Keynesian tradition and the classical/monetarist tradition.

ANSWERS

Trying Out the Terms

1. F
2. A
3. D
4. C
5. E
6. B
7. G

Testing Yourself

Part I: True or False

1. true
2. true
3. true
4. false. The presence of foreign funds reduced the direct competition between government and business borrowing; crowding out was lessened.
5. true
6. false. Barro argues that the method of financing government spending has no impact on private spending.
7. true
8. false. The Phillips curve illustrates the relationship between inflation (or wage growth) and unemployment.
9. false. The long-run Phillips curve is steeper than the short-run Phillips curve.
10. true
11. false. Friedman allows that there is a temporary trade-off, but no permanent trade-off.
12. true
13. false. They are forming adaptive expectations.
14. false. Auction markets are those with many buyers and sellers, good information, and rapid price adjustments.
15. true

Part II: Problem

1. a.

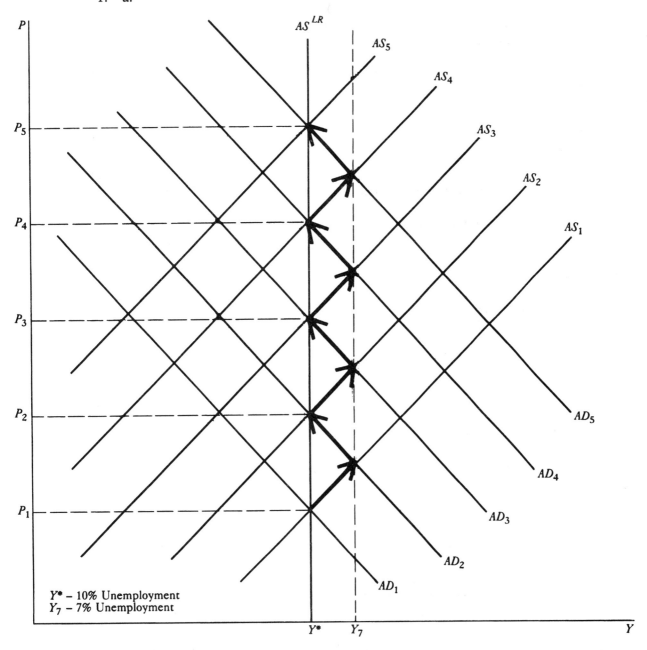

b. The short-run aggregate supply curve is based on expectations of stable prices. When workers realize that the price level has increased, they will demand higher wages for producing the same amount. Business firms will increase prices to cover the rising costs. The short-run aggregate supply curve will shift to the left.

Part III: Multiple Choice

1. a
2. b
3. d
4. d
5. b
6. e
7. b
8. b
9. c
10. d
11. b
12. a
13. c
14. d
15. c

CHAPTER 15 EXERCISES

1. Both of the following graphs show an increase in demand for loanable funds following a change to an expansionary fiscal policy that is financed by deficits.

    a. On the left-hand graph, draw a supply curve for loanable funds that will provide for complete crowding out in the loanable funds market. Label the original equilibrium interest rate and the new equilibrium interest rate.

    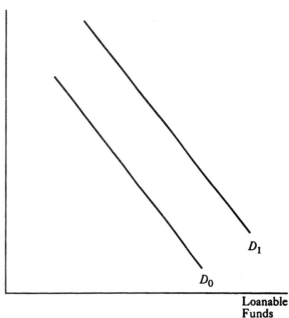

    b. On the right-hand graph, draw a supply curve for loanable funds that allows for partial crowding out. Label the original equilibrium interest rate and the new equilibrium interest rate.

    c. Why isn't crowding out complete in the right-hand graph?

Chapter 15   Current Issues in Stabilization Policy

CHAPTER 16

AGGREGATE SUPPLY, ECONOMIC GROWTH, AND MACROECONOMIC POLICY

CHECKING IN

Previous chapters have discussed aggregate supply, but their focus has been on aggregate demand and the techniques of demand management. This chapter concentrates on policies that can affect the aggregate supply curve.

Debate exists over the shape of the aggregate supply curve. The effects of a shift in the aggregate demand curve depend on the shape of the aggregate supply curve.

Although the idea of a vertical long-run aggregate supply curve is generally accepted, economists disagree about both the shape of the curve in the short run and the length of the short run. The short-run aggregate supply curve may be upward sloping because imperfect market information and rigidities in the system, such as long-term contracts, slow responses to changes in aggregate demand. When expectations are correct and markets adjust quickly, the short run may be very short. A long-run vertical supply curve means that changes in aggregate demand can affect only prices, not output, in the long run.

Economists agree that long-term economic growth requires shifting the aggregate supply curve to the right. This shift has the welcome effects of lower prices and higher output. Changes in the quantity and quality of available resources and improvements in technology can shift the curve. Economists disagree about how to bring about these changes.

Supply side economists call for policies that encourage market efficiency and increased productivity. These policies center on work incentives, saving and investing incentives, and entrepreneurial incentives such as deregulation. Many of the policies enacted during the presidency of Ronald Reagan were supply side in nature.

Another approach to shifting the aggregate supply curve, industrial policy, relies less on the market and more on government intervention. Like supply side policy, industrial policy stresses tax policy and production incentives, but it also gives special attention to selected industries.

TRYING OUT THE TERMS

Match each of the following terms with its definition, and then check your answers. If you are having trouble, go back to the text and find the definition there.

_____ 1. tax wedge

_____ 2. productivity

_____ 3. supply side economics

_____ 4. demand-based growth strategies

_____ 5. innovation

_____ 6. industrial policy

_____ 7. savings rate

_____ 8. real business cycle

A. Policies attempting to increase the level of output over time by shifting the aggregate demand curve to the right.

B. The ratio of combined business, household, and government saving to GDP.

C. The translation of inventions into products and processes that are commercially feasible and cost-effective.

D. A cyclical pattern of economic activity resulting from changes in aggregate supply rather than aggregate demand.

E. A measure of output per worker hour.

F. Branch of economics that advocates a specific group of policies relating to deregulation, tax incentives, and work incentives.

G. The gap between prices paid by buyers and the prices received by sellers.

H. A growth strategy consisting of government programs to identify and encourage promising industries and to ease the decline of old industries.

TESTING YOURSELF

In the next three sections, you will answer questions and work problems that are based on information in the text. Master all of the terms before you begin these sections. Work each section without referring to your notes or the text, and then check your answers.

Part I: True or False

Mark each statement as true or false. Whenever you mark a statement as false, jot down a sentence stating why it is false.

_____ 1. Economic growth is unequivocally good.

_____ 2. When the economy operates below its potential, real output is lost.

_____ 3. In the long run, the aggregate supply curve is upward sloping.

_____ 4. In the short run, people may confuse higher money wages with higher real wages.

_____ 5. If expectations are rational and markets are auction, the short run will be a relatively short period.

_____ 6. The upward slope of the short-run supply curve results from shifts in the aggregate demand curve.

_____ 7. Prices change rapidly in a contract market.

_____ 8. A short-run increase in aggregate demand increases profit opportunities for businesses.

_____ 9. The real business cycle is caused by random shocks to the aggregate demand curve.

_____ 10. A large crop failure might shift the aggregate supply curve to the left.

_____ 11. Spending on education and training can be compared to investment in machinery and equipment.

_____ 12. If the price of copper increases, copper users will probably try to find a substitute.

_____ 13. Supply siders relate tax revenues to tax rates.

_____ 14. Empirical evidence from the early 1980s fails to support many supply side theories.

_____ 15. The United States does not have an industrial policy.

Part II: Problems

1. Ralph Simmons is receiving welfare payments of $200 a week. He is offered a job that pays $350 a week for forty hours of work. If he accepts the job, he will pay about 20 percent of his income in federal income tax, 5 percent in state income tax, and 7.3 percent in Social Security tax.

   a. What is Simmons's marginal tax rate?

   b. How much will he pay in taxes per week?

   c. Do you think he will accept the job?

2. Carol Anderson earns $35,000 a year. She pays 25 percent in federal income tax, 6 percent in state income tax, and 7.3 percent in Social Security tax. She is offered a promotion with many new responsibilities and a raise to $45,000. If she accepts, her marginal federal tax rate will rise to 32 percent and her marginal state tax rate will rise to 8 percent. The Social Security tax rate won't change.

a. What is her current marginal tax rate?

b. If she accepts the promotion, what will her new marginal tax rate be?

c. How much of her raise will Anderson get to take home if she accepts the promotion?

Part III: Multiple Choice

1. The short-run aggregate supply curve has an upward slope because
    a. some resources are immobile.
    b. there are opportunities for short-run profits.
    c. information about changing prices is incomplete.
    d. All three of the above are true.

2. If there are many long-term contracts in place,
    a. the short-run aggregate supply curve is vertical.
    b. the adjustment period from short run to long run will be long.
    c. the aggregate demand curve cannot shift.
    d. firms cannot move along the short-run aggregate supply curve.

3. If there is a rightward shift in the aggregate demand curve,
    a. price will increase and output will be unchanged in the short run.
    b. price and output will both increase in the short run.
    c. price and output will both increase in the long run.
    d. output will increase and price will be unchanged in the long run.

4. If a clothing manufacturer anticipates a new union contract calling for higher wages in July and raises his clothing prices in February,
    a. he may earn short-run profits.
    b. he has a vertical supply curve.
    c. his actions will contribute to a short-run upward sloping aggregate supply curve.
    d. he may earn short-run profits, which will in turn contribute to a short-run upward sloping demand curve.

5. Long-term economic growth requires
    a. steady rightward shifts of the aggregate demand curve.
    b. steady rightward shifts of the aggregate supply curve.
    c. centrally administered industrial policy.
    d. falling prices for natural resources.

6. Which one of the following will *not* shift the aggregate supply curve to the right?
   a. Lower prices for natural resources
   b. A bumper crop of grain
   c. A higher average level of education
   d. A larger defense budget

7. After corrections are made for depreciation,
   a. real net investment since 1965 is unchanged.
   b. real net investment was lower in 1992 than in 1962.
   c. real net investment grew at an average rate of 5 percent since 1960.
   d. real growth in investment has exceeded the rate of economic growth.

8. A higher level of investment should
   a. shift the aggregate demand curve, but not the aggregate supply curve.
   b. shift both the aggregate demand curve and the aggregate supply curve.
   c. cause a movement along the aggregate demand curve and the aggregate supply curve.
   d. cause a movement along the aggregate demand curve and shift the aggregate supply curve.

9. Domestic saving by households and business firms in the 1960s, 1970s, and 1980s
   a. diminished as a percentage of GDP.
   b. grew at about the same rate as GDP.
   c. was increasingly absorbed by private domestic investment.
   d. was increasingly absorbed by private foreign investment.

10. The growth of the labor force during the 1970s
    a. slowed the rightward movement of the aggregate supply curve, because many of the new workers were young and/or unskilled.
    b. caused a large rightward shift of the aggregate supply curve.
    c. caused a leftward shift of the aggregate supply curve.
    d. caused a leftward shift of the aggregate demand curve.

11. Technological change occurs
    a. when both invention and innovations have occurred.
    b. when invention only takes place.
    c. when new products become profitable.
    d. the labor force implements new techniques.

12. Long-term economic growth requires
    a. the aggregate supply curve to shift to the right and the aggregate demand curve to shift to the left.
    b. both the aggregate supply curve and the aggregate demand curve to shift to the right.
    c. the rightward shift of the aggregate supply curve to be larger than the rightward shift of the aggregate demand curve.
    d. the rightward shift of the aggregate supply curve to be smaller than the rightward shift of the aggregate demand curve.

____ 13. Supply siders feel that taxes
   a. are an effective means of increasing supply, since they reduce consumer spending.
   b. create a gap between consumer prices and producer prices and lead to inefficiencies.
   c. are not necessary in an efficient economy.
   d. should always be progressive.

____ 14. Supply siders anticipated that the lower tax rates put into place in 1981 would
   a. result in higher tax revenues.
   b. result in lower tax revenues.
   c. be ineffective, because work effort would diminish.
   d. cause the budget deficit to balloon.

____ 15. Industrial policy as practiced in Japan and many European countries
   a. is a good example of supply side economics.
   b. includes subsidies, tax incentives, and low-interest loans.
   c. leads to government ownership of the primary industries.
   d. is incompatible with international competitiveness.

CHECKING OUT

Now that you have finished studying this chapter, you should be able to:

1. Discuss the importance of the slope of the aggregate supply curve and the length of the short run to demand-based growth strategies.

2. Define real business cycles and explain their relationship to aggregate supply.

3. Identify the sources of economic growth, which are the factors that can shift the aggregate supply curve and improve productivity.

4. Discuss the supply side policies relating to taxes, transfers, and regulation, and evaluate the effectiveness of supply-side policies in the 1980s.

5. Explain what industrial policy is and how it is implemented.

ANSWERS

Trying Out the Terms

1. G   5. C
2. E   6. H
3. F   7. B
4. A   8. D

Testing Yourself

Part I: True or False

1. false. There are trade-offs involved in economic growth, such as redistribution effects, and costs involving leisure, environmental quality, or security.
2. true
3. false. It is vertical.
4. true
5. true
6. false. The slope is the result of market imperfections.
7. false. Because contracts commit buyers and sellers for relatively long periods, prices change slowly in contract markets.
8. true
9. false. Supply disruptions, such as a less experienced labor force, underlie the theory of the real business cycle.
10. true
11. true
12. true
13. true
14. true
15. false. The United States does not have a *formal* industrial policy. It does have an uncoordinated group of policies that affect certain industries both positively and negatively.

Part II: Problems

1. a. His marginal tax rate is 32.3 percent (0.20 + 0.05 + 0.073 = 0.323).
   b. He will pay $113.05 in taxes per week (0.323 × $350).
   c. Very likely, he won't accept the job. His take-home pay would be $236.95. This is less than $40 more than he is receiving in welfare. In effect, for his forty hours of work, Ralph would be gaining less than a dollar an hour.
2. a. Her current marginal rate is 38.3 percent (0.25 + 0.06 + 0.073 = 0.383).
   b. After the promotion, her marginal rate will be 47.3 percent (0.32 + 0.08 + 0.073 = 0.473).
   c. Assuming that Anderson pays the new, higher rates on all of her increase, she will pay $4,730 in taxes and take home $5,270 from her $10,000 raise.

Part III: Multiple Choice

1. d
2. b
3. b
4. d
5. b
6. d
7. b
8. b
9. a
10. a
11. a
12. c
13. b
14. a
15. b

Name _____

CHAPTER 16 EXERCISES

_____ 1. Demand management can have a strong effect on short-run output if
   a. people form appropriate expectations about the future.
   b. people have complete information about current conditions.
   c. prices adjust quickly to changing conditions.
   d. markets are contractual.

_____ 2. In an auction market,
   a. there are many buyers and sellers.
   b. there are infrequent transactions.
   c. most adjustments will be in output.
   d. prices move slowly.

_____ 3. The aggregate supply curve would shift to the left if
   a. an investment tax credit were put into place.
   b. the price of natural resources increased.
   c. more students finished high school.
   d. people started saving more.

_____ 4. When businesses invest in new capital equipment,
   a. workers become more productive, because they have more capital to work with.
   b. workers become more productive, because the new capital embodies new technology.
   c. stagflation may be reduced.
   d. All the above answers are true.

_____ 5. If a vocational nurse returns to college to become a registered nurse and earn more money, he is
   a. becoming more productive.
   b. investing in human capital.
   c. operating in the short run only.
   d. becoming more productive by investing in human capital.

_____ 6. In the United States, expenditures on education
   a. have fallen as a percentage of GNP since 1975.
   b. are greater than expenditures on business investment.
   c. are greater than in any other major industrial country except Switzerland.
   d. are concentrated on post-secondary educational institutions.

_____ 7. Studies done by Kerry Smith and John Krutilla indicate that
   a. there are no good substitutes for most natural resources.
   b. research and development on new methods of natural resource extraction lag badly behind actual need.
   c. low-grade resources are often substituted when high-grade resources are depleted.
   d. because the supply of natural resources is fixed, higher prices will not encourage new sources of supply.

Chapter 16   Aggregate Supply, Economic Growth, and Macroeconomic Policy

_____ 8. Which of the following is more likely to be true of a system with a highly progressive income tax than of an economy with low marginal taxes?
   a. Workers often turn down the opportunity to work extra hours for extra pay.
   b. Saving is encouraged.
   c. Productivity is enhanced.
   d. Entrepreneurial endeavors are less risky.

_____ 9. Which of the following is *not* a policy recommended by Robert Reich to increase productivity in the United States?
   a. Increased government spending on research and development
   b. Increased reliance on market forces
   c. An expenditure tax
   d. Tax incentives for human capital investment

_____ 10. Industrial policy in Japan in the 1970s and 1980s focused on
   a. formation of cartels.
   b. supporting promising industries.
   c. propping up declining industries.
   d. encouraging imports.

CHAPTER 17

THE CHALLENGE OF ECONOMIC DEVELOPMENT

CHECKING IN

This chapter uses basic economic principles to compare relative rates of development among countries and to examine some reasons for these different levels of development. Development economics is concerned with specific solutions to practical problems in less developed countries, rather than with theoretical models.

Less developed countries (LDCs) are usually classified by level of per capita GDP. These countries have many similarities. The main industry in LDCs is agriculture, primarily subsistence agriculture. These countries are mostly in the tropics or subtropics. They have a high rate of population growth and a low rate of investment in human capital. Often they are locked into their economic situations by entrenched cultural values and traditions.

Adam Smith was the first economist to offer a theory of economic development; he believed laissez-faire government policy would let the market create growth. Thomas Malthus predicted that population growth would offset economic growth. W. W. Rostow's historical model sees societies as passing through several stages of growth, from traditional to high mass consumption.

Many strategies for development exist. The big push strategy suggests that all industries in an economy should expand at the same time. This strategy requires government direction and financing. The leading sectors strategy holds that efforts should be directed at successful industries, with linkages to related industries. This strategy also requires government involvement.

There is some controversy over the appropriate role of government in the development process. Some economists believe that government's role is so important that even democracy may need to be sacrificed; many others believe that authoritarian leadership is not necessary. Empirical evidence suggests that private property and market forces (usually found in democracies) are very conducive to economic development.

In practice, developing countries often receive outside assistance. Many of the industrialized nations, including the U.S., provide aid through government agencies and the multinational agencies. Corporations, particularly multinationals, and private groups also provide aid.

TRYING OUT THE TERMS

Match each of the following terms with its definition, and then check your answers. If you are having trouble, go back to the text and find the definition there.

_____ 1. crude birth rate
_____ 2. Agency for International Development (AID)
_____ 3. dualism
_____ 4. big push strategy
_____ 5. dependency ratio
_____ 6. vicious circle of poverty
_____ 7. export promotion
_____ 8. New International Economic Order
_____ 9. crude death rate
_____ 10. leading sectors strategy
_____ 11. import substitution
_____ 12. World Bank
_____ 13. appropriate technology
_____ 14. structural adjustment lending

A. The coexistence of a modern, urban, market-oriented society and a rural, agriculture-based, traditional peasant society, characteristic of many less developed countries.

B. Number of births per thousand population.

C. The percentage of the population not of working age (under fifteen or over sixty-five).

D. Number of deaths per thousand population.

E. A trap in which many low-income countries are caught, in which there is little investment because of a low level of income and a low level of income because of lack of investment.

F. A development strategy calling for a major thrust on all fronts with government leadership and public-private partnership.

G. A development strategy calling for concentration on a few promising sectors, which will then pull along the other sectors in the development process.

H. A development strategy that concentrates on becoming self-sufficient by replacing imported goods with domestic production.

I. A development strategy that calls for developing export industries in order to earn foreign exchange to purchase consumer goods, capital equipment, raw material, and food from abroad.

J. U.S. government agency in charge of U.S. bilateral assistance to foreign countries.

K. Multinational development lending agency that makes low-interest long-term loans to developing countries and provides technical assistance and economic advice.

L. World Bank lending to developing countries that requires specific policy adjustments as a condition of the loan.

M. A proposal from developing nations calling for changes in international economic arrangements so as to benefit poorer nations through trade references, increased aid, and price stabilization for tropical agricultural products.

N. Adapting methods of production to take advantage of the mix of resources available in less developed countries.

TESTING YOURSELF

In the next two sections, you will answer questions that are based on information in the text. Master all of the terms before you begin these sections. Work each section without referring to your notes or the text, and then check your answers.

Part I: True or False

Mark each statement as true or false. Whenever you mark a statement as false, jot down a sentence stating why it is false.

_____ 1. Argentina is an example of a country that not only failed to grow economically but also lost ground for a long period.

_____ 2. A less developed country is usually identified by its level of per capita GDP.

_____ 3. Per capita GDP measures marketed and nonmarketed production.

_____ 4. Baumol's research on convergence indicates a higher level of convergence between rich and poor countries than among the industrialized countries.

_____ 5. In low-income countries, about 70 percent of the labor force works in agriculture.

_____ 6. Most development programs focus on increasing dependence on agriculture as a means of developing the economy.

_____ 7. One advantage of dualism is that urban centers provide large markets for manufactured goods.

_____ 8. Some estimates indicate that about 40 to 60 percent of the developing world population is poor.

_____ 9. Countries with high per capita GDP have higher dependency ratios.

_____ 10. The most important consequence of a high birth rate is that a large percentage of the population is unproductive.

_____ 11. Adam Smith felt that the best approach to encouraging economic development was an attitude of *laissez-faire*.

_____ 12. All countries have somewhat similar development patterns, according to Rostow's stage theory.

_____ 13. The big push strategy of development relies on private incentives and a *laissez-faire* government policy.

_____ 14. One important economic role for the government in a developing country is to define and enforce property rights.

_____ 15. There is no clear evidence that a high level of military spending encourages economic development.

Part II: Multiple Choice

_____ 1. All *but* which one of the following are true of low- and middle-income countries?
   a. More than half of the labor force is engaged in agriculture.
   b. More than one-third of GDP is attributed to agriculture.
   c. Growth in the agricultural sector is faster than growth in other sectors.
   d. Agriculture is basically for subsistence.

_____ 2. The poorest of the low-income countries are found in the
   a. Northern Hemisphere.
   b. Eastern Hemisphere.
   c. tropics and subtropics.
   d. moderate zones.

_____ 3. Why is the crude birth rate high in many less developed countries?
   a. Children are needed for their labor services.
   b. Children are needed as old-age insurance.
   c. Prestige is measured in number of children.
   d. All of the above

_____ 4. According to Table 3 in your textbook, the crude birth rate is highest in
   a. low-income countries.
   b. lower middle-income countries.
   c. upper middle-income countries.
   d. industrial market countries.

_____ 5. The population will remain constant if
   a. the crude birth rate does not exceed 2 percent.
   b. the total fertility rate is 2.1.
   c. the dependency ratio is less than two.
   d. the crude death rate exceeds the crude birth rate.

_____ 6. In a developing country we would expect to observe
   a. the birth rate declining and the death rate increasing.
   b. the birth rate increasing before the death rate increases.
   c. the death rate decreasing before the birth rate decreases.
   d. a constant death rate and an increasing birth rate.

_____ 7. In a dual economy, people in the agricultural sector may remain poor because
   a. they have inappropriate social standards.
   b. they consider the self-denial necessary for adequate investment to be a vice.
   c. they have cultural traits that do not encourage economic growth.
   d. their social systems are too flexible to allow for investment in human capital.

8. Low-income countries tend to invest very little in human capital because
   a. basically agricultural countries have small need for this type of investment.
   b. the need for human capital investment is not recognized.
   c. there are few resources available for investment.
   d. export substitution provides higher returns than investment in human capital.

9. The original theorist of economic development was
   a. Thomas Malthus.
   b. David Ricardo.
   c. W. W. Rostow.
   d. Adam Smith.

10. Rostow's theory of development includes a traditional economy that precedes
    a. tribal communism.
    b. pre-Newtonianism.
    c. feudalism.
    d. a takeoff.

11. According to Rostow's theory of development, the United States and Western European countries are in the _____ stage.
    a. drive to maturity
    b. high mass consumption
    c. capitalistic equilibrium
    d. post-industrial

12. Hirschman's theory of linkage calls for a developing country to develop linkages
    a. with other developing countries that produce complementary products.
    b. forward from successful existing industries.
    c. backward from successful existing industries.
    d. both forward and backward from successful existing industries.

13. The Agency for International Development is the development assistance agency of the
    a. United Nations.
    b. French Republic.
    c. United States.
    d. New International Economic Order.

14. The foreign development aid donations of the United States
    a. amount to 50 percent of all funds given by the Western industrialized nations.
    b. represent the largest amount given by any of the Western industrialized nations.
    c. represent the largest percentage of GDP given by any of the Western industrialized nations.
    d. is administered by the United Nations.

15. Under the Brady Plan, indebted countries
    a. could apply for a World Bank loan if an industrialized nation would co-sign.
    b. surrendered government property to repay bank loans.
    c. exchanged bank loans for marketable bonds.
    d. donated land to environment causes in exchange for debt forgiveness.

CHECKING OUT

Now that you have finished studying this chapter, you should be able to:

1. Describe the distinctive characteristics of less developed countries.

2. Analyze the role of population growth and lack of investment in human capital in creating a vicious circle of poverty.

3. Explain the following theories and strategies for economic development: classical *laissez-faire,* Rostow's stages of growth, big push versus leading sectors, and export promotion versus import substitution.

4. Summarize the opposing views on the role of the national government in promoting economic development.

5. Discuss the role of the developed countries in promoting and encouraging development through foreign aid, the World Bank, the New International Economic Order, and multinational corporations.

ANSWERS

Trying Out the Terms

1. B
2. J
3. A
4. F
5. C
6. E
7. I
8. M
9. D
10. G
11. H
12. K
13. N
14. L

Testing Yourself

Part I: True or False

1. true
2. true
3. false. It measures only output that goes through the market. For this reason, per capita GDP is often understated.
4. false. Convergence is higher among the industrial nations.
5. true
6. false. Development programs seek to reduce dependence on agriculture.
7. false. In a dual economy, the urban market is too small to provide markets for manufactured goods.
8. true
9. false. High dependency ratios are generally found where GDP is low.
10. true
11. true
12. true
13. false. The big push strategy must be conducted by the government because there is little incentive otherwise for entrepreneurs to expand production.
14. true
15. true

Part II: Multiple Choice

1. c	5. b	9. d	13. c
2. c	6. c	10. d	14. b
3. d	7. c	11. b	15. c
4. a	8. c	12. d	

Name _____

CHAPTER 17 EXERCISES

Answer each of the following questions in one or two paragraphs.

1. Explain how per capita income might fall in a country with a growing GDP.

2. Suppose you have been hired as an economic consultant to a less developed country that subscribes to Hirschman's linkage theory. This country's main export is peanuts. Describe some of the forward and backward linkages you might suggest.

3. "Economic development will be more successful under an authoritarian government than under a democratic one." Discuss the theories and evidence supporting and disputing this statement.

CHAPTER 18

POLICY APPLICATIONS OF SUPPLY AND DEMAND

CHECKING IN

This chapter demonstrates how economic and social issues are analyzed. You get a chance to practice applying the basic supply and demand model from Chapter 3 before going on to new microeconomic challenges. This model gives you the tools to explain how the market works and, sometimes, doesn't work.

People typically weigh costs and benefits before undertaking an action, even when that action is illegal. If the costs of committing a crime are raised by increasing the penalty or the probability of apprehension or if the benefits of committing a crime are reduced, then crime will decrease. This is true whether the crime is littering or treason.

When a market is allowed to function freely, it will reach an equilibrium price and quantity. This was the important lesson of Chapter 3. At times, an equilibrium price doesn't seem fair to everybody, and attempts are made to set either a price floor (above the equilibrium price) or a price ceiling (below the equilibrium price) to make things better. The price does change then, but other interesting things occur, because the price controls interfere with market allocation. We observe surpluses, shortages, or black markets. These situations arise frequently. Rent control is an example of a price ceiling. Minimum wage laws and agricultural supports are examples of price floors.

Over the last century, farmers in the United States have become highly productive. So productive, in fact, that they have produced too much. Agricultural prices have fallen, and farmers have found it difficult to remain in business. In addition to this long-run problem of increased productivity, farmers face short-run problems of strong competition, highly inelastic demand, and unpredictable weather.

The federal government and, to a limited extent, state governments have undertaken a variety of programs to aid the agricultural industry; most of these are pointed toward retaining jobs in agriculture and preserving family farms. Although most of these programs are designed to reduce supply, some are intended to increase the demand for agricultural products. Because there are many programs initiated over a long period of time, it is hard to measure the success of U.S. agricultural policy.

TRYING OUT THE TERMS

Match each of the following terms with its definition, and then check your answers. If you are having trouble, go back to the text and find the definition there.

_____ 1. agricultural support program

_____ 2. soil bank program

_____ 3. price ceilings

_____ 4. target prices

_____ 5. rent control

_____ 6. parity

_____ 7. marketing orders

_____ 8. price floors

_____ 9. Commodity Credit Corporation (CCC)

_____ 10. payment in kind (PIK) program

_____ 11. black markets

_____ 12. Food Security Act

_____ 13. minimum wage

_____ 14. Soil Conservation Service

_____ 15. shortage

_____ 16. surplus

_____ 17. support prices

_____ 18. acreage allotment

_____ 19. Conservation Reserve Program (CRP)

A. Markets in which people illegally buy and sell goods and services at prices above government-imposed price ceilings.

B. Upper limits on prices imposed by a governmental unit. The ceiling is a price that cannot be exceeded.

C. Minimum limits on prices established by a governmental unit. The floor is a price that cannot be undercut.

D. The amount by which the quantity consumers wish to purchase at some price exceeds the quantity suppliers wish to supply at that price. A shortage can occur on a lasting basis only when a price ceiling is in effect.

E. A price ceiling imposed by a governmental unit on housing rents.

F. The amount by which the quantity suppliers wish to supply at some price exceeds the quantity consumers wish to purchase at that price. A surplus can occur on a lasting basis only when a price floor is in effect.

G. A U.S. government agency that makes loans to farmers as part of federal price support programs.

H. A price floor imposed by the federal government in the labor market.

I. Attempts by the federal government to achieve parity for farmers through the use of price supports.

J. A one-to-one ratio between the average prices of farm products and the prices of what farmers buy.

K. Price floors for agricultural products maintained by the government, which purchases any surplus to keep the price from falling.

L. A limit set by the government on the number of acres that can be used to produce a specific crop, based on past production levels.

M. A federal program that pays farmers to remove land from production for ten years or more.

N. A federal program that establishes producer cartels that control the supply of certain agricultural products not subject to price supports.

O. A federal agricultural program beginning in the 1950s under which farmers were paid to let their land lie idle in order to reduce their supply of farm products.

P. A federal program under which grants were given to encourage farmers to contract production by fallowing fields, contour plowing, and other conservation techniques.

Q. Prices the government considers to be fair for farmers, used to determine subsidy payments.

R. A federal agricultural program similar to the soil bank program, but with payments made in surplus commodities rather than in money.

S. A 1985 federal law that sets target prices and requires farmers to agree to keep part of their land idle.

TESTING YOURSELF

In the next three sections, you will answer questions and work problems that are based on information in the text. Master all of the terms before you begin these sections. Work each section without referring to your notes or the text, and then check your answers.

Part I: True or False

Mark each statement as true or false. Whenever you mark a statement as false, jot down a sentence stating why it is false.

_____ 1. Tax-financed victim compensation would be an effective deterrent to crime.

_____ 2. The death penalty is an effective deterrent to crime because it increases the expected cost of committing death-penalty crimes.

_____ 3. Models that indicate the outcome or consequence of a policy action are called subjective models.

_____ 4. If a traffic ticket costs $50 and you believe that your chances of getting caught are one in two (50 percent), the estimated cost of the ticket is $50.

_____ 5. If a price ceiling is set below the equilibrium market price, a shortage will occur.

_____ 6. Surpluses are caused by setting a price floor below the equilibrium market price.

_____ 7. If the equilibrium price of compact discs is $12 but a price ceiling of $9 is imposed, there is likely to be a surplus of compact discs.

_____ 8. If the equilibrium price of compact discs is $12 but a price ceiling of $9 is imposed, we are likely to see a black market arise for compact discs.

_____ 9. Whenever a good is scarce, there will be a shortage.

_____ 10. Price floors are imposed to raise the market price above the equilibrium level.

_____ 11. According to some studies, an increase in the minimum wage will lead to a decrease in the level of unemployment.

_____ 12. Most U.S. farm policies are designed to increase agricultural efficiency.

_____ 13. A bumper crop may mean lower revenues for farmers.

_____ 14. Increasing farm output may provide the key to solving the farm problem.

_____ 15. If one state passes restrictive farm ownership laws, its neighboring states stand to gain.

Part II: Problems

1. Consider the following supply and demand schedules for cloth.

Quantity Demanded (in yds.)	Price (per yd.)	Quantity Supplied (in yds.)
100	$10.00	3,100
300	9.00	2,800
500	8.00	2,500
700	7.00	2,200
900	6.00	1,900
1,100	5.00	1,600
1,300	4.00	1,300
1,500	3.00	1,000
1,700	2.00	700
1,900	1.00	400

   1. a. If the market is allowed to function without interference, what quantity will be traded? What will the price be?

b. Suppose the government decides to make clothing readily available to poverty-level school children by imposing a price ceiling of $3. What will happen?

c. Suppose the government decides to protect the income of poverty-level cotton farmers by setting a price floor at $8. What will happen?

d. In the figure below, graph the situation described in Exercise 1c. Label any surplus or shortage.

2. Consider the market for croissants, illustrated in the figure below.

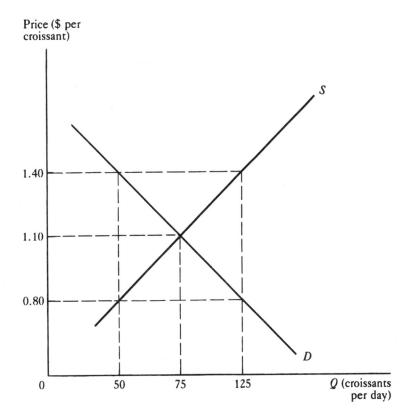

a. At a price of $0.80, how many croissants will be sold? Is there a shortage or a surplus?

b. If there is a persistent surplus of 75 croissants, what sort of market interference is occurring?

c. If the market is operating freely and without interference, what quantity will be traded? What will the price be?

Part III: Multiple Choice

____ 1. The expected cost of a crime can be measured by the
   a. length of the prison sentence plus the amount of the fine.
   b. average penalty assessed for that crime over the last ten years.
   c. penalty for the crime plus the cost of apprehension.
   d. penalty for the crime adjusted for the probability of apprehension and conviction.

____ 2. After an increase in the number of basketball referees in a game, the number of fouls per game
   a. decreased.
   b. increased by a smaller percentage than the percentage increase in referees.
   c. increased by the same percentage as the percentage increase in referees.
   d. was unchanged.

____ 3. The work of William Trumbull indicates that
   a. the best deterrent to crime is severe punishment.
   b. certainty of punishment is a greater deterrent than severity.
   c. severe punishment is not effective as a deterrent.
   d. the presence of legal alternatives has no effect on the crime rate.

____ 4. If the equilibrium price (with no price controls) of milk is $0.75 per gallon and a price ceiling of $0.60 per gallon is imposed, we would expect
   a. nothing to happen, since the price ceiling is lower than the equilibrium price.
   b. increased production of milk, leading to increased consumption.
   c. a shortage to occur, since the price ceiling is lower than the equilibrium price.
   d. a surplus to occur, since there is an increased incentive to suppliers.

____ 5. Black markets usually arise when
   a. goods are scarce.
   b. there is a price ceiling.
   c. there is a price floor.
   d. goods are in excess supply.

____ 6. A good example of a price floor is
   a. rent control on apartments in major cities.
   b. general admission tickets to concerts.
   c. the minimum wage law.
   d. food stamp regulations.

____ 7. The economic model of supply and demand indicates that an increase in the minimum wage would lead to
   a. increased incomes.
   b. higher employment among workers over twenty five.
   c. higher teenage unemployment.
   d. no change in the unemployment rate.

8. At the equilibrium price of $3.50 a bushel, with no price controls, 10,000 bushels of oats are sold. If the government imposes a price floor of $4.50, we would expect
   a. nothing to happen, since the price floor is above the equilibrium price.
   b. farmers to continue to supply 10,000 bushels of oats.
   c. the quantity of oats sold to consumers to fall below 10,000 bushels.
   d. a shortage of oats to exist.

9. Government programs to assist the farming industry
   a. cause farmers to grow more and thus cause surpluses to accumulate.
   b. restrict the supply of food in order to raise prices.
   c. require that surpluses of certain agricultural products be destroyed.
   d. All of the above

10. The government has attempted to manage agricultural production in the United States by setting
    a. minimum prices.
    b. acreage allotments.
    c. target prices.
    d. All of the above

11. Most state regulation of agriculture is designed to
    a. encourage increased production.
    b. help farmers decide which crop to plant.
    c. preserve family farms.
    d. encourage the development of new agricultural industries.

12. In 1993, the budget costs for federal agricultural programs were
    a. the smallest in two decades.
    b. more than $1,000 for every nonfarm family in the United States.
    c. more than $1,500 for every nonfarm family in the United States.
    d. smaller than the off-budget transfers to farmers.

13. Government agricultural programs result in a transfer of income from
    a. taxpayers to farmers.
    b. foreigners to farmers.
    c. farmers to city dwellers.
    d. farmers to the government.

14. European Community agricultural policy focuses on
    a. payment for production.
    b. acreage reduction.
    c. output restrictions.
    d. direct welfare payments to farmers.

15. After post-World War II price restrictions were relaxed in Germany
    a. black markets increased.
    b. farm families moved to the city.
    c. railroad travel decreased.
    d. food prices fell.

TAKING ANOTHER LOOK

The text states that black markets spring up almost inevitably when price ceilings are imposed. We frequently hear about black markets for goods that are prohibited by law: marijuana and other controlled substances; alcoholic beverages during the 1920s, or even today in certain areas of the country; medicines not approved by the FDA, such as cancer cures and diet pills. How do these black markets relate to price ceilings?

They relate exactly the same way as black markets for other goods, except that now the ceiling price is equal to zero. People are prohibited from selling such a good at any price. The result is a huge shortage at $0.00 and lots of incentive for illegal sales. In the graph shown below, the equilibrium price is the one that would prevail in a legal market. The black market price would likely be even higher, since the black marketeer would insist on being compensated for the risk involved in this operation. (Remember the costs and benefits of crime in the first section of this chapter?)

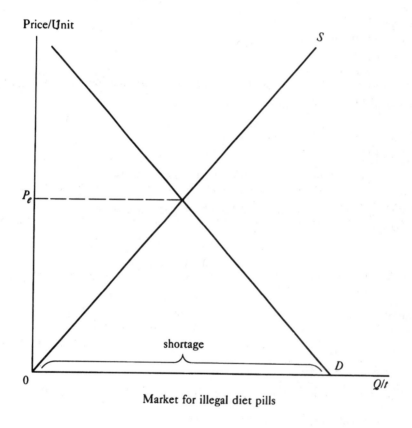

Market for illegal diet pills

CHECKING OUT

Now that you have finished studying this chapter, you should be able to:

1. Demonstrate a simple economic model by calculating the expected cost of a crime given the probability of arrest and conviction, and the penalty.

2. Describe and diagram the economic effects of rent control, the minimum wage, and price supports in agriculture.

3. Discuss how markets allocate scarce resources.

4. Use U.S. agricultural policy to investigate how intervention in markets creates incentives that further affect the market process.

ANSWERS

Trying Out the Terms

1. I	5. E	9. G	13. H	17. K
2. O	6. J	10. R	14. P	18. L
3. B	7. N	11. A	15. D	19. M
4. Q	8. C	12. S	16. F	

Testing Yourself

Part I: True or False

1. false. This would not be a good deterrent, because it does not increase the expected cost of committing the crime.
2. true
3. false. They are called positive models.
4. false. It is $25 (0.5 × $50).
5. true
6. false. A price floor set above the equilibrium price will have no effect. If it is set *above* the equilibrium price, a surplus will occur.
7. false. There is likely to be a shortage, since the ceiling price is below the equilibrium price.
8. true
9. false. Shortages occur on a lasting basis only when a price ceiling is set below the equilibrium price.
10. true
11. false. It is much more likely that the level of unemployment will increase.
12. false. Most policies are designed to protect the income of farmers and to prevent a decline in the number of farmers,
13. true
14. false. Excess farm output is one cause of the farm problem.
15. true

Part II: Problems

1. a. The quantity will be 1,300 yards, and the price will be $4 per yard.
   b. The quantity sold will be 1,000 yards. This is all that suppliers are willing to supply at a price of $3. There will be a shortage of 500 yards (the difference between what demanders are willing to buy and what suppliers are willing to provide).
   c. The quantity sold will be 500 yards. This is all that demanders are willing to purchase at a price of $8.00. There will be a surplus of 2,000 yards (the difference between what demanders are willing to buy and what suppliers are willing to provide).

d.

2. a. At $0.80, 50 croissants will be sold. This is all that suppliers are willing to supply at that price. There will be a shortage of 75 croissants.
   b. A price floor of $1.40 must be in place. Suppliers are willing to supply 125 croissants, but at this price demanders will buy only 50.
   c. The quantity sold will be 75 croissants, at $1.10 each.

Part III: Multiple Choice

1. d
2. a
3. b
4. c
5. b
6. c
7. c
8. c
9. d
10. d
11. c
12. b
13. a
14. a
15. c

Name _____

CHAPTER 18 EXERCISES

1. Consider the following supply and demand schedule.

Quantity Demanded	Price	Quantity Supplied
10	$7	40
15	6	35
20	5	30
25	4	25
30	3	20
35	2	15

   a. If there are no price controls, what will be the equilibrium price and quantity?

   b. If a price ceiling of $6 is imposed, what will be the price and the quantity? Is there a surplus or a shortage?

   c. If a price floor of $6 is imposed, what will be the price and the quantity? Is there a surplus or a shortage?

   d. If a price ceiling of $3 is imposed, what will be the price and the quantity? Is there a surplus or a shortage?

Chapter 18   Policy Applications of Supply and Demand

2. The graphs below show the dairy industry and the beef industry before implementation of the Dairy Termination Program. Show the effects of this program on each market.

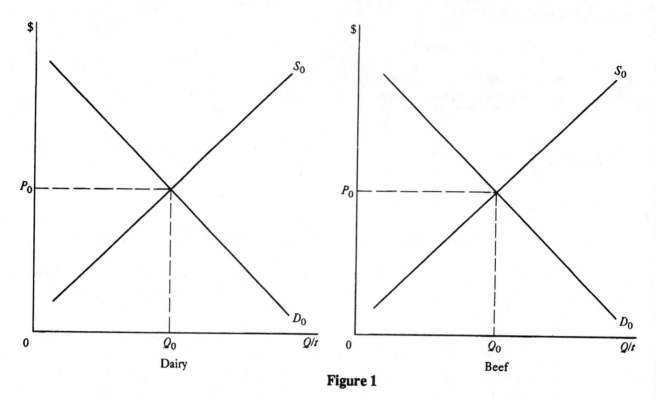

Figure 1

CHAPTER 19

ELASTICITY: THE MEASURE OF RESPONSIVENESS

CHECKING IN

The law of demand states that when price decreases, the quantity demanded increases. What it does not tell us is how much quantity responds to the change in price. Does it fall drastically or by a negligible amount? The degree of responsiveness of demand (or supply) to a change in a determinant is called *elasticity*.

Price elasticity of demand measures the responsiveness of the quantity demanded of a good to a change in its price. The coefficient of price elasticity of demand is the ratio of the percent change in quantity demanded of a good to the percent change in price. If this ratio is less than one, demand is said to be *inelastic*. If the ratio is greater than one, demand is *elastic*. Price elasticity of demand is not necessarily constant. Along a linear demand curve, elasticity will range from elastic (at higher prices) to inelastic (at lower prices), unless the curve is horizontal or vertical.

When the demand for a good is price elastic, a small change in price will cause a large change in the quantity demanded. One possible reason for this is that the good has many substitutes. If the price goes up, consumers have many other goods that they can switch to. The length of time consumers have to adjust also affects the price elasticity of a good. If they have a long time to search out new substitutes and options, their demand for the good will be elastic. If the decision to purchase must be made immediately, however, they may opt to pay the higher price; demand will be price inelastic.

Total revenue depends on price elasticity of demand. When price changes, according to the law of demand, the quantity demanded responds. If the change in quantity demanded outweighs the change in price, total revenue moves in the opposite direction from the price change, and demand is price elastic. For example, price falls and total revenue increases. If price and total revenue change in the same direction, demand is price inelastic.

We know that both supply and demand respond not only to changes in price but also to changes in other nonprice determinants (the *ceteris paribus* factors). Income elasticity of demand measures the responsiveness of demand to a change in income. If the quantity demanded of a good increases when income increases, the good is normal; if it falls when income increases, then the good is inferior. Cross elasticity of demand measures the responsiveness of demand for one good to a change in the price of another good. This measure can be used to determine whether goods are complements, substitutes, or independent.

Price elasticity of supply measures the responsiveness of changes in the quantity supplied of a good to changes in its price. The primary determinant of this measure is time. The longer the time period allowed for adjustment, the more price elastic the supply curve will be.

Adding the knowledge of elasticity to the basic concepts of supply and demand allows us to study many interesting applications of economics. One very important application is the determination of tax incidence (where the burden of any tax actually falls). The more inelastic the demand for a good or service and the more elastic the supply, the greater the amount of any excise tax on the good or service that is paid by consumers. The converse is also true. The more elastic the demand and the more inelastic the supply, the greater the amount of the tax paid by suppliers.

TRYING OUT THE TERMS

Match each of the following terms with its definition, and then check your answers. If you are having trouble, go back to the text and find the definition there.

____ 1. coefficient of price elasticity of demand (E_d)

____ 2. elasticity

____ 3. arc elasticity

____ 4. tax incidence

____ 5. total revenue (*TR*)

____ 6. income elasticity of demand

____ 7. perfectly inelastic demand

____ 8. unit elastic demand

____ 9. cross elasticity of demand

____ 10. price elasticity of supply

____ 11. perfectly elastic demand

____ 12. point elasticity

____ 13. coefficient of price elasticity of supply (E_s)

____ 14. excise tax

____ 15. price elasticity of demand

A. The measure of the sensitivity or responsiveness of quantity demanded or quantity supplied to changes in price (or other factors).

B. The measure of the responsiveness of the quantity demanded to changes in price.

C. The numerical measure of price elasticity of demand, equal to the percent change in quantity demanded of a good divided by the percent change in its price.

D. Demand represented by a vertical demand curve with a coefficient of price elasticity of demand that is equal to zero. There is no response in quantity demanded to changes in price.

E. Demand represented by a horizontal demand curve with a coefficient of price elasticity of demand that is equal to infinity. The quantity demanded responds in an infinite way to a change in price.

F. The situation where the coefficient of price elasticity of demand is unitary (equal to one).

G. The elasticity at the midpoint between two points on a demand curve.

H. The elasticity at a particular point on a demand curve.

I. The amount of money a firm takes in, equal to the quantity of the good or service sold multiplied by its price.

J. The measure of the responsiveness of demand to changes in income.

K. The measure of the responsiveness of changes in the demand for one good to changes in the price of another.

L. The measure of the responsiveness of the quantity supplied to changes in the price.

M. The numerical measure of price elasticity of supply, equal to the percent change in the quantity supplied of a good divided by the percent change in its price.

N. A tax on the purchase of a particular good, such as liquor, cigarettes, or electricity, or a broad class of goods, such as food.

O. The place where the burden of a tax actually falls after all shifting has occurred.

TESTING YOURSELF

In the next three sections, you will answer questions and work problems that are based on information in the text. Master all of the terms before you begin these sections. Work each section without referring to your notes or the text, and then check your answers.

Part I: True or False

Mark each statement as true or false. Whenever you mark a statement as false, jot down a sentence stating why it is false.

_____ 1. When the quantity demanded falls by 15 percent in response to a 10 percent increase in price, demand is perfectly elastic.

_____ 2. A local restaurant chain runs some low-price weekend specials and finds that total revenues fall. This indicates that demand is inelastic.

_____ 3. The price elasticity of a rectangular hyperbola is not constant, but varies over the range of prices.

_____ 4. If Jane knows that the price elasticity of demand for the Christmas decorations she makes and sells is equal to 1.6, she can increase her total revenues by lowering her price.

_____ 5. If new substitutes for a good appear on the market, we would expect the price elasticity of demand for that product to increase.

_____ 6. You would expect the demand for food to be more inelastic than the demand for cookies.

_____ 7. When consumers are given a long time to respond to a change in price, demand becomes more price inelastic.

_____ 8. If Eleanor's income increases by 10 percent and she increases her purchases of clothing by 5 percent, then clothing is a normal good for Eleanor.

_____ 9. If the coefficient of income elasticity of demand is positive, an increase in income will shift the demand curve to the left.

_____ 10. If the coefficient of cross elasticity of demand for two goods is equal to zero, those two goods are perfect substitutes.

_____ 11. We would expect the cross elasticity of demand for canned tuna and canned salmon to be positive.

_____ 12. A vertical supply curve indicates a fixed quantity.

_____ 13. If a tax is placed on a good with an upward-sloping supply curve and a perfectly inelastic demand curve, the tax incidence will be entirely on the consumer.

_____ 14. During the period of rising gasoline prices, we might expect the demand curve for automobiles to shift to the left.

_____ 15. If braces are normal goods, then the income of orthodontists should rise during a recession.

Part II: Problems

1. For each interval along this demand schedule, find the coefficient of price elasticity of demand and state whether demand is elastic, unit elastic, or inelastic.

DEMAND FOR COFFEE MUGS

Price	Quantity Demanded	E_d (coefficient)	E_d (using total revenue)
$1.00	12	_____	_____
2.00	10	_____	_____
3.00	8	_____	_____
4.00	6	_____	_____
5.00	4	_____	_____
6.00	2	_____	_____

2. Suppose that you are a farmer who runs a roadside fruit stand. You have a bumper crop of tomatoes this year, so many that you are afraid they will rot in the field if sales don't increase. You have read that the price elasticity of demand for fresh tomatoes is 4.60. Assume that this figure is valid in your market.

   a. By what percentage must you lower your price in order to increase sales by 100 percent?

   b. If you lower your price from $2.25 a pound to $1.75 a pound, by what percentage would you expect quantity demanded to increase? Use the formula for arc elasticity.

3. For each situation given, show how the changes will affect the demand curves and explain why.

   a. The price of a substitute increases; the good is normal.

   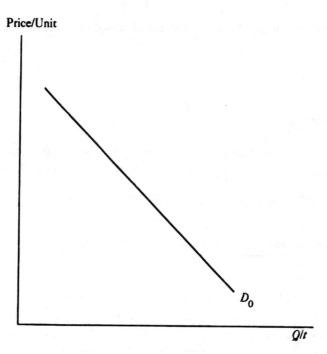

   b. The income of the consumer increases; the good is inferior.

   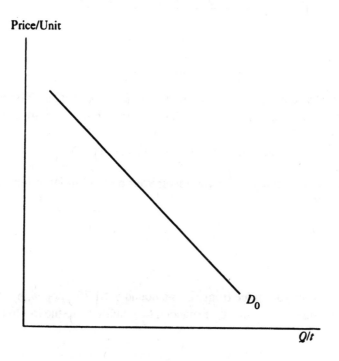

c. The price of a complement increases at the same time that income of the consumer falls; the good is normal.

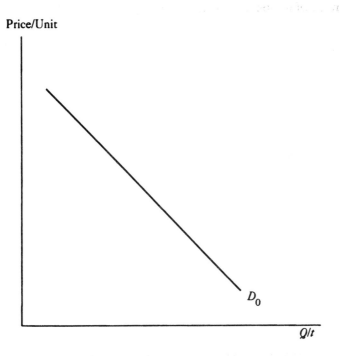

d. The price of a substitute falls at the same time that income of the consumer falls; the good is inferior.

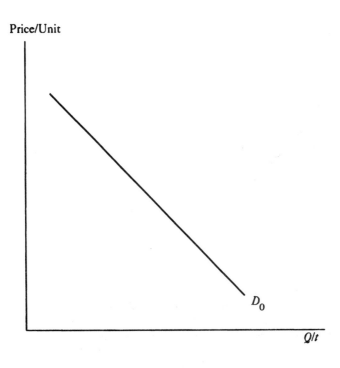

Part III: Multiple Choice

_____ 1. The formula for the coefficient of price elasticity of demand is
   a. the change in the quantity supplied of a good divided by the change in the quantity demanded.
   b. the unit change in the quantity supplied of a good divided by the unit change in price.
   c. the percent change in the quantity demanded of a good divided by the percent change in price.
   d. the percent change in price divided by the percent change in the quantity demanded.

_____ 2. If the demand for a good is elastic, then the percent change in quantity demanded is
   a. greater than the percent change in price but less than infinite.
   b. less than the percent change in price but greater than zero.
   c. the same as the percent change in price, and both are greater than zero.
   d. unchanged when prices increase.

_____ 3. The price of a product decreases by 12 percent, and the quantity demanded falls by 30 percent. What is the coefficient of price elasticity of demand (approximately)?
   a. 3.00
   b. 2.50
   c. 2.00
   d. Indeterminate

_____ 4. The price of a product increases from $10 to $14, and the quantity demanded falls from 100 to 50. According to the formula for arc elasticity, what is the coefficient of price elasticity of demand?
   a. 3.5
   b. 3.0
   c. 2.5
   d. 2.0

_____ 5. If an exclusive private kindergarten raises its price and finds that its total revenue from tuition decreases, this is an indication that demand for this school is
   a. perfectly inelastic.
   b. inelastic.
   c. unit elastic.
   d. elastic.

_____ 6. Price elasticity of demand varies over the range of prices when the demand curve
   a. is a downward-sloping straight line.
   b. has a positive slope.
   c. is a rectangular hyperbola.
   d. is a horizontal straight line.

7. If a price decrease results in a fall in total revenue, then demand is
   a. unit elastic.
   b. inelastic.
   c. elastic.
   d. indeterminate.

8. If the coefficient of price elasticity of demand is 1.35, then
   a. demand is inelastic.
   b. demand is perfectly elastic.
   c. a price increase of 1 percent will result in a decrease in quantity demanded of 135 percent.
   d. a price decrease of 10 percent will result in an increase in quantity demanded of 13.5 percent.

9. A demand curve that is perfectly inelastic is
   a. horizontal.
   b. vertical.
   c. downward sloping.
   d. upward sloping.

10. Stella receives a pay increase of 25 percent after she directs a tremendously successful ad campaign. She immediately trades her Hyundai in on a Corvette. For Stella, cars are
    a. positive goods.
    b. normal goods.
    c. price inelastic.
    d. perfect substitutes.

11. If cross elasticity of demand for two goods is negative, then those two goods are
    a. complements.
    b. substitutes.
    c. unrelated goods.
    d. inferior goods.

12. The formula for the coefficient of price elasticity of supply is
    a. the change in the quantity supplied of a good divided by the change in the quantity supplied.
    b. the unit change in the quantity supplied of a good divided by the unit change in price.
    c. the percent change in the quantity supplied of a good divided by the percent change in price.
    d. the percent change in the price of a good divided by the percent change in quantity supplied.

For Questions 13–15, use the information in Figure 1.

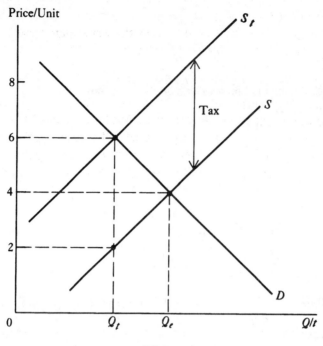

Figure 1

_____ 13. What is the amount of tax in Figure 1?
   a. $6
   b. $4
   c. $2
   d. $0

_____ 14. The amount received by the producer before the tax is imposed is _____, whereas the amount received after the tax is imposed is _____.
   a. $2, $4
   b. $6, $4
   c. $4, $2
   d. $4, $6

_____ 15. The incidence of this tax is on
   a. the government.
   b. the consumer.
   c. the supplier.
   d. the consumer and the supplier.

TAKING ANOTHER LOOK

The next time you fix frozen orange juice, look at the listing of ingredients. You will probably find that it contains some juice from Brazil, even if the word *Florida, Texas,* or *California* figures prominently in the brand name. A great deal of orange juice sold in the United States is imported from Brazil. During a recent winter, the citrus-growing regions of Brazil suffered a severe drought, and the orange crop was smaller than anticipated. How would this fall in the supply of oranges in Brazil affect the price of orange juice in the United States?

A financial analyst appearing on a television news show speculated that it would cause prices to rise less than they had after similar events in the past. This, she said, was because the demand for orange juice had become more elastic in the last few years as consumers began to realize that there were more substitutes for orange juice.

One example she cited was the presence on the market of soft drinks that contain some percentage of fresh juices. At one time, people drank orange juice only for breakfast. Now, many regard it as a good refreshment at any time of day. Of course, in this context, it has many substitutes: water, milk, other juices, and soft drinks (particularly those containing fruit juice). It is interesting that at the same time orange juice prices were rising, Coca-Cola began to market its cola drinks as good breakfast drinks.

CHECKING OUT

Now that you have finished studying this chapter, you should be able to:

1. Review the most important concepts in supply and demand analysis.

2. Define elasticity as a relationship between variables.

3. Define and calculate the coefficient of elasticity price elasticity of demand.

4. Define and calculate the income elasticity of demand and the cross elasticity of demand.

5. Define and calculate the price elasticity of supply.

6. Determine the incidence of an excise tax.

ANSWERS

Trying Out the Terms

1. C	5. I	9. K	13. M
2. A	6. J	10. L	14. N
3. G	7. D	11. E	15. B
4. O	8. F	12. H	

Testing Yourself

Part I: True or False

1. false. Demand is elastic (the coefficient is greater than one) but less than perfectly elastic (the percent change in quantity demanded is less than infinity). In this case, the coefficient of price elasticity of demand is 1.5.
2. true
3. false. The price elasticity of a rectangular hyperbola is equal to one at all points; a straight-line, downward-sloping demand curve has varying price elasticities of demand.

Chapter 19 Elasticity: The Measure of Responsiveness

4. true
5. true
6. true
7. false. A longer time period gives consumers more time to find substitutes. Demand becomes more elastic.
8. true
9. false. It will shift the demand curve to the right. When income increases, demand for the good also increases.
10. false. Those goods have independent demand and are completely unrelated.
11. true
12. true
13. true
14. true
15. false. Their income should fall. When income falls during a recession, people buy less of a normal good.

Part II: Problems

1.

DEMAND FOR COFFEE MUGS

Price	Quantity Demanded	E_d (coefficient)	E_d (using total revenue)
$1.00	12	—	—
2.00	10	0.273	inelastic
3.00	8	0.555	inelastic
4.00	6	1.000	unit elastic
5.00	4	1.800	elastic
6.00	2	3.667	elastic

2. a. $4.60 = \dfrac{100\%}{\%\Delta P}$

   $4.60(\%\Delta P) = 100\%$

   $\%\Delta P = \dfrac{100\%}{4.60} = 21.7\%$

   b. $\Delta P = \dfrac{\$2.25 - \$1.75}{\dfrac{\$2.25 + \$1.75}{2}} \times 100\%$

   $\$\Delta P = \left(\dfrac{\$0.50}{\$200}\right) \times 100\% = 25\%$

   $4.60 = \dfrac{\%\Delta Q}{25\%}$

   $\%\Delta Q = 4.60 \times 25\% = 115\%$

3. a. The demand curve will shift to the right as consumers substitute more of this good for its now-more-expensive substitute.

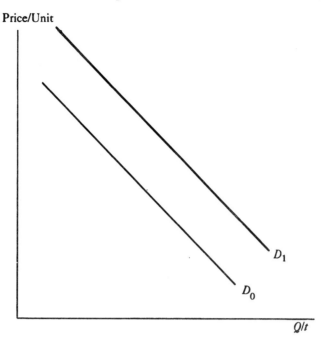

b. The demand curve will shift to the left, because the demand for an inferior good decreases when income increases.

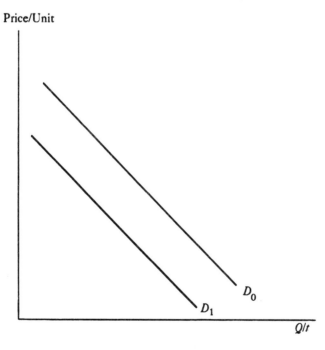

c. The demand curve will shift to the left. As the price of a complement increases, less of this good is demanded; this shift is reinforced by the fall in income, which decreases demand for a normal good.

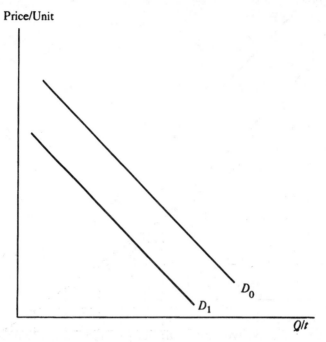

d. It is impossible to determine the outcome. The fall in the price of a substitute would cause the demand curve to shift to the left, but the falling income would cause the demand curve for an inferior good to shift to the right. The final outcome will depend on the relative sizes of the two shifts.

Part III: Multiple Choice

1. c
2. a
3. b
4. d

5. d
6. a
7. b
8. d

9. b
10. b
11. a
12. c

13. b
14. c
15. d

CHAPTER 19 EXERCISES

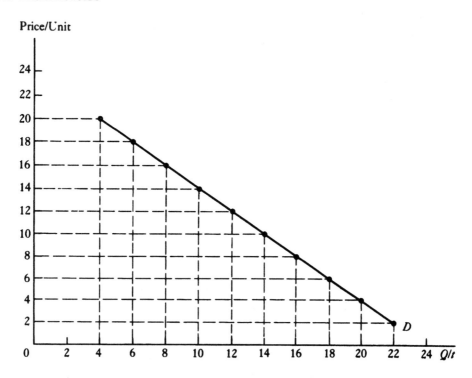

1. According to the above graph, what is the total revenue received by this firm at each of the following prices?

Price	Total Revenue	Price	Total Revenue
$2	_____	$12	_____
4	_____	14	_____
6	_____	16	_____
8	_____	18	_____
10	_____	20	_____

2. On the graph, label the area where price elasticity of demand is elastic and the area where it is inelastic.

Chapter 19 Elasticity: The Measure of Responsiveness

3. Use the formula for arc elasticity to determine the coefficient of price elasticity of demand for each interval.

Price	E_d	Price	E_d
$2	_____	$12	_____
4	_____	14	_____
6	_____	16	_____
8	_____	18	_____
10	_____	20	_____

4. Suppose this firm is presently charging a price of $6 and wishes to maximize its revenue. What price should it charge? How would you justify a lower level of sales to the management?

CHAPTER 20

DEMAND AND CONSUMER CHOICE

CHECKING IN

The law of demand tells us that price and quantity are inversely related. The market demand curves that you studied in previous chapters all obeyed this law of demand. In this chapter, you will study the individual demand curves that make up these market demand curves and discover why consumers behave according to the law of demand.

When price falls, the quantity demanded increases, *ceteris paribus*. Utility theory offers one explanation of this law of demand. People get satisfaction from the goods that they purchase and consume. This satisfaction is called *utility*. Total utility increases as a consumer acquires more and more of a good, but marginal utility (utility per additional item) decreases. Consumers decide what to buy based on the marginal utility they expect to receive for each dollar spent. Utility is maximized when the marginal utility per dollar for each good consumed is equal. If prices change, consumers will rearrange their purchases. They can get greater marginal utility per dollar by buying more of a good with a lower price. This explains the downward-sloping demand curve. There are many criticisms of utility theory, but it does a very good job of explaining how consumers behave.

Another way of understanding the law of demand is through the substitution and income effects. As one good becomes relatively cheaper, people buy more of it and less of other goods; this is the substitution effect. The income effect occurs when the price of a good falls. The same amount may now be bought for a lower price, thus increasing the consumer's real income. When income rises, consumers purchase more normal goods. When price increases, these effects work in the opposite direction.

Consumers are willing to pay a high price for the first few items they buy and a lower price for subsequent items with lower marginal utility. The difference between the benefit that a consumer derives from a purchase and the price that the consumer actually pays is called *consumer surplus*. It is a kind of bonus in utility or increase in real income.

The Appendix to this chapter develops indifference theory, an alternative approach to consumer behavior. An indifference map shows combinations of goods that yield equal amounts of satisfaction. Consumers are restrained by their budgets from consuming all they want of all goods; therefore, they find the maximum possible utility by choosing the combination of goods represented by the indifference curve that is tangent to the budget line. A price-consumption curve shows the way consumers change their behavior when prices change. The demand curve can be derived from the price-consumption curve. Consumer response to changing income can also be explained with indifference theory.

TRYING OUT THE TERMS

Match each of the following terms with its definition, and then check your answers. If you are having trouble, go back to the text and find the definition there.

Part I

____ 1. utility function

____ 2. budget constraint

____ 3. diamond-water paradox

____ 4. consumer surplus

____ 5. utility maximization

____ 6. substitution effect

____ 7. principle of diminishing marginal utility

____ 8. interpersonal utility comparisons

____ 9. income effect

____ 10. marginal utility (*MU*)

____ 11. util

____ 12. utility

A. The fact that diamonds, although less useful than water, are more expensive than water. That is, things with the greatest value in exchange (price) often have little value in use.

B. The satisfaction that an individual expects to receive from consuming a good or service.

C. An arbitrary unit used to measure individual utility.

D. A relationship expressing a consumer's desire to consume differing amounts of a good.

E. The fact that the additional utility declines as quantity consumed increases. Less satisfaction is obtained per additional unit as more units are consumed.

F. The amount of utility that one more or less unit of consumption adds to or subtracts from total utility.

G. A given level of income that determines the maximum amount of goods that may be purchased by an individual.

H. The process by which a consumer adjusts consumption, given a budget constraint and a set of prices, in order to attain the highest total amount of satisfaction.

I. Attempts to compare the utility of one individual with that of another (or others).

J. An increase in the quantity demanded of a good (or service) because its price has fallen and it becomes a better substitute for all other goods.

K. An increase in demand for a good (or service) when its price falls, *ceteris paribus,* because the household's real income rises and the consumer buys more of all normal goods.

L. The extra utility derived from a purchase that has a value to the consumer greater than the market price.

Part II

These terms are found in the Appendix to the chapter.

_____ 1. indifference analysis   _____ 5. income-consumption curve

_____ 2. price-consumption curve   _____ 6. indifference map

_____ 3. marginal rate of substitution (*MRS*)   _____ 7. indifference set

_____ 4. indifference curve   _____ 8. principle of diminishing marginal rates of substitution

A. A curve that uses parallel budget lines to show changes in consumer equilibrium when income changes.

B. An approach to analyzing consumer behavior based on ranking the utility of choices relative to one another.

C. A plot of all combinations of goods that the consumer is indifferent among.

D. A curve that shows changes in consumer equilibrium when the price of one good on an indifference curve changes.

E. Any number of combinations of goods among which the individual consumer is indifferent (has no preference).

F. A set of indifference curves. Higher curves represent higher levels of utility.

G. The fact that as more of one good is consumed, more and more of the other must be given up to maintain indifference between the two.

H. The trade-off ratio along an indifference curve.

TESTING YOURSELF

In the next three sections, you will answer questions and work problems that are based on information in the text. Master all of the terms before you begin these sections. Work each section without referring to your notes or the text, and then check your answers.

Part I: True or False

Mark each statement as true or false. Whenever you mark a statement as false, jot down a sentence stating why it is false. Statements 13–15 are based on material in the Appendix.

_____ 1. Choice is made necessary by the competing options offered by markets.

_____ 2. Classical economists had trouble analyzing utility because they assumed that a numerical calculation of utility was impossible.

_____ 3. Alfred Marshall held that price is determined by the interaction of supply and demand.

_____ 4. When a good or service can be obtained for some positive price in the marketplace, it has utility.

_____ 5. The diamond-water paradox was solved by Adam Smith.

_____ 6. As an individual consumes more of any one good, its marginal utility usually increases.

_____ 7. If Ralph continues to buy chocolates even after the price of chocolates goes up, his total utility of chocolates is increasing, because he is willing to pay more to get the same amount.

_____ 8. Frito, a cat, refuses to eat any more sardines, even though there are plenty in her dish. This indicates that the marginal utility of one more sardine is negative.

_____ 9. If marginal utility is falling, it is an indication that total utility is falling.

_____ 10. Susan finds that the marginal utility per dollar of earrings is greater than the marginal utility per dollar of rings. Susan should buy more rings until the marginal utility per dollar for each good is equal.

_____ 11. If the price of movie tickets goes up, the substitution effect will cause people to rent more videotapes.

_____ 12. Karen had planned to buy six doughnuts. However, she bought seven, because an in-store special on doughnuts left her with extra change. This is an example of the income effect.

_____ 13. The marginal rate of substitution is measured along an indifference curve.

_____ 14. A consumer is maximizing utility when she is at a point where her indifference curve is tangent to the budget line.

_____ 15. If the price of good A increases when all other prices are unchanged, in the new equilibrium the consumer of good A will be on a new budget line and the same indifference curve.

Part II: Problems

Problem 3 is based on the Appendix.

1. Kenny has the following utility functions for three goods, *A*, *B*, and *C*.

GOOD A: $P_A = \$3$

Units	Total Utility (TU)	Marginal Utility (MU)	MU/P
1	27	_____	_____
2	51	_____	_____
3	72	_____	_____
4	90	_____	_____
5	105	_____	_____
6	117	_____	_____
7	126	_____	_____
8	132	_____	_____
9	135	_____	_____
10	138	_____	_____

GOOD B: $P_B = \$7$

Units	Total Utility (TU)	Marginal Utility (MU)	MU/P
1	70	_____	_____
2	133	_____	_____
3	189	_____	_____
4	238	_____	_____
5	280	_____	_____
6	315	_____	_____
7	343	_____	_____
8	364	_____	_____
9	378	_____	_____
10	385	_____	_____

GOOD C: $P_C = \$5$

Units	Total Utility (TU)	Marginal Utility (MU)	MU/P
1	60		
2	110		
3	150		
4	185		
5	215		
6	240		
7	260		
8	275		
9	290		
10	295		

a. Complete the tables.

b. If Kenny has a budget of $87, how many of each good will he purchase? What is his total utility?

c. Suppose Kenny's budget rises to $102 and he buys 3 more units of good C. Has he increased his total utility? Has he maximized his total utility?

2. Jane's demand schedule for dry cleaning each month is shown below.

Price/Garment	Number of Garments
$7.00	0
6.50	1
6.00	2
5.50	3
5.00	5
4.50	7
4.00	10
3.50	13

a. Graph Jane's demand curve below.

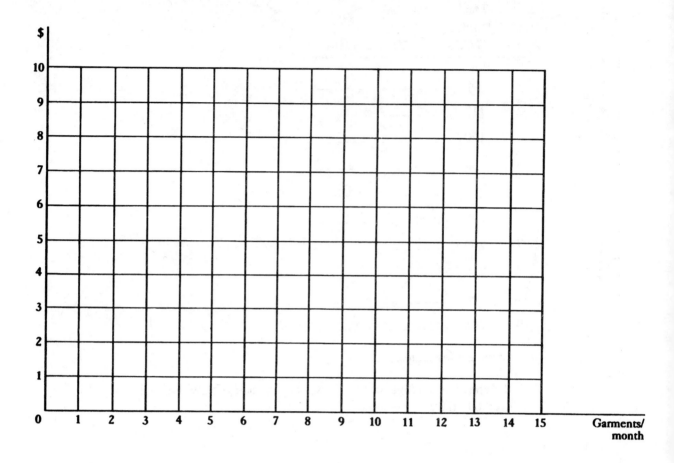

b. The current price is $5.00. Mark the area of Jane's consumer surplus on the graph.

c. Explain how the substitution effect makes Jane's demand curve downward sloping.

3. Use the figure below to answer the following questions.

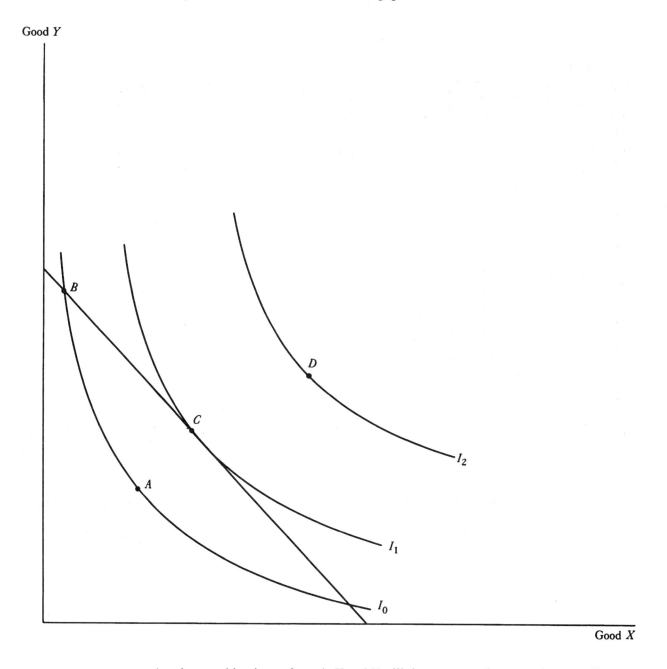

a. At what combinations of goods X and Y will the consumer have maximum utility?

b. Explain why the rational consumer would never choose point B or D.

c. Suppose the consumer has an increase in income and can now maximize consumption at point D. Draw the new budget line and income-consumption curve on your graph.

Part III: Multiple Choice

Questions 14 and 15 are based on material in the Appendix.

For Questions 1–3, use the following table.

Quantity	Total Utility
5	45
6	50
7	54
8	57
9	59

_____ 1. This table is an example of
   a. a budget line.
   b. an indifference curve.
   c. an indifference map.
   d. a utility function.

_____ 2. The table illustrates
   a. irrational behavior on the part of the consumer.
   b. increasing total utility.
   c. diminishing marginal utility.
   d. both increasing total utility and diminishing marginal utility.

_____ 3. What is the marginal utility associated with the eighth unit of the good described?
   a. 206
   b. 149
   c. 3
   d. 12

_____ 4. If the marginal utilities associated with the first four units of consumption of good Y are 10, 12, 9, and 7, respectively, what is the total utility associated with the third unit?
   a. 38
   b. 31
   c. 3
   d. An amount that cannot be determined from marginal utilities

_____ 5. If the price of peanut butter decreases and Patricia buys more as a result, then
   a. total utility will likely increase.
   b. marginal utility per dollar will likely increase.
   c. the budget line will be unchanged.
   d. both total utility and marginal utility per dollar are likely to increase.

_____ 6. The sum of the marginal utilities up to one point is known as
   a. total utility.
   b. average utility.
   c. maximum utility.
   d. an indifference curve.

_____ 7. When total utility is at a maximum, marginal utility is
   a. at a maximum.
   b. falling.
   c. equal to zero.
   d. rising.

_____ 8. Suppose Steven's *MU* per dollar spent on books is 65 and his *MU* per dollar spent on movies is 80. Steven
   a. can increase his total utility by going to more movies and buying fewer books.
   b. is maximizing his total utility.
   c. can increase his total utility only if he can increase his total income.
   d. can increase his total utility by buying more books and going to fewer movies.

_____ 9. As a general rule, marginal utility will be less
   a. as less of the good is consumed.
   b. as more of the good is consumed.
   c. when average utility is at a maximum.
   d. only when the good is inferior.

_____ 10. Terry believes in the principle of diminishing marginal utility. If he wants to sell more hats in his hat shop, he will
   a. offer a wider variety of hats.
   b. advertise more.
   c. lower his prices.
   d. raise his prices.

_____ 11. Terry has done a consumer survey and believes that the demand curve for his hats is

Price	Quantity
$45	0
40	2
30	4
20	8

If Terry sets a price of $30,
a. he is not allowing his customers to maximize utility.
b. his customers have a total consumer surplus of $20.
c. his customers have a total consumer surplus of $70.
d. his price is too high.

_____ 12. The price of running shoes increases; as a result, the fall in real income causes fewer running shoes to be sold. This is an example of
a. diminishing utility.
b. the income effect.
c. the budget effect.
d. the substitution effect.

_____ 13. Sylvia's income is $800 a month. The price of chicken increases. What will happen?
a. The substitution effect will cause Sylvia to buy more tuna fish, which is cheaper.
b. The income effect will cause Sylvia to buy more chicken, since she thinks of chicken as a normal good.
c. Sylvia's consumer surplus for chicken will get bigger.
d. Sylvia's real income will rise.

_____ 14. As an individual moves from one point on an indifference curve to another point that is higher and to the left,
a. total utility decreases.
b. marginal utility decreases.
c. total utility remains the same.
d. the income effect becomes stronger.

_____ 15. If Randy's income goes down,
a. his budget line will shift to the left.
b. he can maximize utility only on a lower indifference curve.
c. he will move to a higher indifference curve.
d. his budget line will shift to the left and he will maximize utility on a lower indifference curve.

TAKING ANOTHER LOOK

The diamond-water paradox continues to puzzle many people. Apparently, some of the utility a person gets from owning a good depends on intangible attributes, such as the identity of a former owner. Following the death of the Duchess of Windsor, her jewels were auctioned off at spectacularly and unexpectedly high prices. Not long after that auction, some of Cary Grant's possessions also turned up on the auction block. An expert had estimated the value of one cigarette case when new at about $5,000. It sold for $13,200. Of course, it bore the inscription "Merci, January 18, 1942"; it had been a gift to Grant from his then-wife, Barbara Hutton.

CHECKING OUT

Now that you have finished studying this chapter, you should be able to:

1. Define utility, income effects, substitution effects, and consumer surplus and then derive an individual demand curve for a good based on the equation for maximizing total utility and the principle of diminishing marginal utility.

2. Explain the solution to the diamond-water paradox based on marginal utility and total utility.

3. Identify and describe the concept of consumer surplus.

4. Describe how advertising affects utility.

5. Describe experimental economics.

In addition, if your instructor assigned the material in the Appendix, you should be able to:

1. Define the following elements of indifference curve analysis: indifference curve, budget line, the equilibrium point in terms of the slope of the budget line, and the marginal rate of substitution.

2. Using indifference curve analysis, derive an income-consumption curve, a price-consumption curve, and a demand curve.

ANSWERS

Trying Out the Terms

Part I

1. D
2. G
3. A
4. L
5. H
6. J
7. E
8. I
9. K
10. F
11. C
12. B

Part II

1. B
2. D
3. H
4. C
5. A
6. F
7. E
8. G

Testing Yourself

Part I: True or False

1. false. Choice is made necessary by scarcity.
2. false. Classical economists did not seem too concerned about the measurability of utility.
3. true
4. false. Utility is the satisfaction a consumer anticipates getting from a good or service. The good may be available, but that doesn't necessarily mean that people are willing to buy it.
5. false. It was solved by Jevons, Menger, and Walras.
6. false. Total utility usually increases, but marginal utility decreases.
7. true
8. true
9. false. If marginal utility is positive (whether rising or falling), total utility is rising. Total utility falls when marginal utility is negative.
10. false. She should buy more earrings and fewer rings until the marginal utility per dollar is equal for each item.
11. true
12. true
13. true
14. true
15. false. The consumer will be on a new budget line and a new, lower indifference curve.

Part II: Problems

1. a.   Good A: $P_A = \$3$

Units	Total Utility (TU)	Marginal Utility (MU)	MU/P
1	27	27	9
2	51	24	8
3	72	21	7
4	90	18	6
5	105	15	5
6	117	12	4
7	126	9	3
8	132	6	2
9	135	3	1
10	138	3	1

Good B: $P_B = \$7$

Units	Total Utility (TU)	Marginal Utility (MU)	MU/P
1	70	70	10
2	133	63	9
3	189	56	8
4	238	49	7
5	280	42	6
6	315	35	5
7	343	28	4
8	364	21	3
9	378	14	2
10	385	7	1

Good C: $P_C = \$5$

Units	Total Utility (TU)	Marginal Utility (MU)	MU/P
1	60	60	12
2	110	50	10
3	150	40	8
4	185	35	7
5	215	30	6
6	240	25	5
7	260	20	4
8	275	15	3
9	290	15	3
10	295	5	1

b. Kenny will buy 5 units of good *A*, 6 units of good *B*, and 6 units of good *C*. His total utility is 660.

c. Total utility increases by 50 to 710. To maximize total utility, he should have bought one more of each good; then total utility would increase by 60 to 720.

2. a., b.

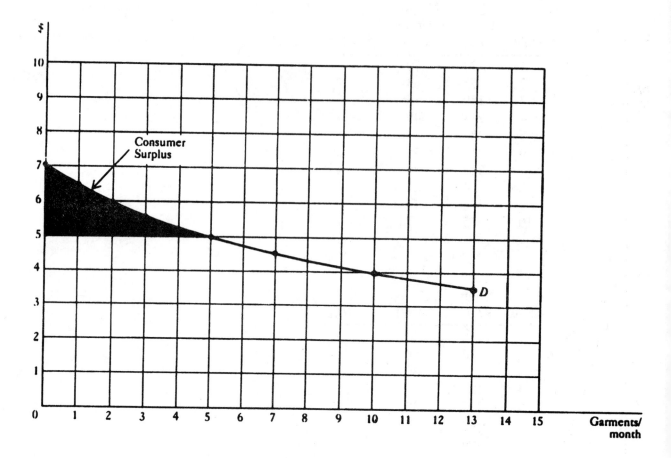

c. As the price goes down, Jane will begin to substitute dry cleaning for washing her clothes herself. She may, over time, begin to substitute "dry clean only" garments for garments that can be washed at home.

3. a. The consumer will maximize utility at point C.
   b. The consumer would not maximize utility at point B. It would exhaust the budget, but he or she could move to a higher indifference curve (I_1) by buying more of X and less of Y. Point D is unattainable, given the current budget constraints.

c.

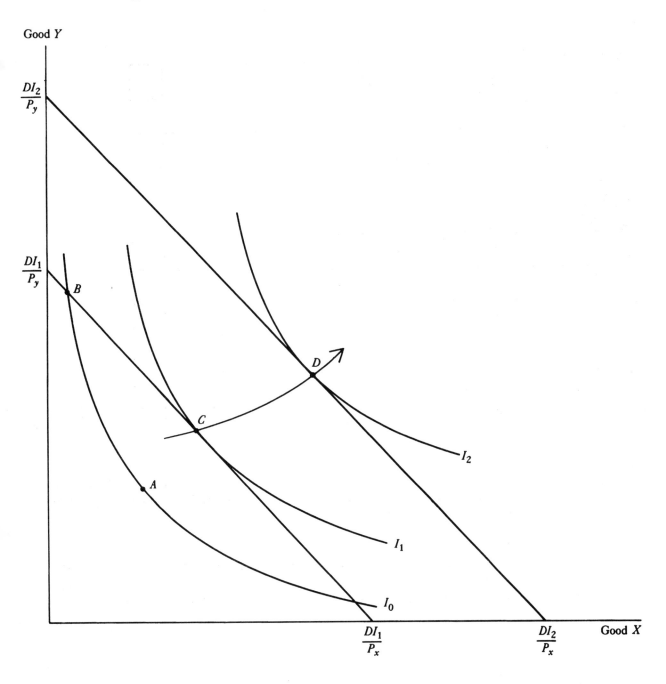

Part III: Multiple Choice

1. d
2. d
3. c
4. b
5. d
6. a
7. c
8. a
9. b
10. c
11. b
12. b
13. a
14. c
15. d

Name _____

CHAPTER 20 EXERCISES

1. a. Complete the following table.

Units of Good	Total Utility (TU)	Marginal Utility (MU)
1	20	_____
2	23	_____
3	25	_____
4	23	_____
5	20	_____
6	16	_____
7	11	_____
8	5	_____
9	0	_____
10	−2	_____

b. Where does diminishing marginal utility set in?

c. Where is total utility at a maximum?

d. If this good were free, how much would this consumer use?

2.

Unit/Fun	Marginal Utility (MU)	Unit/Games	Marginal Utility (MU)
1	10	1	32
2	8	2	24
3	5	3	20
4	3	4	12
5	1	5	8

a. Suppose that Fred has $15 to spend. Fun is free, but games cost $4 per unit. How much fun will Fred have? How many games will he buy? He can't buy part of a game.

b. Now suppose that fun costs $1 per unit and games still cost $4 per unit. How will Fred divide up his budget?

c. What is Fred's total utility at this point?

d. If Fred's income goes up to $20, how will he spend his income?

CHAPTER 21

FIRMS AND PRODUCTION

CHECKING IN

Goods and services are supplied to the market by firms. In this chapter and the next, you will learn how firms obtain and pay for the inputs used in production.

Entrepreneurs seeking to make a profit combine inputs to produce goods and services. Nonprofit firms, both private and governmental, also produce goods and services; however, they have different incentives and do not attempt to maximize profits.

The greatest number of firms in the United States are organized as sole proprietorships. Many former sole proprietorships and partnerships are now registering as S corporations because this type of firm enjoys some of the advantages of corporate organization while avoiding double taxation on income. Corporations account for about 85 percent of annual U.S. business sales.

One way firms attempt to maximize profits is by producing in an economically efficient manner. This is done by combining inputs so that a certain level of output can be produced for the least possible cost. A firm's production opportunities can be illustrated by a production function, which gives the technical relationship between inputs and output. In the short-run production function, some inputs are fixed and others are variable. In the long-run production function, all inputs are variable. As more and more variable inputs are added to the fixed inputs in the short run, the total output increases in smaller and smaller quantities. This is known as the principle of diminishing returns. This principle does not hold for the long run. In the long run, firms can increase production by varying all inputs. The combination of inputs is based on relative prices and cost constraints.

The Appendix to this chapter analyzes production and cost decisions using isoquant curves and isocost lines. These are very similar to indifference curves and budget lines.

TRYING OUT THE TERMS

Match each of the following terms with its definition, and then check your answers. If you are having trouble, go back to the text and find the definition there.

Part I

_____ 1. industry
_____ 2. production
_____ 3. stock
_____ 4. horizontally integrated firms
_____ 5. stockholders
_____ 6. shirk
_____ 7. partnership
_____ 8. vertically integrated firms
_____ 9. board of directors
_____ 10. corporation
_____ 11. conglomerates
_____ 12. sole proprietorship
_____ 13. S corporation
_____ 14. transaction costs
_____ 15. business firm
_____ 16. teams
_____ 17. bond
_____ 18. limited liability
_____ 19. residual claimant

A. The process of transforming inputs into marketable outputs.

B. Firms that perform many sequential steps in a production process.

C. Firms that perform many similar production operations in the same industry.

D. Firms that perform many unrelated operations or produce in many different industries.

E. Costs associated with gathering information about markets (prices and quantities supplied) for consuming or producing.

F. Groups of employees that work together to produce something.

G. To put forth less effort than agreed on.

H. An organization formed by an entrepreneur to combine inputs in order to produce marketable outputs.

I. A group of firms producing similar or related products.

J. A form of enterprise in which no legal distinction is made between the firm and its owner.

K. A form of enterprise in which there is more than one owner, and the firm does not have a legal existence separate from the owners.

268   Chapter 21   *Firms and Production*

L. A form of enterprise in which stockholders are the owners of the firm but have limited liability.

M. The owners of a corporation.

N. Individual or group of individuals who shares in the profits of an enterprise.

O. The individuals elected by the stockholders of a corporation to select the managers and oversee the management of the corporation.

P. Interest-earning certificate issued by governments or corporations in exchange for borrowed funds and has a fixed face value, annual interest payment, and maturity date.

Q. A certificate of ownership in a corporation.

R. A hybrid type of corporation that passes income directly to the owners, avoiding the double taxation of corporate profits.

S. The fact that the stockholders of a corporation cannot be sued for failure of the corporation to meet its obligations.

Part II

(Terms 12 and 13 are found in the Appendix.)

____ 1. economic efficiency
____ 2. fixed inputs
____ 3. long run
____ 4. short run
____ 5. technical efficiency
____ 6. average product (*AP*)
____ 7. variable inputs
____ 8. marginal product
____ 9. production function
____ 10. principle of diminishing returns
____ 11. total product (*TP*)
____ 12. isocost line
____ 13. isoquant

A. A curve that shows all combinations of quantities of two inputs that can be used to produce a given quantity of output.

B. A line that shows the amounts of inputs that can be purchased with a fixed sum of money (a firm's budget line).

C. The basis for minimizing the inputs to a production method according to some specific rule (an engineering concept).

D. The least-cost method of production.

E. A description of the amounts of output expected from various combinations of inputs.

F. The productive resources that cannot be varied in the short run.

G. The productive resources that can be increased or decreased in the short run.

H. The period of time that is too short to vary all the inputs.

I. The period of time in which all inputs, including plant and equipment, can be varied.

J. The fact that as more and more units of a variable input are added to a set of fixed inputs, the resulting additions to output eventually become smaller.

K. The change in total output that is produced by a unit change in an input.

L. The total product (output) divided by the number of units of input used.

M. The amount of output that a firm produces.

TESTING YOURSELF

In the next three sections, you will answer questions and work problems that are based on information in the text. Master all of the terms before you begin these sections. Work each section without referring to your notes or the text, and then check your answers.

Part I: True or False

Mark each statement as true or false. Whenever you mark a statement as false, jot down a sentence stating why it is false. (Questions 14 and 15 are based on material in the Appendix.)

_____ 1. If it is more efficient for them to produce than to purchase, households will not buy certain goods from firms.

_____ 2. A firm that owns three grocery stores in one state and three farms and a bakery in another state is vertically integrated.

_____ 3. Ronald Coase contends that there are different sizes and forms of firms because firms can't get enough information to operate efficiently.

_____ 4. Firms exist so that they can combine inputs to produce marketable outputs.

_____ 5. Shirking would most likely be observed in a sole proprietorship.

_____ 6. The residual claimant gets what is paid after the stockholders' claims are met.

_____ 7. Production changes inputs into outputs.

_____ 8. In the short run, some inputs are variable and some are fixed.

_____ 9. According to the principle of diminishing returns, adding more and more units of a variable input to a set of fixed inputs will eventually result in increasingly smaller additions to output.

_____ 10. If the marginal product (*MP*) is greater than the average product (*AP*), we know that *AP* is at a maximum.

_____ 11. The change in total output per unit change in an input is the average product.

_____ 12. When the total product is at a maximum, the marginal product is equal to zero.

_____ 13. Firms maximize profits by choosing a mix of inputs so that the marginal product of a dollar's worth of each input is equal to the marginal product of a dollar's worth of every other input.

_____ 14. An isoquant is a line that shows the amounts of two inputs that can be purchased with equal total cost.

_____ 15. When a firm changes its choice of inputs because the price of one of them has changed, the firm is moving along an expansion path.

Part II: Problems

1. Consider the following production function.

Capital	Number of Workers	Total Product	Marginal Product	Average Product
10	0	0	_____	_____
10	1	90	_____	_____
10	2	200	_____	_____
10	3	330	_____	_____
10	4	440	_____	_____
10	5	540	_____	_____
10	6	630	_____	_____
10	7	700	_____	_____
10	8	720	_____	_____

a. Complete the table.

b. Is this firm operating in the short run or the long run? How can you tell?

c. In terms of number of workers, where do diminishing marginal returns begin?

2. You are given the following information about factor inputs and their marginal products. Also, $P_L = \$2$ and $P_K = \$4$.

Labor Units	MP_L	Capital Units	MP_K
1	12	1	20
2	10	2	16
3	8	3	12
4	6	4	8
5	4	5	4

a. What combinations of inputs fulfill the requirement that $MP_L/P_L = MP_K/P_k$?

b. If the budget is $20, what combination of inputs will be used? Why is this combination preferable to any of the others that fulfill the requirement?

Chapter 21 Firms and Production

3. (Problem 3 is based on the Appendix.) Consider the isoquant map below.

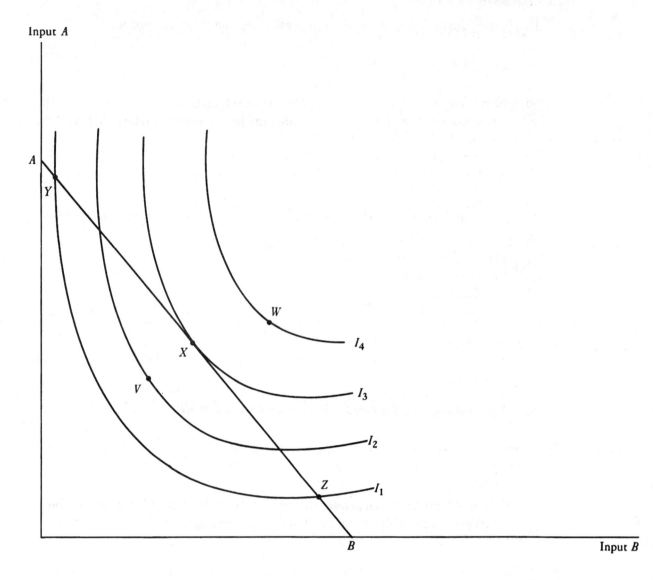

a. If the firm's total cost is given by isocost line AB, where will the firm operate? Explain why this point is preferable to any of the other marked points.

b. Suppose the price of input B falls while the price of input A remains unchanged. Draw the new isocost line on the graph, and trace the firm's expansion path. You do not need to know amounts; just show the direction of change.

Part III: Multiple Choice

_____ 1. When Steve Eliot bakes a cake instead of buying one at the bakery, he is
   a. misallocating his resources.
   b. acting like a firm.
   c. involved in household production.
   d. both acting like a firm and involved in household production.

_____ 2. A vertically integrated firm might own
   a. a ski factory, an Alpine resort hotel, and a hospital.
   b. several plants that manufacture skis of different qualities.
   c. a ski factory, a cigar manufacturer, and a carpet factory.
   d. several ski-manufacturing plants in different countries.

_____ 3. Which of the following is *not* a basic legal form for a firm?
   a. Sole proprietorship
   b. Chartered organization
   c. Partnership
   d. Corporation

_____ 4. How can a partnership raise funds?
   a. Borrowing from a bank
   b. Issuing bonds
   c. Selling common stock
   d. Selling restricted stock

_____ 5. S corporations became popular during the late 1980s because this form of business organization
   a. facilitates the merger of large firms.
   b. offers some of the advantages of corporate structure to small businesses.
   c. provided a way to avoid capital gains tax.
   d. allows foreigners to invest in U.S. securities.

_____ 6. When inputs are combined so that total production has the lowest possible cost, we are observing
   a. technical efficiency.
   b. optimal engineering.
   c. economic efficiency.
   d. average-cost production.

_____ 7. If Anne Morris buys wood and ivory (synthetic, of course) every month to manufacture pianos in the plant she has leased for four years, Anne is operating
   a. in the long run.
   b. without a production function.
   c. in the short run.
   d. a vertically integrated firm.

8. A production function
   a. is the technical relationship between inputs and outputs.
   b. indicates whether a plant is operating at technical efficiency.
   c. indicates the various costs of different levels of production.
   d. indicates both the various costs of different levels of production and whether a plant is operating at technical efficiency.

9. In the short run
   a. all inputs are variable.
   b. some inputs are variable and some are fixed.
   c. all inputs are fixed.
   d. the time period cannot exceed one year.

10. When Adam hires Nancy to work in the box factory, output goes from 1,000 boxes to 1,200 boxes; when Adam then hires Rachel, output increases to 1,350 boxes. This example demonstrates that
    a. the factory is operating in the short run.
    b. Rachel is not as good a boxmaker as Nancy.
    c. the factory is operating inefficiently.
    d. the factory is not on its production function.

11. When the box factory has 12 workers, total output is 1,200. When the factory has 13 workers, total output is 1,350. Which of the following is true?
    a. The factory is operating in the long run.
    b. The average product of 12 workers is 100 boxes.
    c. The marginal product of 12 workers is 1,000 boxes.
    d. The plant should reduce production.

12. Joanna runs a shoe repair shop. When she has 4 employees, total output is 80 pairs of shoes a day. After she hires a fifth worker, total output rises to 95 pairs a day. Which of the following is true?
    a. Total product has increased.
    b. Average product has decreased.
    c. Marginal product is greater than average product.
    d. Total product has increased while average product has decreased.

(Questions 13-15 are based on material in the Appendix.)

13. Output can be increased without increasing cost if a firm is operating at a point
    a. on an isoquant curve that is beyond the isocost curve.
    b. on an isoquant curve that intersects the isocost curve.
    c. on an isoquant curve that is tangent to the isocost curve.
    d. anywhere along the isocost curve.

14. When the slope of the isocost curve changes, the
    a. slope of the isoquant curve will also change.
    b. firm is operating on a new production function.
    c. price of at least one of the inputs has changed.
    d. firm will find it necessary to change the level of production.

____ 15. If isoquant B lies below and to the left of isoquant A,
  a. costs will be higher along isoquant B.
  b. isoquant B is preferable to isoquant A.
  c. isoquant A and isoquant B have the same level of output with different levels of inputs.
  d. output will be lower along isoquant B.

TAKING ANOTHER LOOK

Shareholders don't have to wait for the annual meeting to communicate displeasure with the managers of their firm; they do so through the movement of share prices in the stock market. Although many forces affect prices, stock prices remain the fundamental evaluation of what buyers and sellers think the firm is worth. If earnings (profits) fall, stock prices usually respond quickly. This is the shareholders' way of telling management, "We are not receiving the profits we expect from this firm, so we are going to reallocate our resources elsewhere."

CHECKING OUT

Now that you have finished studying this chapter, you should be able to:

1. Explain why firms come into existence.
2. Define the various types of firms and list the advantages and disadvantages of each business organization.
3. Describe the difference between a for-profit firm and a nonprofit firm.
4. Calculate the least-cost method of production to determine economic efficiency.
5. Use a production function to explain increasing and diminishing marginal returns.
6. Show how a firm chooses its mix of inputs to maximize output.

In addition, if your instructor assigned the material in the Appendix, you should be able to:

1. Define isoquant, isocost, and the highest level of production along an isocost line.
2. Derive an expansion path using isoquant-isocost analysis.

ANSWERS

Trying Out the Terms

Part I

1. I
2. A
3. Q
4. C
5. M
6. G
7. K
8. B
9. O
10. L
11. D
12. J
13. R
14. E
15. H
16. F
17. P
18. S
19. N

Part II

1. D	5. C	9. E	13. A
2. F	6. L	10. J	
3. I	7. G	11. M	
4. H	8. K	12. B	

Testing Yourself

Part I: True or False

1. true
2. true
3. false. Coase contends that different sizes and forms of firms more efficiently reduce transaction costs for different kinds of production activities.
4. true
5. false. It is most likely to be observed in nonprofit organizations.
6. false. A residual claimant is one who shares in the profits of the firm; therefore, stockholders are residual claimants.
7. true
8. true
9. true
10. false. If MP is greater than AP, then AP is increasing.
11. false. The change in total output per unit change of resource use is the marginal product.
12. true
13. true
14. false. This is the definition of the isocost line. An isoquant curve shows all combinations of two inputs that can be used to produce a given output.
15. true

Part II: Problems

1. a.

Capital	Number of Workers	Total Product	Marginal Product	Average Product
10	0	0	—	—
10	1	90	90	90
10	2	200	110	100
10	3	330	130	110
10	4	440	110	110
10	5	540	100	108
10	6	630	90	105
10	7	700	70	100
10	8	720	20	90

    b. The firm is operating in the short run because capital is fixed and the MP is decreasing (beyond three workers).
    c. Beginning with the fourth worker, marginal product is diminishing.

2. a. 2 labor units and 1 capital unit; 3 labor units and 2 capital units; 4 labor units and 3 capital units; and 5 labor units and 4 capital units.
   b. The firm will use 4 units of labor (costing $8) and 3 units of capital (costing $12). None of the other combinations have a cost equal to the budget.
3. a. The firm will operate at point X. Points Y and Z will exhaust the budget, but the firm can produce more for the same cost at point X. Point V will not exhaust the budget. Point W is unattainable with the current budget.
   b.

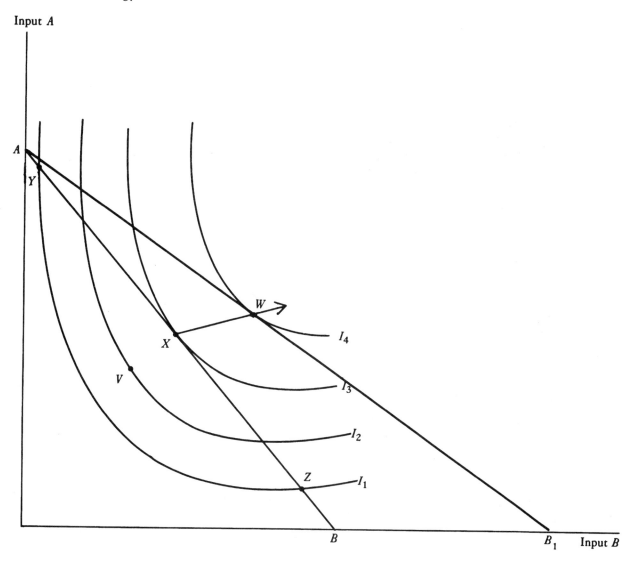

Part III: Multiple Choice

1. d
2. a
3. b
4. a
5. b
6. c
7. c
8. a
9. b
10. a
11. b
12. d
13. b
14. c
15. d

CHAPTER 21 EXERCISES

1. Complete the following short-run production function.

Units of Labor	AP_L	TP_L	MP_L
1	150		
2	170		
3	180		
4	190		
5	180		
6	170		
7	160		
8	150		
9	140		
10	130		
11	120		
12	110		

2. Graph this production function on the graph on the next page. Mark the area of increasing returns and diminishing returns on your graph.

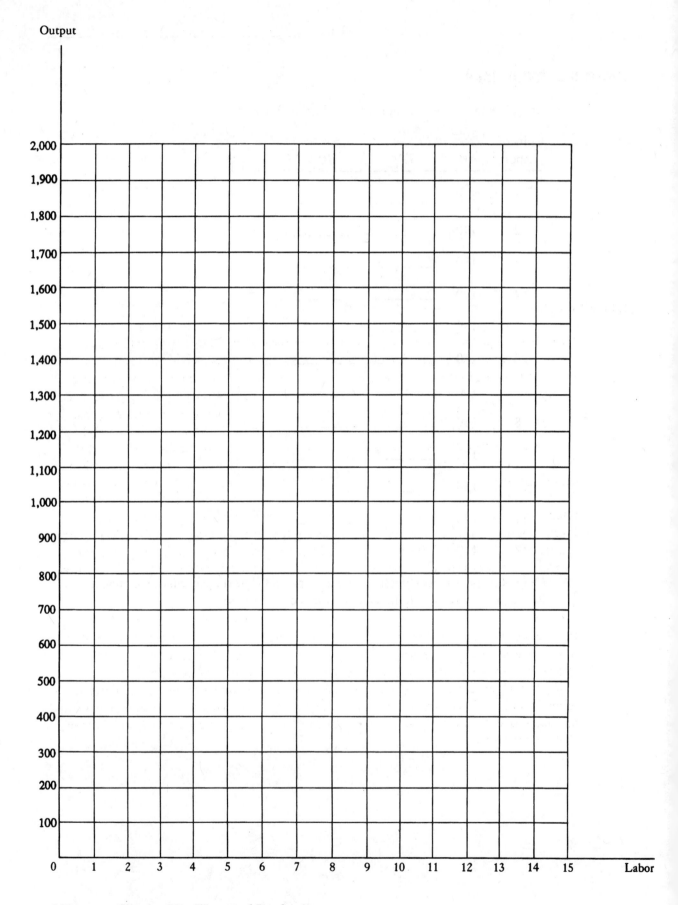

CHAPTER 22

COSTS AND PROFITS

CHECKING IN

Firms have to pay for the inputs that they use as in production. These payments are costs to the firms. Sometimes it is difficult to find all the costs, since not all costs are explicit, or expressed in dollar terms. Some costs are implicit; they are opportunity costs that must be recognized, even when they do not represent a dollar outlay. Normal profits represent one implicit cost. If the owners of capital and the entrepreneur do not receive some minimum return, they will leave the industry for another. In economics, normal profits are thought of as a cost; only profits greater than normal are considered economic profits.

Because decisions about production and costs are interrelated, the analysis in this chapter closely parallels the previous chapter's analysis of production. In the short run, as variable factors are added to fixed factors, firms may experience increasing returns, but marginal returns eventually begin to diminish. As a result, marginal costs may fall at low output levels, but marginal costs will increase as returns diminish. Increasing and then decreasing returns account for the U shape of the short-run average cost and average variable cost curves. In the long run, all factors can be varied. As a result, the average cost of production may either increase or decrease, depending on whether the firm or industry has economies of scale or diseconomies of scale.

Firms do not wish to merely make a profit or have revenue in excess of costs. They want to *maximize* the difference between total revenues and total costs. To do this, firms will produce at the level of output where marginal cost and marginal revenue are equal. This choice ensures that every possible profit-contributing unit will be produced.

Two problems encountered by entrepreneurs are valuing future payments and costs in terms of today's dollars and incorporating risk into decision making. Using present value calculations and employing insurance, diversity, and information can provide amelioration of these problems.

TRYING OUT THE TERMS

Match each of the following terms with its definition, and then check your answers. If you are having trouble, go back to the text and find the definition there.

_____ 1. diseconomies of scale
_____ 2. total cost (TC)
_____ 3. long-run average cost (LRAC) curve
_____ 4. planning curve
_____ 5. risk loving
_____ 6. discounting
_____ 7. implicit costs
_____ 8. average total cost (AC)
_____ 9. marginal revenue (MR)
_____ 10. total fixed costs (TFC)
_____ 11. economic profit
_____ 12. natural monopoly
_____ 13. marginal cost (MC)
_____ 14. normal profit
_____ 15. optimal-size plant
_____ 16. average fixed cost (AFC)
_____ 17. economies of scale
_____ 18. average variable cost (AVC)
_____ 19. risk averse
_____ 20. total variable cost (TVC)
_____ 21. accounting profit
_____ 22. total revenue (TR)
_____ 23. explicit costs
_____ 24. risks neutral
_____ 25. present value (PV)

A. Accounting costs or money outlays.

B. Costs measured by the value of alternatives given up.

C. The difference between total sales and explicit costs.

D. The difference between total sales and the total of explicit and implicit costs of production.

E. The opportunity cost of capital and enterprise, or the rate of return that is necessary for a firm to remain in a competitive industry.

F. The sum of all the costs of production for a given level of output.

G. The costs of the fixed inputs of production, which can't be avoided in the short run.

H. The total of costs that vary directly with output, increasing as more output is produced.

I. Total costs of producing a level of output divided by the number of units of output.

J. Total fixed costs of production divided by number of units of output.

K. Total variable costs of production divided by the number of units of output.

L. The change in total cost from producing one more (or one less) unit of output.

M. The long-run average cost curve used in the planning stage.

N. A curve tangent to all the possible short-run cost curves and representing the lowest attainable average cost of producing any given output.

O. The plant represented by the short-run average cost curve with the lowest attainable per-unit costs.

P. Declines in long-run average cost that are due to increased plant size.

Q. Increases in long-run average cost that are due to increased plant size.

R. A monopoly that emerges because economies of scale mean that there is room for only one firm in the market.

S. The change in total revenue from selling one more (or one less) unit.

T. The value of a future payment or series of future payments discounted to the present.

U. The technique of calculating present values by adjusting for interest that would be earned between now and some specified future time.

V. The price an item sells for multiplied by the number of units sold.

W. The preference for a certain outcome to a risky outcome with the same expected value.

X. Indifference between outcomes with the same expected values.

Y. The preference for an expected value that is lower, but has a higher variance.

TESTING YOURSELF

In the next three sections, you will answer questions and work problems that are based on information in the text. Master all of the terms before you begin these sections. Work each section without referring to your notes or the text, and then check your answers.

Part I: True or False

Mark each statement as true or false. Whenever you mark a statement as false, jot down a sentence stating why it is false.

_____ 1. When a firm earns a return that is greater than both explicit and implicit costs, it is earning excessive profits.

_____ 2. Jennifer owns a launderette. She doesn't pay herself, since she gets to keep all the profits. This means she has only explicit costs.

_____ 3. Jim's video shop has accounting profits of $25,000, but Jim figures his economic profits are $3,000. This means that Jim's implicit costs are $22,000.

_____ 4. Normal profit is the required return to capital and enterprise.

_____ 5. An explicit cost is the same as an accounting cost.

_____ 6. When fixed costs are subtracted from total costs, the remainder is marginal cost.

_____ 7. *AVC* equals *TVC* divided by *Q*.

_____ 8. In the short run, all costs are fixed.

_____ 9. When marginal costs are added up, they are equal to total costs.

_____ 10. Average fixed costs are constant.

_____ 11. An upward-sloping planning curve indicates that an industry has economies of scale.

_____ 12. If *LRAC* is tangent to the minimum point on *AC*, then plant size is optimal.

_____ 13. A wise professional athlete will insist on being paid the present value of a contract up front, in a lump sum, instead of being paid a larger amount over time.

_____ 14. Jermaine can work in one of two businesses. If he joins his mother's insurance agency, he can expect a certain income of $25,000 a year; if he sells real estate, the expected value of his earnings is only $20,000 but it may range between $5,000 and $100,000. Jermaine goes with the real estate company. He is risk loving.

_____ 15. Japan followed the infant industry argument in the period after World War II.

Part II: Problems

1.

Output (Q)	Total Cost (TC)	Average Cost (AC)	Marginal Cost (MC)
0	$25	—	—
1	30	_____	_____
2	36	_____	_____
3	45	_____	_____
4	60	_____	_____
5	80	_____	_____
6	108	_____	_____
7	147	_____	_____

a. Complete the cost schedule on the previous page.

b. What are the total fixed costs?

c. When output is 5, what are the average variable costs?

d. When output is 6, what are the averaged fixed costs?

2. Label the graph below correctly.

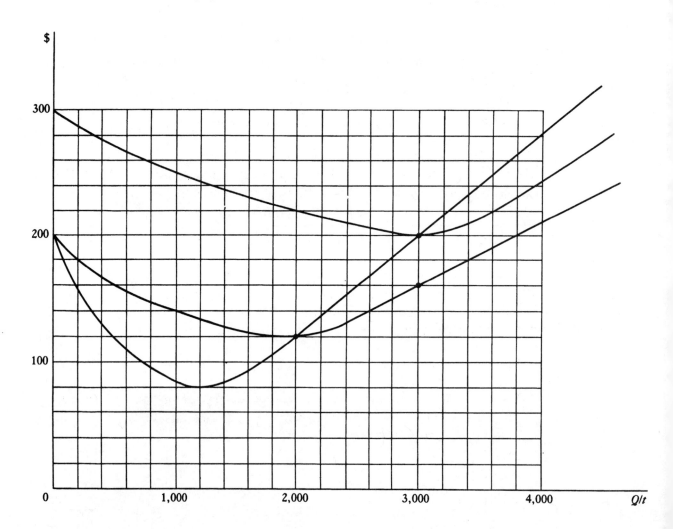

b. What are the total fixed costs at an output of 3,000?

c. At what output is marginal cost equal to average variable cost? to average cost?

d. Explain why the output at which $MC = AVC$ is lower than the output at which $MC = AC$.

Part III: Multiple Choice

1. Ralph's Travel Agency had accounting profits of $50,000 and implicit costs of $30,000. What were economic profits?
   a. $50,000
   b. $30,000
   c. $20,000
   d. An amount that cannot be determined from the given information

2. The Southern Tree Trimming Corporation reported accounting profits of $35,000 and a normal rate of return of 15 percent on capital and enterprise valued at $30,000. The opportunity cost of labor is $15,500. What is the economic profit?
   a. $110,500
   b. $19,500
   c. $15,000
   d. $5,000

3. The costs of alternatives given up that do not carry dollar cost are
   a. not of interest to a business enterprise.
   b. assigned dollar values and recorded as explicit costs.
   c. considered implicit costs.
   d. part of economic profits.

4. Martha has opened a temporary employment service and is earning twice as much as she did when she ran a successful newspaper delivery service. She is
   a. earning an economic profit.
   b. earning normal profits only.
   c. suffering an economic loss.
   d. charging too much.

5. Total costs are the sum of
   a. marginal costs and average costs.
   b. average fixed costs and average variable costs.
   c. variable costs and fixed costs.
   d. implicit costs and marginal costs.

6. If marginal costs are rising,
   a. total costs are falling.
   b. fixed costs are at a minimum.
   c. average variable costs are at a maximum.
   d. average variable costs may be falling or rising.

7. The short-run marginal cost curve falls and then rises because of
   a. fixed costs.
   b. diseconomies of scale.
   c. diseconomies and economies of scale.
   d. the principle of diminishing returns.

8. Ajax Better-Bilt Furniture shows average cost as $540, and the marginal cost of the last increase in production was $560. Ajax is anticipating further expansion; management should expect
   a. marginal cost to fall.
   b. average cost to be constant.
   c. average cost to rise.
   d. total fixed cost to fall.

9. Last spring, Coil Spring Co. reported that average fixed costs had increased, but average variable costs were unchanged. This indicates that
   a. marginal costs are less than *AVC* but greater than *AC*.
   b. fixed costs have increased.
   c. output is declining.
   d. marginal costs have increased.

For Questions 10 and 11, use Figure 1.

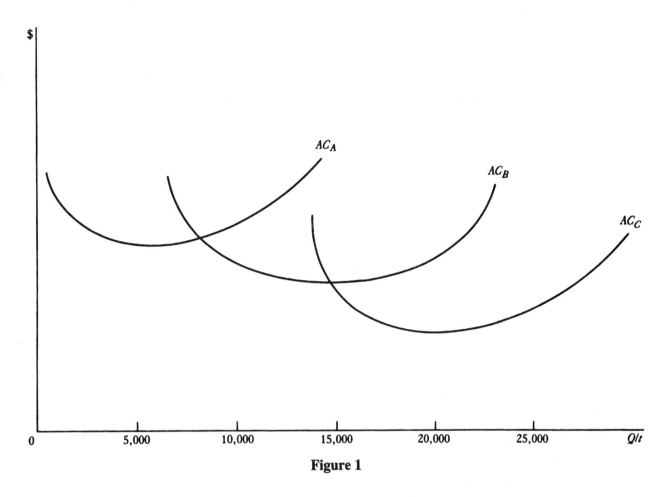

Figure 1

____ 10. Which average cost curve shows that production of 10,000 units is possible in the plant?
   a. AC_A
   b. AC_B
   c. AC_C
   d. Both AC_A and AC_B

____ 11. According to the graph, this firm has
   a. economies of scale.
   b. diseconomies of scale.
   c. long-run diminishing returns.
   d. increasing average cost.

____ 12. If a firm is operating at the point where marginal cost is equal to marginal revenue, it should
   a. leave the level of production unchanged.
   b. increase production.
   c. decrease production but remain in operation.
   d. decrease production to zero.

13. The _____ the interest rate, the _____ the present value of future payments.
    a. higher; higher
    b. lower; lower
    c. lower; higher
    d. None of the alternatives is true.

14. What is the approximate present value of a payment of $150 to be made in two years if the interest rate is 10 percent?
    a. $182
    b. $150
    c. $124
    d. $115

15. The argument in favor of trade protection for infant industries is that
    a. some industries must operate on a smaller scale than others, and they deserve to be protected.
    b. some industries will eventually enjoy economies of scale, but only if they are protected from competition while they are growing.
    c. new industries are less likely to suffer from diminishing marginal productivity.
    d. research and development won't occur unless the government forces trading partners to pay for it.

TAKING ANOTHER LOOK

In the long run, all costs are variable. The firm may change all factors as it attempts to maximize profits by lowering costs. Usually, we think of the decisions as being between larger and smaller plants or between higher and lower technology. Sometimes, however, the long-run changes may be drastic, involving entirely new methods and techniques.

Several years ago, for example, the government of Singapore commissioned a study to find new ways of producing food at lower costs to the densely populated city. One plan suggested a sea-going, self-contained dairy farm. About 600 cows would live aboard a ship. The cows would eat grass grown on deck and drink converted sea water. The power for the ship would come from manure-generated methane gas.

CHECKING OUT

Now that you have finished studying this chapter, you should be able to:

1. Define and explain the difference between accounting profit and economic profit.

2. Calculate the various short-run cost curves and illustrate their relationships graphically.

3. List the reasons for economies and diseconomies of scale.

4. Determine the profit-maximizing level of production.

5. Calculate the present value of a future stream of income.

6. Discuss how risk and uncertainty affect decision making and determine what can be done to reduce this risk and uncertainty.

ANSWERS

Trying Out the Terms

1. Q
2. F
3. N
4. M
5. Y
6. U
7. B
8. I
9. S
10. G
11. D
12. R
13. L
14. E
15. O
16. J
17. P
18. K
19. W
20. H
21. C
22. V
23. A
24. X
25. T

Testing Yourself

Part I: True or False

1. false. It is earning economic profits.
2. false. The wages she could earn somewhere else are an implicit (opportunity) cost.
3. true
4. true
5. true
6. false. The remainder is variable costs.
7. true
8. false. In the short run, there are both fixed and variable costs.
9. false. They are equal to total variable costs.
10. false. They decline as production increases.
11. false. It has diseconomies of scale; average cost increases as the size of the operation increases on an upward-sloping curve.
12. true
13. false. Either will have the same value.
14. true
15. true

Part II: Problems

1. a.

Output (Q)	Total Cost (TC)	Average Cost (AC)	Marginal Cost (MC)
0	$25	—	—
1	30	$30	$5
2	36	18	6
3	45	15	9
4	60	15	15
5	80	16	20
6	108	18	28
7	147	21	39

   b. Total fixed costs are $25.
   c. When output is 5, total variable costs are $80 − $25, or $55. Average variable costs are $55/5, or $11.
   d. When output is 6, average fixed costs are $25/6, or $4.17.

2. a.

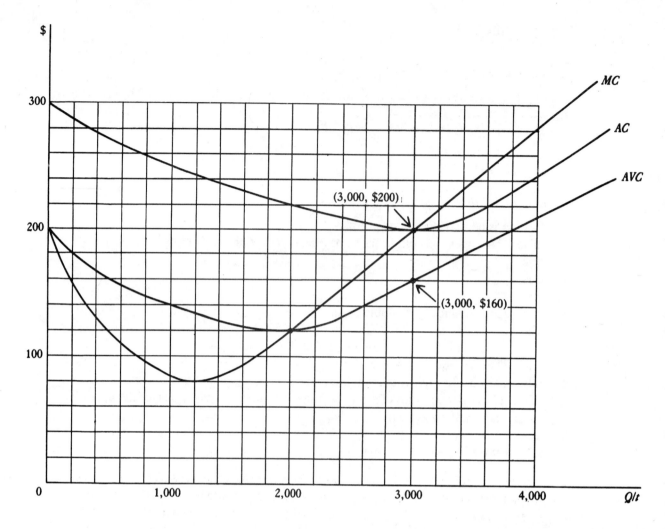

b. $120,000. At an output of 3,000, AC is $200 and AVC is $160. The $40 is AFC. Remember, AFC × output = TFC, so TFC is $40 × 3,000, or $120,000.
c. AVC = MC at 2,000; AC = MC at 3,000.
d. Average costs include fixed costs; variable costs do not. Therefore, the minimum of AC is greater than the minimum of AVC.

Part III: Multiple Choice

1. c
2. c
3. c
4. a
5. c
6. d
7. d
8. c
9. b
10. d
11. a
12. a
13. c
14. c
15. b

Name _____

CHAPTER 22 EXERCISES

1. Fixed costs are $130. Fill in the table.

Q	MC	TVC	TC
0	—	—	—
1	30		
2	25		
3	18		
4	23		
5	29		
6	36		
7	44		
8	53		
9	63		
10	74		

2. Randy is going to tape some TV shows this weekend. He decides that he will need two blank tapes and stops to buy them on his way home. While he is in the store, the manager announces a 15-minute special. One blank tape is free with the purchase of another for $6. Randy gets two tapes for $6 and goes home. Later that evening, his neighbor calls and asks if he has a blank videotape she can buy from him right now. She needs to tape a show for her sociology class. Randy tells her, "Sure, you can have it for my cost." Should Randy charge her $6, $3, or give it to her for free?

CHAPTER 23

PERFECT COMPETITION

CHECKING IN

Firms maximize profits (or minimize losses) by considering both the costs of production and forecasted revenues. Although all firms face similar cost curves, forecasted revenues depend on the industry. This chapter and the two chapters that follow consider the various forms of market structure and explain how firms make their production decisions.

The basic market model is that of perfect competition. This model provides the standard by which we can evaluate other models. Perfect competition has six basic characteristics: a large number of sellers, a large number of buyers, a homogeneous product, free entry into and exit from the industry, perfect knowledge, and perfect mobility of resources. A firm in an industry with these characteristics will have a perfectly elastic demand curve. This type of firm is known as a price taker. It can sell all it wants at the price set in the market, but it has no influence on price.

Such firms will maximize profits or minimize losses by choosing the output level where $MC = MR = P$, as long as the firm is covering its fixed costs. This means that above the minimum point of the AVC curve, the MC curve is the short-run supply curve for a perfectly competitive firm. In the short run, a firm may earn economic profits or normal profits, or it may sustain losses. In long-run equilibrium, each firm in the industry will be earning a normal profit. If there are short-run economic profits, more firms will enter the industry (easy entry is a characteristic of perfect competition). Losses, on the other hand, will cause firms to leave the industry.

Perfectly competitive industries may have long-run supply curves that are upward sloping, downward sloping, or horizontal, depending on how the factor market responds to changes in demand. If the entry of new firms into an industry drives factor prices up, the industry has increasing costs, which will be reflected in an upward-sloping supply curve. As the industry expands, costs may remain constant (a horizontal supply curve) or decline (a downward-sloping supply curve). In a perfectly competitive industry, the long-run equilibrium will have $P = AC = LRAC = LRMC$. This gives both allocative efficiency and least-cost production. All other industry equilibria are compared to this ideal standard. Sometimes it appears that some firms in perfect competition earn persistent economic profits. This case is not a violation of the model. These returns are economic rent (payments in excess of opportunity cost) to specific factors of production.

TRYING OUT THE TERMS

Match each of the following terms with its definition, and then check your answers. If you are having trouble, go back to the text and find the definition there.

_____ 1. short-run supply curve
_____ 2. perfect competition
_____ 3. decreasing cost industry
_____ 4. shutdown point
_____ 5. market power
_____ 6. economic rent
_____ 7. price taker
_____ 8. constant cost industry
_____ 9. average revenue (AR)
_____ 10. representative firm
_____ 11. increasing cost industry

A. The market structure in which there are many sellers and buyers, firms produce a homogeneous product, and there is free entry into and exit out of the industry.

B. The ability of buyers or sellers to affect price.

C. A seller (or buyer) in perfect competition that has no influence on price and can sell any amount at the market-clearing price.

D. Total revenue divided by the quantity sold, or the revenue per unit sold (the price).

E. A typical firm in perfect competition, one of the many identical firms in the market.

F. The supply curve for the period in which the size of the plant cannot be varied (in perfect competition, the same as the short-run marginal cost curve).

G. The minimum point on the average variable costs (AVC) curve, or the level of output at which a firm minimizes its losses by ceasing operation.

H. An industry in which expansion of output does not cause average costs to rise in the long run.

I. An industry in which expansion of output causes average cost to rise in the long run.

J. An industry in which expansion of output causes average cost to fall in the long run.

K. A payment to a productive resource in excess of its opportunity cost.

TESTING YOURSELF

In the next three sections, you will answer questions and work problems that are based on information in the text. Master all of the terms before you begin these sections. Work each section without referring to your notes or the text, and then check your answers.

Part I: True or False

Mark each statement as true or false. Whenever you mark a statement as false, jot down a sentence stating why it is false.

_____ 1. A homogeneous product is characteristic of perfect competition.

_____ 2. The basic assumptions of perfect competition were developed by David Ricardo.

_____ 3. If a perfectly competitive firm increases output, it will have marginal revenue that is less than price.

_____ 4. A typical firm in the industry can be called a representative firm.

_____ 5. If a new, low-cost technique for harvesting tomatoes is developed, the short-run effect in a perfectly competitive market will be a lower price and a higher output of tomatoes.

_____ 6. John Evans sells his products in a perfectly competitive market. If he can maximize profits by producing at a level where marginal cost is $45, he will also have a selling price of $45.

_____ 7. Because the demand curve for a firm in perfect competition is perfectly elastic, the firm can increase revenue and sales by lowering price.

_____ 8. In the short run, a firm can avoid paying fixed costs by closing down.

_____ 9. Sloan is operating her vegetable farm at a level where $MC = MR = \$55$ and $AC = \$30$. She is making an economic profit.

_____ 10. If a firm is making zero economic profits, it will operate in the short run and close down in the long run.

_____ 11. An increasing cost industry has a long-run supply curve that is positively sloped.

_____ 12. In perfect competition, if P is greater than MC, not enough of the product is being produced.

_____ 13. The theory of differential rents was developed by Adam Smith.

_____ 14. Differential rent is an economic profit and should not be viewed as a cost.

_____ 15. Some cultures view risk-taking as unacceptable; therefore, it is difficult for an entrepreneurial class to develop in those cultures.

Part II: Problems

1. a. Complete the table. (Round your answer to the nearest dollar.)

Output (Q)	Average Revenue (AR)	Average Fixed Cost (AFC)	Average Variable Costs (AVC)	Total Cost (TC)	Marginal Cost (MC)
1	$35	$120.00	$35.00	_____	_____
2	35	60.00	27.50	_____	_____
3	35	40.00	23.33	_____	_____
4	35	30.00	21.25	_____	_____
5	35	24.00	22.00	_____	_____
6	35	20.00	23.33	_____	_____
7	35	17.14	25.00	_____	_____
8	35	15.00	26.88	_____	_____
9	35	13.33	28.89	_____	_____
10	35	12.00	31.00	_____	_____

b. Where will this firm operate in order to maximize profits or minimize losses?

c. At this point, will the firm have an economic profit, a normal profit, or an economic loss? What is the amount?

d. What is the level of output at the firm's shutdown point?

e. What will this firm do if the market price rises to $45? What will be the economic profit or loss?

Chapter 23   Perfect Competition

2. Use the figure below to answer the following questions.

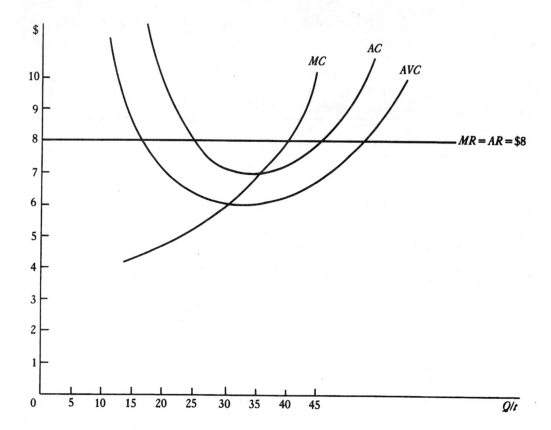

a. If $P = \$8$ and this firm is maximizing profits or minimizing losses, how many units will it produce?

b. What is the shutdown point for this firm?

c. Suppose that the market price falls to $7. Draw the new demand curve for the firm on the graph. How many units will it produce now? Will it make a profit?

3. The firm shown in the figure below is initially in equilibrium at (P_1, x_1), but then market demand increases.

   a. On the graph, mark the short-run adjustment for the representative firm.

(a) Firm

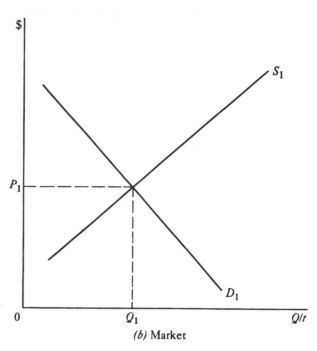
(b) Market

   b. This is an increasing cost industry. Draw the firm's new AC and MC. What will happen to the market supply curve and the equilibrium price? Show this on your graph.

   c. Show the long-run market supply curve on your graph.

Part III: Multiple Choice

1. For a perfectly competitive firm, the demand curve is
    a. the marginal revenue curve.
    b. perfectly inelastic.
    c. always equal to marginal cost.
    d. the same as the market demand curve.

2. Which of the following is *not* a basic characteristic of perfect competition?
    a. A homogeneous product
    b. Large number of sellers
    c. Resource immobility
    d. Absence of market power

3. Anna sells timber in a perfectly competitive market. Incomes increase, and many people buy new homes; the market demand curve shifts to the right. In the short run, she should expect
    a. the price of timber to be unchanged.
    b. profits to fall.
    c. the price of timber to rise.
    d. firms to leave the timber business.

4. A firm that must sell at market price if it wishes to sell at all is called a
    a. price taker.
    b. price seeker.
    c. marginal firm.
    d. loss taker.

5. Average revenue (AR)
    a. occurs when $MC = MR$.
    b. equals TR/Q.
    c. is greater than price when economic profits are present.
    d. does not appear in the model of perfect competition.

6. The marginal cost curve above the minimum AVC
    a. indicates points where the firm will realize an economic profit.
    b. covers the area where a firm should shut down.
    c. is equal to the firm's marginal revenue curve.
    d. is the firm's short-run supply curve.

7. Economic profits equal zero when
    a. $P = AVC = TC$.
    b. $P = AR = MR = AC$.
    c. normal profits are absent.
    d. market demand increases in the short run.

8. If $P = \$25$, $MR = \$25$, $MC = \$25$, $AVC = \$35$, and $AC = \$50$, the firm should
   a. increase output.
   b. decrease output but continue to produce.
   c. increase price.
   d. shut down.

9. An equilibrium price of $9.50 in a perfectly competitive industry means that the MR for a firm in that industry will be
   a. equal to $9.50.
   b. greater than $9.50.
   c. equal to AVC and equal to $9.50.
   d. greater than its average revenue of $9.50.

10. A profit-maximizing (or loss-minimizing) firm in perfect competition will set its output where
    a. it is operating at capacity.
    b. its total cost is equal to its total revenue.
    c. its average variable cost is equal to its average revenue.
    d. its marginal cost is equal to its marginal revenue.

11. If a firm has $P > AC$, it
    a. should reduce output.
    b. is losing money.
    c. is earning an economic profit.
    d. should shut down.

12. At its profit-maximizing output, a perfectly competitive firm has an AVC of $3.19 and an AC of $4.23. What is its total fixed cost?
    a. $1.04
    b. $(\$4.23 - \$3.19) \times Q$
    c. The same as its total revenue
    d. $7.42

13. A perfectly competitive industry experienced a decrease in demand. In response, some firms left the industry. The original equilibrium price was $3.90; the new equilibrium price is $4.05. This industry has
    a. increasing costs.
    b. decreasing costs.
    c. inefficiencies.
    d. a vertical long-run supply curve.

14. A firm is using the least-cost method of production when
    a. $MC = AR$.
    b. $P = AC = MC$.
    c. $TR = (AR)Q$.
    d. $MC = MR$.

Chapter 23 Perfect Competition 305

15. Economic rent occurs
    a. when some factors of production are used more intensely than others.
    b. when land is the only input.
    c. when the payment to a factor of production is greater than its opportunity cost.
    d. only in the short run; in the long run, there can be only normal rent.

TAKING ANOTHER LOOK

All firms, large or small, have to face the necessity of closing down when variable costs cannot be covered. In 1980, with high hopes and an optimistic marketing forecast, RCA launched its version of the videodisc player. RCA was able to sell its player to distributors for about $250 (retail price was around $500). The variable costs of production were estimated to be about $150. In 1984, RCA withdrew from the market. It had seriously overestimated demand by not taking competition from VCRs into account. In 1984, RCA was receiving about $100 for each unit it sold to a distributor. RCA couldn't cover its variable costs, so it left the business with a loss of more than $500 million. A decade later, videodiscs became popular and were marketed successfully.

CHECKING OUT

Now that you have finished studying this chapter, you should be able to:

1. List the assumptions of perfect competition.

2. Diagram the relationship between a firm and the total market. Calculate profits, given quantity, marginal revenue, marginal cost, average cost, and price. Identify the profit-maximizing level of output.

3. Define the shutdown point in terms of price and average variable costs or total fixed costs and losses.

4. Describe the long-run supply curve for a constant cost industry, an increasing cost industry, and a decreasing cost industry.

5. Identify the long-run equilibrium for the firm and the industry under perfect competition.

6. Explain how economic rent might exist in perfect competition, even in long-run equilibrium.

ANSWERS

Trying Out the Terms

1. F
2. A
3. J
4. G
5. B
6. K
7. C
8. H
9. D
10. E
11. I

Testing Yourself

Part I: True or False

1. true
2. false. They were developed by Adam Smith.
3. false. For perfectly competitive firms, price and marginal revenue are always equal.
4. true
5. true
6. true
7. false. A perfectly competitive firm can sell all it wants at the prevailing price. $P = MR$, so lower prices would mean lower revenue.
8. false. Fixed costs must be paid, even if output equals zero. A firm can avoid paying variable costs by closing down.
9. true
10. false. The firm is at a long-run equilibrium and is making normal profits. A firm will not close down until it is actually losing money.
11. true
12. true
13. false. It was developed by David Ricardo.
14. false. Differential rent is a payment to better factors of production and should be considered a cost.
15. true

Part II: Problems

1. a.

Output (Q)	Average Revenue (AR)	Average Fixed Cost (AFC)	Average Variable Costs (AVC)	Total Cost (TC)	Marginal Cost (MC)
1	$35	$120.00	$35.00	$155	$35
2	35	60.00	27.50	175	20
3	35	40.00	23.33	190	15
4	35	30.00	21.25	205	15
5	35	24.00	22.00	230	25
6	35	20.00	23.33	260	30
7	35	17.14	25.00	295	35
8	35	15.00	26.88	335	40
9	35	13.33	28.89	380	45
10	35	12.00	31.00	430	50

(To find total cost, find TVC and TFC; then add them together.)

    b. To maximize profits or minimize losses, this firm will produce 7 units at a price of $35. This is the output where $MC = MR$. (Remember, in perfect competition $MC = AR$.)
    c. The firm will have an economic loss of $50 (TR − TC = $245 − $295).
    d. The level of output at the shutdown point is 4 units, where AVC is at its minimum ($21.25).
    e. The firm will sell 9 units and make an economic profit of $25.

2.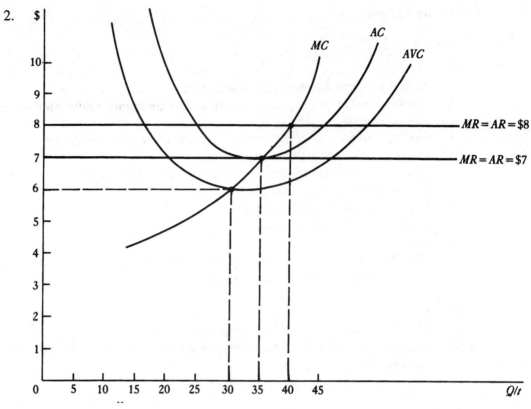

a. The firm will produce 40 units. This is where $MR = MC$.
b. The shutdown point is at 30 units, where $AVC = \$6$.
c. The firm will produce 35 units and make a normal profit.

3.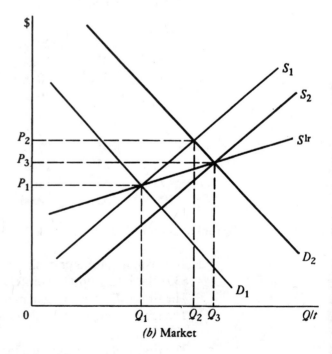

a. In the short run, firms will move along the MC curve to MC = P2. They will earn an economic profit.
b. The economic profit will attract new firms into the industry. The market supply curve shifts to the right, and market price falls. However, it does not fall to its original level, because the new firms bid up the factor prices, and all firms now face new, higher cost curves. Firms will earn normal profits only with a higher market price.
c. The long-run supply curve intersects the old and new equilibrium points on graph (b).

Part III: Multiple Choice

1. a
2. c
3. c
4. a
5. b
6. d
7. b
8. d
9. a
10. d
11. c
12. b
13. b
14. b
15. c

CHAPTER 23 EXERCISES

1. Fill in the tables. Mark the profit-maximizing (loss-minimizing) output using the $MR = MC$ approach. Is it at the same level as the $TR - TC$ approach?

Total Output (Q)	Total Revenue (TR)	Cost (TC)	Profit (Loss)
0	$0	$24	_____
1	15	32	_____
2	30	36	_____
3	45	42	_____
4	60	52	_____
5	75	70	_____
6	90	96	_____
7	105	133	_____

Output (Q)	Marginal Cost (MC)	Marginal Revenue (MR)	Average Variable Costs (AVC)	Average Cost (AC)
1	_____	_____	_____	_____
2	_____	_____	_____	_____
3	_____	_____	_____	_____
4	_____	_____	_____	_____
5	_____	_____	_____	_____
6	_____	_____	_____	_____
7	_____	_____	_____	_____

2. Graph *AC*, *AVC*, *MC*, and *MR* on the following figure. Mark the profit-maximizing output level and the shutdown point.

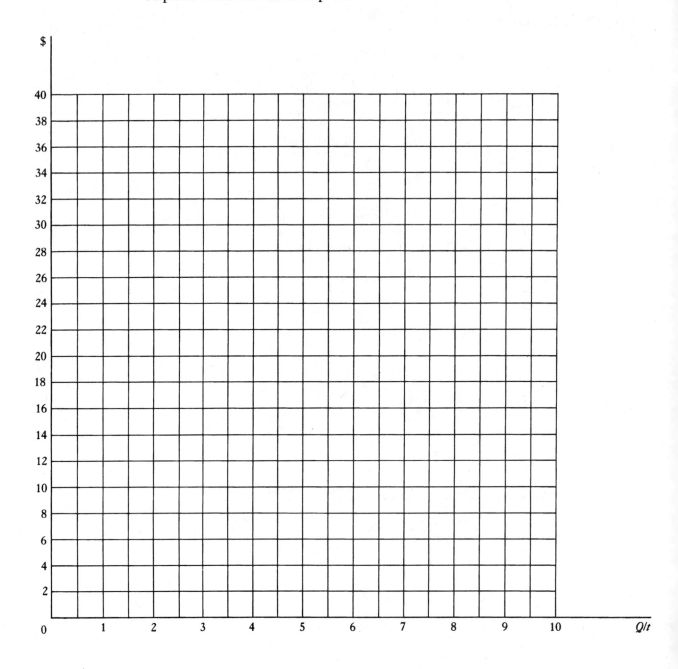

312   Chapter 23   Perfect Competition

CHAPTER 24

MONOPOLY

CHECKING IN

Monopoly is at the other end of the market continuum from perfect competition. Monopoly exists when there is but one seller in a market for a product with no close substitutes. Such a firm faces a downward-sloping demand curve with a marginal revenue curve that lies beneath it.

Like a firm in perfect competition, a monopoly firm maximizes profit by operating where $MC = MR$, but because $MR < P$, price is greater than marginal cost. This is a different result from that of perfect competition. In the short run, monopolists may make economic profits or normal profits, or they may sustain losses. A monopolist making economic profits attempts to keep them by erecting barriers to entry that will prevent other firms from entering the industry and taking a share of the profits. Some barriers to entry are natural, such as economies of scale; other barriers are artificial. It is hard for a firm to maintain artificial barriers to entry; the government may help by passing legislation favorable to the monopolist.

Monopolies may try to increase their revenues, and hence their profits, by practicing price discrimination. To do this, the firm must be able to divide its customers into groups with different price elasticities of demand. The firm then raises the price for the customers with inelastic demand and lowers the price for those customers with more elastic demand. This practice works only when the group paying a lower price can be prevented from reselling the product to the other group.

There are costs associated with monopoly that are not present in the model of perfect competition. Monopoly misallocates resources, causes a loss of a portion of consumer surplus (deadweight loss), wastes resources in monopoly rent seeking, and often suffers from x-inefficiency, or slack management due to monopoly power and the lack of market discipline.

There are few examples of a true monopoly in the real world. In the United States, monopoly is prohibited, except for a few regulated cases of natural monopoly. Most of the firms that approach the monopoly model are publicly held corporations. In these firms, there is a separation of ownership and management. Often, the managers of these firms will not attempt to maximize profits. Rather, they may satisfy the shareholders by seeking some acceptable profit target. They may also attempt to maximize sales rather than profits.

TRYING OUT THE TERMS

Match each of the following terms with its definition, and then check your answers. If you are having trouble, go back to the text and find the definition there.

_____ 1. dumping

_____ 2. long-run profit maximization

_____ 3. monopoly

_____ 4. monopoly rent seeking

_____ 5. constrained sales maximization

_____ 6. barriers to entry

_____ 7. contestable markets

_____ 8. *x*-inefficiency

_____ 9. monopoly power

_____ 10. price searcher

_____ 11. deadweight loss

_____ 12. separation of ownership and control

_____ 13. satisficing hypothesis

_____ 14. price discrimination

_____ 15. local monopoly

A. The market structure in which there is a single seller of a product that has no close substitutes.

B. The ability to exercise some of the economic effects predicted in the model of monopoly by restricting output.

C. A firm that sets price in order to maximize profits and thus has monopoly power.

D. Natural or artificial obstacles that keep new firms from entering an industry.

E. A firm that has monopoly power in a geographic region because of the large distance from other suppliers of its product (or substitutes).

F. The practice of charging different prices to different consumers or to a single consumer for different quantities purchased.

G. The practice of selling in foreign markets at lower prices than in domestic markets (a form of price discrimination).

H. The lost consumer surplus due to monopolistic restriction to output.

I. The efforts and resources expended by those attempting to establish monopolies to earn monopoly profits.

J. The inefficiency associated with the "slack" management of monopoly firms because of the lack of market discipline.

K. The idea that large firms are controlled by hired managers, not the owners, and the managers might have different goals from those of the owners.

L. The argument that managers do not seek to maximize profits but rather seek target levels of output and profits that are satisfactory to the ownership interests.

M. The hypothesis that managers' primary goal is to increase the sales of the firm because they will be rewarded by stockholders for increasing the firm's relative share of the market.

N. The argument that even if managers seem to behave in accord with satisficing or constrained sales maximization, they only do so because it leads to higher profits in the long run.

O. Markets composed of large firms that are nevertheless efficient because easily reversible entry into the market is possible.

TESTING YOURSELF

In the next three sections, you will answer questions and work problems that are based on information in the text. Master all of the terms before you begin these sections. Work each section without referring to your notes or the text, and then check your answers.

Part I: True or False

Mark each statement as true or false. Whenever you mark a statement as false, jot down a sentence stating why it is false.

_____ 1. Monopoly is on one end of the market continuum, and perfect competition is on the other.

_____ 2. A monopolist is a price taker with a perfectly elastic demand curve.

_____ 3. A monopolist selling the eighth unit of a product for $150 should expect a marginal revenue greater than $150.

_____ 4. A monopolistic firm with costs identical to those of a firm in perfect competition will charge a higher price than the perfectly competitive firm.

_____ 5. A monopolist can increase revenue by lowering prices when operating in the elastic range of the demand curve.

_____ 6. Monopolists always earn high profits.

_____ 7. The monopolist's supply curve is the short-run marginal cost curve.

_____ 8. If the value placed on an item by the consumer exceeds the opportunity cost of producing that item, then $P > MC$.

_____ 9. If a monopoly firm is earning more than its opportunity costs, it is earning a normal profit.

_____ 10. Economies of scale are a natural barrier to entry.

_____ 11. A monopolist is charging a price of $34.89. If the firm is in equilibrium, this is a point where $MC = MR$ will be less than $34.89.

_____ 12. Because a monopoly industry is so big, it is usually more efficient than a perfectly competitive industry.

_____ 13. Consumer surplus cannot exist in the presence of monopoly.

_____ 14. A price-discriminating monopolist can increase profits by lowering prices for consumers with elastic demand and raising prices for consumers with inelastic demand.

_____ 15. The separation of ownership and management may lead to satisficing behavior by firm managers.

Part II: Problems

1. a. Fill in the table.

Output (Q)	Price (P)	Total Revenue (TR)	Marginal Revenue (MR)
0	$24	$0	—
1	22	____	____
2	20	____	____
3	18	____	____
4	16	____	____
5	14	____	____
6	12	____	____
7	10	____	____
8	8	____	____

b. Name the region where demand is price elastic.

Chapter 24 Monopoly   317

c. The following table gives the marginal costs for the output levels in the table in a. If the marginal cost for this firm is given by MC_1, what is the profit-maximizing price and quantity?

Output (Q)	MC_1	MC_2
0	—	—
1	$8	$7
2	11	8
3	14	9
4	17	10
5	20	11
6	23	12
7	26	13
8	29	14

d. Suppose the firm finds a new, lower cost producer and now faces MC_2. What is the new profit-maximizing price and quantity?

2. On each of the following graphs, draw the appropriate demand and marginal revenue curves for a profit-maximizing or loss-minimizing monopoly firm.

   a. A monopoly firm earning an economic profit.

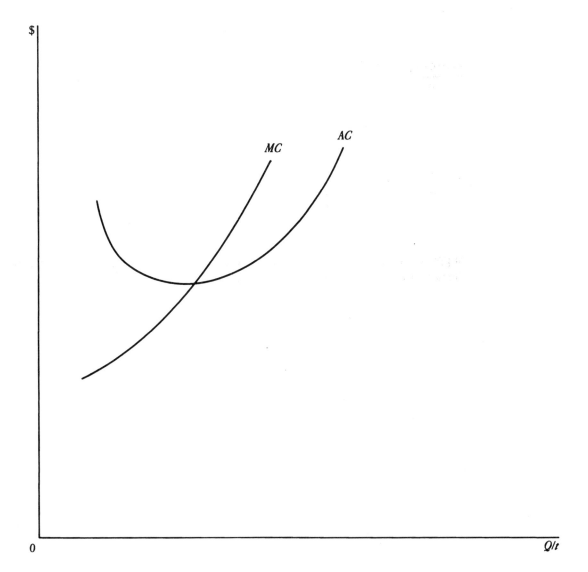

Chapter 24 Monopoly   319

b. A monopoly firm earning normal profits.

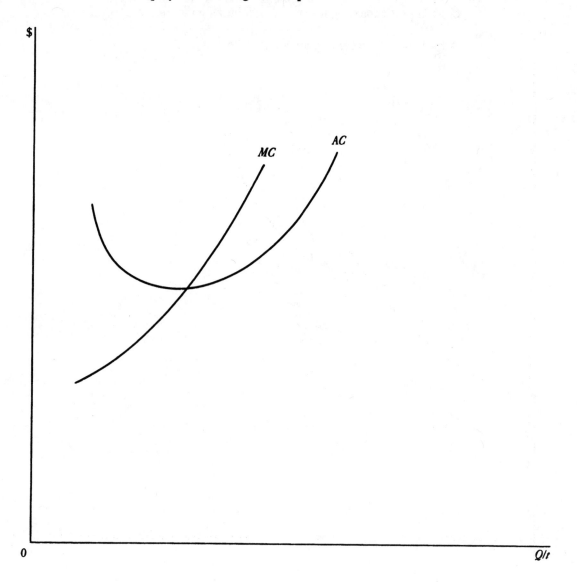

c. A monopoly firm sustaining short-run losses.

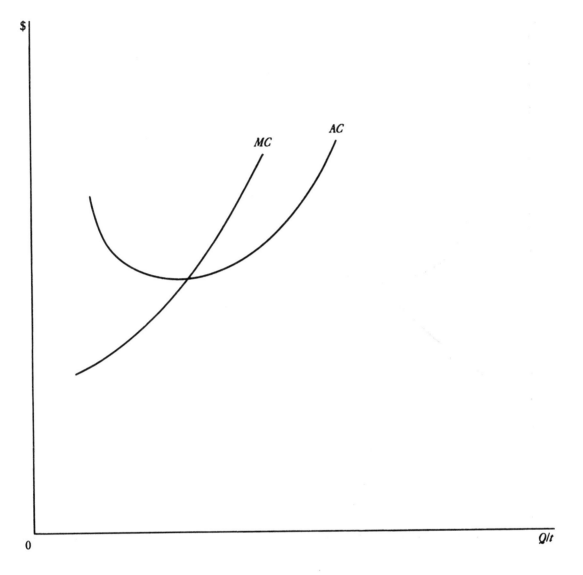

Part III: Multiple Choice

_____ 1. A monopolist will have a marginal revenue curve that is
   a. identical to the demand curve.
   b. identical to the marginal cost curve.
   c. below the demand curve.
   d. above the marginal cost curve.

_____ 2. A monopolist will try to operate
   a. where marginal cost equals marginal revenue.
   b. in the inelastic range of the demand curve.
   c. where average revenue equals marginal revenue.
   d. at the highest price on the demand curve.

3. A monopoly firm is selling eight units of output for a price of $95. In order to sell a ninth unit, it must expect to receive a price
   a. equal to $95.
   b. less than $95.
   c. greater than $95.
   d. less than the marginal revenue on the eighth unit.

4. Compared to a perfectly competitive firm with the same cost structure, a monopoly firm will charge a
   a. higher price and sell more.
   b. lower price and sell more.
   c. higher price and sell less.
   d. lower price and sell less.

5. Along a downward-sloping monopoly demand curve,
   a. marginal revenue is greater than price.
   b. elasticity of demand is constant.
   c. marginal revenue decreases when price decreases.
   d. marginal revenue is equal to zero when price is equal to zero.

6. If a monopoly firm observes an increase in total revenue after a price increase, it must be true that
   a. $MR > 0$.
   b. $MR < 0$.
   c. $MR = 0$.
   d. $MR = TR$.

7. If a monopoly firm produces an output where $MC < MR$, it can increase profit by
   a. decreasing fixed costs.
   b. decreasing production until $AC = AR$.
   c. increasing production until TR is at a maximum.
   d. increasing production until $MC = MR$.

8. In the short run, a monopolist may experience
   a. economic profits.
   b. normal profits.
   c. losses.
   d. economic profits, normal profits, or losses.

9. Which of the following is *not* a barrier to entry?
   a. Economies of scale
   b. Patents and controls over material
   c. Easy entry into the industry
   d. Government regulations

_____ 10. If a profit-maximizing monopoly firm experiences an increase in marginal costs, it will
   a. increase price and reduce output.
   b. increase price and maintain output.
   c. decrease price and decrease output.
   d. remain at the same point.

_____ 11. When a firm charges different people different prices for the same good, it is engaging in
   a. price fixing.
   b. price discrimination.
   c. market manipulation.
   d. vertical monopoly.

_____ 12. A profit-maximizing monopoly firm will operate with $P > MC$. This is indicative of
   a. economies of scale.
   b. long-run normal profits.
   c. misallocation of resources.
   d. price discrimination.

_____ 13. The cost of monopoly in terms of management problems stemming from the lack of competition is called
   a. allocative inefficiency.
   b. x-inefficiency.
   c. satisficing.
   d. disadvantage of scale.

_____ 14. It takes time, effort, and resources to establish a monopoly. Such activity is called
   a. imperialism.
   b. price searching.
   c. monopoly market allocation.
   d. monopoly rent seeking.

_____ 15. The theory of contestable markets holds that
   a. monopoly profits will not persist if monopolists are subject to pro-competitive legislation.
   b. monopoly profits will be present in small firms as well as large firms.
   c. economic efficiency can exist in a monopoly market if there is easy entry.
   d. monopolies cannot exist in a market economy.

TAKING ANOTHER LOOK

While no true monopoly exists in this country, we observe many instances of monopoly-like behavior. The next time you take an automobile trip, notice the price of gasoline in towns of various sizes. In most instances, you will observe higher prices in smaller towns. This is because people have few alternatives to buying locally. Prices will be particularly high in small towns with only one or two station owners. If you live in a town 70 miles from Atlanta where all three gas stations are named "The Jones Boys'," you ought to fill up in Atlanta before you head home.

CHECKING OUT

Now that you have finished studying this chapter, you should be able to:

1. Define monopoly and calculate average revenue and marginal revenue, given data on price and output. Diagram average revenue, marginal revenue, marginal cost, and average cost curves for a monopolistic firm making an economic profit, a loss, and finally, a normal profit.

2. Explain the economic role of natural and artificial barriers to entry into an industry.

3. Describe price discrimination.

4. Discuss how a monopolist misallocates resources in terms of price and costs.

5. Describe the costs associated with monopoly.

6. Discuss why managers may pursue goals other than profit maximization.

7. Explain facts and fallacies of monopoly organization.

8. Evaluate the concept of contestable markets.

ANSWERS

Trying Out the Terms

1. G
2. N
3. A
4. I
5. M
6. D
7. O
8. J
9. B
10. C
11. H
12. K
13. L
14. F
15. E

Testing Yourself

Part I: True or False

1. true
2. false. A monopolist is a price searcher with a demand curve that is also the downward-sloping demand curve for the industry.
3. false. For the monopolist, marginal revenue is less than price.
4. true
5. true
6. false. Monopolists may earn economic profits or normal profits, or they may sustain losses, depending on demand.
7. false. The monopolist's supply curve cannot be determined.
8. true
9. false. It is earning an economic profit.
10. true
11. true

12. false. The higher monopoly price indicates an inefficient allocation of resources, and there is no competition to drive the monopolist into least-cost production.
13. false. Some consumer surplus exists, some is transferred to the monopolist as economic profit, and some (but not all) is lost. The part that is lost is the deadweight loss.
14. true
15. true

Part II: Problems

1. a.

Output (Q)	Price (P)	Total Revenue (TR)	Marginal Revenue (MR)
0	$24	$0	—
1	22	22	$22
2	20	40	18
3	18	54	14
4	16	64	10
5	14	70	6
6	12	72	2
7	10	70	−2
8	8	64	−6

b. The elastic range is the region where marginal revenue is positive, from ($P = \$24$, $Q = 0$) to ($P = \$12$, $Q = 6$).
c. With MC_1, the firm will produce 3 units and charge $18.
d. With MC_2, the firm will produce 4 units and charge $16.

2. a. Average revenue (price) is greater than average cost, and the monopoly firm is earning an economic profit.

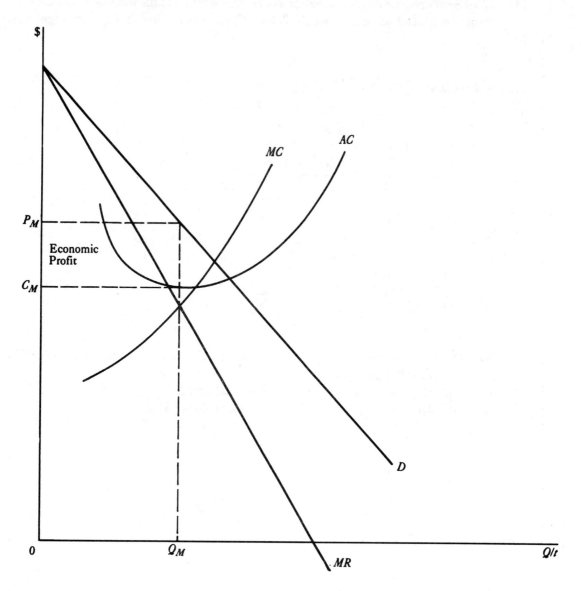

b. Average revenue (price) is equal to average cost, and the monopoly firm is earning normal profits.

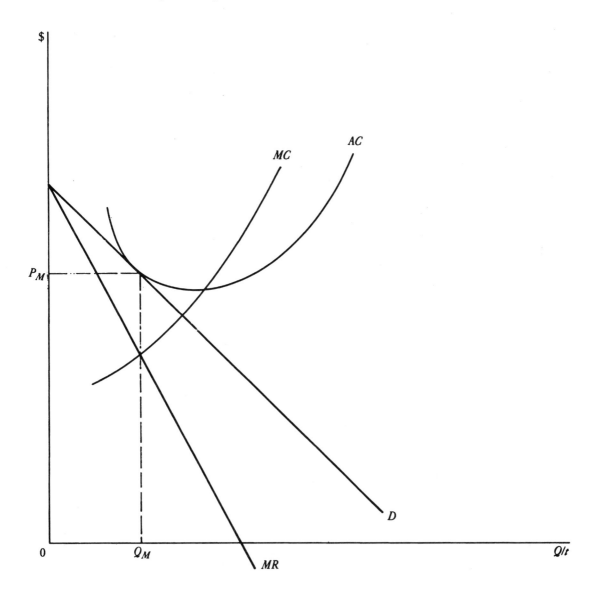

c. Average revenue (price) is less than average cost, and the monopoly firm is sustaining short-run losses.

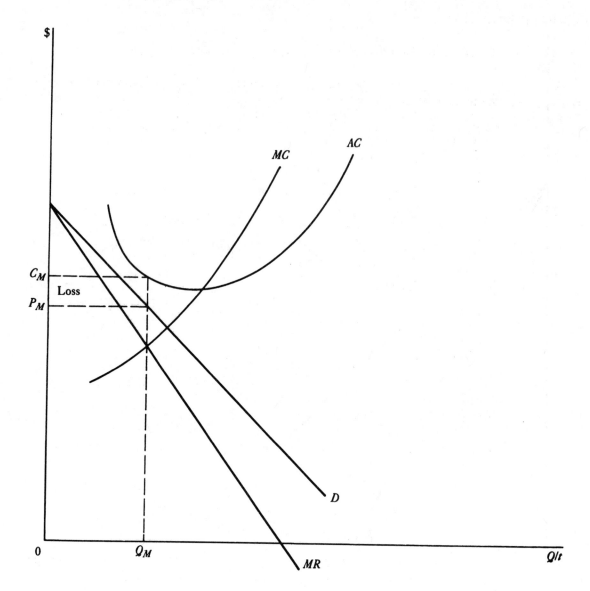

Part III: Multiple Choice

1. c
2. a
3. b
4. c

5. c
6. b
7. d
8. d

9. c
10. a
11. b
12. c

13. b
14. d
15. c

Name _____

CHAPTER 24 EXERCISES

1. Consider the following revenue and cost data for a monopoly firm.

Output (Q)	Price (P)	Total Revenue (TR)	Marginal Revenue (MR)	Total Cost (TC)	Marginal Cost (MC)
0	$22,500	_____	—	$10,000	—
1	22,000	_____	_____	20,000	_____
2	21,500	_____	_____	32,000	_____
3	21,000	_____	_____	46,000	_____
4	20,500	_____	_____	62,000	_____
5	20,000	_____	_____	80,000	_____
6	19,500	_____	_____	100,000	_____
7	19,000	_____	_____	122,000	_____

a. Complete the table.

b. If this is a profit-maximizing monopoly firm, what quantity will be produced? What will the price be?

c. Demonstrate that your answer to b is correct by finding the profit levels at one unit more and one unit less than the profit-maximizing level.

d. On the following page, graph the demand, marginal cost, and marginal revenue curves from the table. Label the profit-maximizing price and quantity.

Chapter 24   Monopoly   329

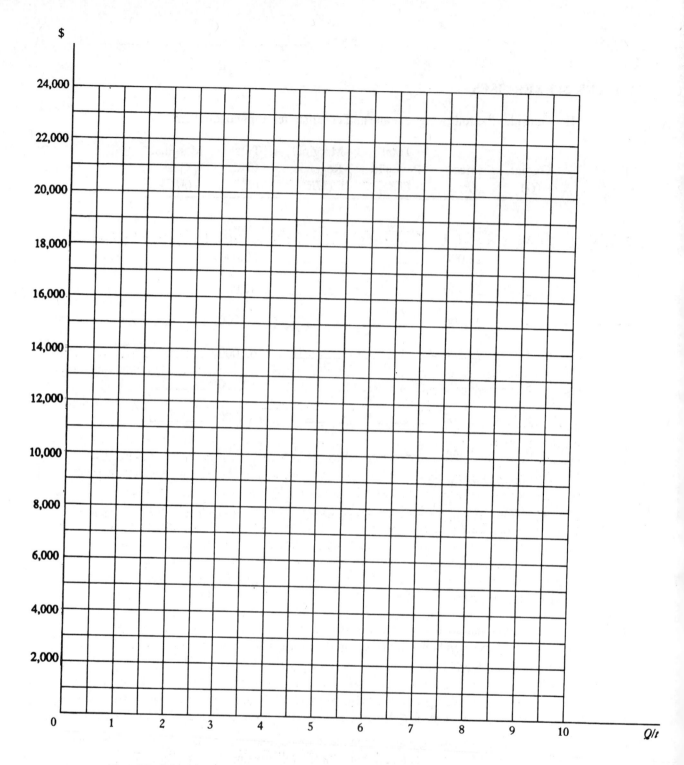

2. Explain why a monopoly firm does not have a supply curve.

CHAPTER 25

MONOPOLISTIC COMPETITION AND OLIGOPOLY

CHECKING IN

Most real-world firms can be classified as either monopolistic competitors or oligopolists. These two models lie between the two extremes of perfect competition and monopoly, and they are referred to as imperfect competition.

Monopolistic competition has many of the characteristics of perfect competition: a large number of producers, easy entry into the industry, and, in the long run, zero economic profits for the firm. However, there are important differences between perfect competition and monopolistic competition. In monopolistic competition, the product is differentiated. Firms compete in many ways as they attempt to stress the differences between their products. Because of differentiation, firms do not have the perfectly elastic demand curves of perfect competitors. Instead, they have downward-sloping demand curves resembling those of monopolists. Like monopolists, monopolistic competitors seek the output where marginal revenue is equal to marginal cost. Price, then, is greater than marginal cost in both the short run and the long run. In the long run, each firm earns only a normal profit, and price is equal to average cost. A least-cost method of production is not used; therefore, there is excess capacity in the industry.

Industries with only a few firms are called oligopolies. They may produce either homogeneous or differentiated goods. When there are only a few firms in an industry, those firms are interdependent. Each firm must consider the other firms' behavior when making decisions about prices and output. An oligopoly may act as a cartel (this is illegal in the United States); it may pursue some imperfect methods of joint action; or the firms in the oligopoly may behave independently and only be able to guess at what other firms are doing. Oligopolies are much like monopolies: there are strong barriers to entry, and there may be long-run economic profits.

Successful cartels are able to act as if they were monopolists; however, cartels tend to fall apart because of strong incentives for members to chisel. Cartels are threatened if new firms enter the industry. The more firms there are in a cartel, the more likely it is to fall apart.

TRYING OUT THE TERMS

Match each of the following terms with its definition, and then check your answers. If you are having trouble, go back to the text and find the definition there.

_____ 1. monopolistic competition
_____ 2. pure oligopoly
_____ 3. excess capacity
_____ 4. game theory
_____ 5. price leadership
_____ 6. cartel
_____ 7. differentiated product
_____ 8. oligopoly
_____ 9. kinked demand curve
_____ 10. tacit collusion
_____ 11. communication

_____ 12. nonprice competition
_____ 13. competitive fringe
_____ 14. coordination
_____ 15. product group
_____ 16. shared monopoly
_____ 17. dominant firm
_____ 18. differentiated oligopoly
_____ 19. price clusters
_____ 20. collusion
_____ 21. chiseling
_____ 22. name brand capital

A. A good or service that has real or imagined characteristics that are different from those of other goods or services.

B. A market for a set of goods that are differentiated but have a large number of close substitutes.

C. The unutilized part of existing production facilities by a monopolistically competitive firm.

D. Competing with rival firms through advertising, style changes, color changes, and techniques other than lowering price.

E. The market structure in which a few firms compete imperfectly and recognize their interdependence.

F. The model of oligopoly that says that oligopolists coordinate and share markets to act as a monopoly.

G. An oligopoly that produces heterogeneous products that are very close substitutes.

H. An oligopolistic industry that produces a homogeneous product.

I. Groupings of prices for similar, but not homogeneous, products.

J. Firms' ability to signal their intentions to each other.

K. Firms' ability to relate their production decisions to those made by other firms in an industry.

L. Agreements between firms in an industry to set a certain price or to share a market in certain ways.

M. A group of independent firms that agree not to compete but rather to determine prices and output jointly.

N. Cheating on a cartel agreement by lowering prices in an attempt to capture more of the market.

O. Unorganized and unstated attempts by informally coordinated oligopolies to practice joint actions.

P. The form of tacit collusion in an oligopolistic industry in which one firm, the price leader, sets the price or initiates price changes and the other firms follow that lead.

Q. The most influential firm in an industry, usually the largest firm.

R. The smaller competitors in informally coordinated markets with one large, dominant firm.

S. A mathematical theory about rational decision making under conditions of uncertainty that can provide insight into oligopolistic behavior.

T. A demand curve with a bend in it at the price settled on in an oligopolistic industry because other firms' price cuts, but not price increases, are matched.

U. The value that consumers place on a product because of experience, reputation, or image.

V. The market structure in which a large number of firms sell differentiated products.

TESTING YOURSELF

In the next three sections, you will answer questions and work problems that are based on information in the text. Master all of the terms before you begin these sections. Work each section without referring to your notes or the text, and then check your answers.

Part I: True or False

Mark each statement as true or false. Whenever you mark a statement as false, jot down a sentence stating why it is false.

_____ 1. Monopolistic competition and oligopoly are examples of imperfect competition.

_____ 2. When the representative firm in a monopolistically competitive industry is sustaining losses, some firms will leave the industry. This will shift the demand curve of the remaining firms to the left.

_____ 3. Industries in both perfect competition and monopolistic competition produce homogeneous products.

_____ 4. A highly differentiated product will have a more elastic demand curve than a less differentiated product.

_____ 5. In monopolistic competition, the long-run equilibrium is $P = AC$.

_____ 6. A firm with an output that does not fully utilize its plant size has excess capacity.

_____ 7. Trademarks are used as a means of product differentiation.

_____ 8. The grocery stores in a city are an example of an oligopolistic industry.

_____ 9. Joan Robinson developed a theory of monopolistic competition.

_____ 10. A pure oligopoly is one composed of three or fewer firms.

_____ 11. Organized collusive activity in private industry is prohibited in the United States.

_____ 12. Barriers to entry are low in oligopolistic industries.

_____ 13. Cartels often break up because of chiseling by member firms.

_____ 14. Oligopolies are marked by mutual independence.

_____ 15. Price clusters may appear just above and just below the kink in a kinked demand curve.

Part II: Problems

1. Use the table below to answer the following questions.

Output (Q)	Average Revenue (AR)	Average Cost (AC)	Average Variable Cost (AVC)
1	$5	$6.00	$5.00
2	4	4.25	3.75
3	3	3.00	2.67
4	2	2.50	2.25
5	1	3.50	3.30

   a. What is the TFC of producing 2 units of output?

   b. What is the profit or loss from producing 5 units of output?

c. What would be the long-run equilibrium for a monopolistically competitive firm?

d. What would be the long-run equilibrium for a perfectly competitive firm?

e. What would be the excess capacity in this representative monopolistically competitive firm?

2. Use the figure below to answer the following questions.

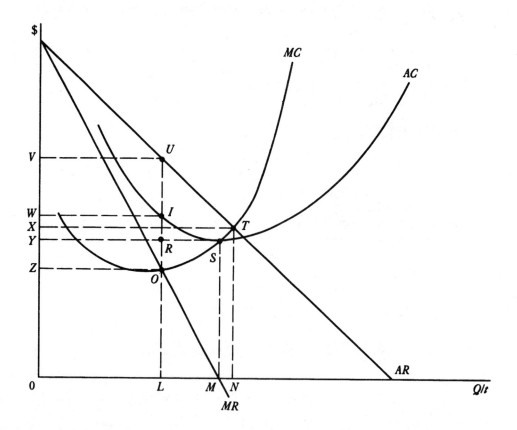

a. What is the profit-maximizing price and quantity for this monopolistically competitive firm?

b. At this price and quantity, is this firm operating in the short run or the long run?

c. Does the firm have profits or losses? How much?

d. What would the long-term equilibrium price and quantity be if the industry were perfectly competitive?

Part III: Multiple Choice

1. A firm in a monopolistically competitive industry faces a downward-sloping demand curve because
    a. the product is homogeneous.
    b. the product is differentiated.
    c. nonprice competition is missing.
    d. barriers to entry are high.

2. A firm in a(n) _____ industry will have the most elastic demand curve.
    a. monopolistic
    b. oligopolistic
    c. monopolistically competitive
    d. perfectly competitive

3. Jane's Malt Shop is in short-run equilibrium, with $P = \$1.50$, $AC = \$0.90$, and $MC = MR$ at $\$0.75$. Jane should
    a. expect other, similar shops to open in the area.
    b. lower her price to increase profits.
    c. increase prices until $AC = P$.
    d. close down.

4. Sydney's Super Toys is operating at an output where $MC = \$4.50$ and $MR = \$3.76$. Sydney should
    a. be happy with a profit of $\$0.74$.
    b. increase output.
    c. decrease output.
    d. decrease output and lower prices.

5. Monopoly and monopolistically competitive industries share the characteristic of
   a. making long-run economic profits.
   b. being able to sustain long-run losses without closing down.
   c. facing downward-sloping demand curves.
   d. having $MR = AR$.

6. One way a monopolistically competitive firm can cause its demand curve to shift to the right is by
   a. lowering price.
   b. advertising.
   c. encouraging entry of new firms.
   d. making the product more homogeneous.

7. The long-run equilibrium of a monopolistically competitive firm will differ from that of a firm in perfect competition because, in a monopolistically competitive long-run equilibrium,
   a. $MC < MR$.
   b. $AC > P$.
   c. $P = MR$.
   d. $P > MR$.

8. Monopolistic competition is less efficient that perfect competition because of the long-run presence of
   a. homogeneous products.
   b. excess capacity.
   c. profit-maximizing behavior.
   d. strong barriers to entry and exit.

9. If an oligopoly produces a homogeneous product, it is called a
   a. pure oligopoly.
   b. monopolistic oligopoly.
   c. cartel.
   d. differentiated oligopoly.

10. A small group of firms trying to maximize joint profits is called
    a. monopolistic competition.
    b. a cartel.
    c. a price searcher group.
    d. a pure oligopoly.

11. There is an oligopoly with three firms all charging a price of $400. If firm A raises its price to $450, the kinked demand curve theory would predict that firms B and C would
    a. follow firm A's price leadership and raise their prices to $450.
    b. lower prices to some level below $400.
    c. do nothing.
    d. endure economic losses equal to $50 a unit.

_____ 12. Cartels are destroyed by
   a. chiseling.
   b. inelastic demand.
   c. new entry.
   d. either chiseling or new entry.

_____ 13. In an oligopoly with a dominant firm,
   a. price is set by the dominant firm at its profit-maximizing price, and firms on the competitive fringe accept this price as the market price.
   b. the dominant firm makes a normal profit, and the firms on the competitive fringe make a profit that is less than normal.
   c. the presence of the competitive fringe causes an excess supply in the market.
   d. the output level is the same as if the industry were a monopoly.

_____ 14. Which of the following is likely to prolong the life of a cartel?
   a. Fluctuating demand
   b. Many firms
   c. A homogeneous product
   d. Weak entry barriers

_____ 15. George Stigler disagrees with the kinked demand curve models because he feels that
   a. oligopolists will always cheat.
   b. long-run prices in oligopoly are not necessarily more stable than prices in other industries.
   c. there are too many firms in an oligopoly.
   d. it is impossible to prevent collusion.

TAKING ANOTHER LOOK

I. Fast-food restaurants are in a monopolistically competitive industry. There is lots of nonprice competition and a seemingly endless variety of food choice. In their advertising, these firms stress speed and convenience. In the 1990s, people stay at home more cocooning. Two reasons for this may be the growing number of VCRs and better frozen meals. In response, an increasing number of fast-food restaurants offer delivery service, a practice formerly limited to very large cities. One enterprising firm offers to not only deliver dinner but also bring along a videotape. It says it can do everything but the dishes—and you can throw those away.

II. Everyone knows Mr. Peanut. He's been the symbol of Planters' Peanuts since 1916, and he's a good example of name brand capital. As such, he's worth a lot to Nabisco, which owns Planters'. In 1993, Nabisco's market researchers decided the old boy wasn't appealing to younger consumers, and management made a marketing policy decision: Mr. Peanut underwent a makeover emerging as "a '90s kind of guy" lying on the beach and kicking around in cowboy boots. He got to keep the top hat, though.

CHECKING OUT

Now that you have finished studying this chapter, you should be able to:

1. Describe the characteristics of monopolistic competition.
2. Explain why interdependence is unique to oligopoly.
3. Understand why government policy is often necessary to assure the success of a cartel.
4. Use game theory to understand oligopolistic behavior.
5. Describe how and why equilibrium price and output under monopolistic competition and oligopoly differ from that of perfect competition.

ANSWERS

Trying Out the Terms

1. V
2. H
3. C
4. S
5. P
6. M
7. A
8. E
9. T
10. O
11. J
12. D
13. R
14. K
15. B
16. F
17. Q
18. G
19. I
20. L
21. N
22. U

Testing Yourself

Part I: True or False

1. true
2. false. The market will be divided among a smaller number of firms; therefore, the demand curve of each remaining firm will shift to the right.
3. false. In monopolistic competition, the product is differentiated.
4. false. A highly differentiated product has fewer substitutes; hence, a less elastic demand curve.
5. true
6. true
7. true
8. false. They are closer to the model of monopolistic competition.
9. true
10. false. A pure oligopoly is one that produces a homogeneous product.
11. true
12. false. There are usually strong barriers to entry in these industries.
13. true
14. false. Oligopolies are marked by mutual interdependence.
15. false. Price clusters are groups of prices for similar, but not homogeneous, products.

Part II: Problems

1. a. $1
   b. loss of $12.50
   c. $P = \$3$, $Q = 3$
   d. $P = \$2.50$ and Q is between 3 and 4 (where AC is at its minimum).
   e. The excess capacity is between 0 and 1 unit of output.

2. a. price = V; quantity = L
   b. The firm is operating in the short run, because it is making economic profits.
   c. The firm is making an economic profit equal to the area $WIUV$.
   d. price = Y; quantity = M

Part III: Multiple Choice

1. b	5. c	9. a	13. a
2. d	6. b	10. b	14. c
3. a	7. d	11. c	15. b
4. c	8. b	12. d	

CHAPTER 25 EXERCISES

____ 1. In which market structure do firms face the flattest (most elastic) demand curve?
   a. Perfect competition
   b. Monopolistic competition
   c. Oligopoly
   d. Monopoly

____ 2. A highly elastic, downward-sloping demand curve is most representative of
   a. monopoly.
   b. industry.
   c. oligopoly.
   d. perfect competition.
   e. monopolistic competition.

____ 3. A wide variety of styles, colors, qualities, and brands is provided by
   a. monopoly.
   b. monopsony.
   c. monopolistic competition.
   d. perfect competition.
   e. All of the above

____ 4. Which of the following is *not* implied by the excess capacity of monopolistically competitive industries?
   a. Many firms will be operating at a loss.
   b. The consumer pays for the greater differentiation between goods.
   c. The same total output could have been produced by fewer firms at a lower cost.
   d. Price will be higher than it would be for the same industry operating in perfect competition.
   e. In long-run equilibrium, average cost will be higher for monopolistically competitive firms than for perfectly competitive firms producing the same output.

____ 5. In striving for joint profit maximization, it is necessary for a cartel to
   a. set prices, outputs, and market areas.
   b. reduce the profits of each of its members.
   c. force each member to produce more.
   d. force each member to set $P < AC$.

____ 6. An oligopoly that produces resources that will be used by other firms would probably be
   a. a differentiated oligopoly.
   b. a pure oligopoly.
   c. a genuine oligopoly.
   d. not an oligopoly at all.
   e. the dominant firm.

7. Which model assumes that competitors will not follow price increases but will follow price cuts?
   a. Price leadership
   b. Dominant firm
   c. Kinked demand curve
   d. Competitive fringe
   e. Price discrimination

8. The presence of name brand capital
   a. allows consumers to participate in the ownership of the firm.
   b. encourages the entry of new firms.
   c. is most prevalent in perfect competition.
   d. is prohibited by law in the United States.
   e. can act as a barrier to entry in oligopolistic industries.

CHAPTER 26

REGULATION, DEREGULATION AND ANTITRUST POLICY

CHECKING IN

You have studied the four theoretical models of market structure. Now it is time to discuss the ways firms actually behave. As you have learned, groups of firms operate in an industry. But what is an industry? The Commerce Department classifies firms by means of the Standard Industrial Classification (SIC) system. The firms within one four-digit code group are considered an industry.

The degree of concentration in an industry can be measured to estimate the degree of monopoly power. A four-firm concentration ratio measures the concentration in a particular industry by comparing the sales of the top four firms with total industry sales. A Herfindahl Index accounts for all of the firms in an industry by totaling the squares of the market shares of all the firms in that industry. Many consider the Herfindahl Index a better measure of monopoly power than a simple concentration ratio.

Although concern exists about the degree of monopoly power in the United States, there is no conclusive evidence that the degree of concentration is increasing. In fact, it appears to be relatively stable. Because of a wave of merger and acquisition activities, there was serious concern about increasing concentration in the 1980s. Mergers in the 1990s appear to be based on the desire of firms to become more internationally oriented.

There is considerable debate about the performance of highly concentrated industries, including such issues as whether these industries engage in monopoly pricing and whether pricing in these industries is as flexible as in the economy as a whole. Some people argue that a highly concentrated structure results in the antisocial behavior and unsatisfactory performance expected of a monopoly (the market concentration doctrine). Others argue that the presence of monopoly on both sides of the market (countervailing power) controls monopoly excesses and that concentrated industries are conducive to innovation.

Sometimes natural monopolies are permitted to exist with regulation. Usually, regulators allow such monopolies to engage in cost-plus pricing. However, this type of pricing is inefficient, because it provides little incentive for firms to minimize costs. Another alternative for regulators is to tax the monopoly profits; this practice, however, does not affect price or output.

U.S. law prohibits most monopolies and highly concentrated industries. Congress passed the first antitrust law, the Sherman Act, in 1890. In the succeeding years, there have been many other antitrust laws, usually in response to prevailing business practices. These laws are enforced by the Justice Department and the Federal Trade Commission. Presidential administrations since 1890 have enforced these laws with varying degrees of enthusiasm and success. Lawsuits can take a long time and do not often result in a more competitive situation. Politics play an important role in antitrust prosecution.

TRYING OUT THE TERMS

Match each of the following terms with its definition, and then check your answers. If you are having trouble, go back to the text and find the definition there.

Part I

_____ 1. number equivalent

_____ 2. Lerner Index of monopoly power (LMP)

_____ 3. Standard Industrial Classification (SIC) system

_____ 4. trusts

_____ 5. countervailing power

_____ 6. cost-plus pricing

_____ 7. concentration ratio

_____ 8. industry studies

_____ 9. fair rate of return

_____ 10. market concentration doctrine

_____ 11. marginal cost pricing

_____ 12. Herfindahl Index

_____ 13. administered prices

_____ 14. holding companies

_____ 15. industry

A. A group of firms producing similar or related products.

B. Investigations of specific industries to determine the degree of competitive behavior.

C. A code devised by the U.S. Census Bureau for classifying industries using about 400 four-digit numbers.

D. A measure of the distribution of economic power among firms in an oligopolistic market.

E. A summed index of concentration that takes into account all the firms in an industry.

F. A measure of the theoretical number of equal-sized firms that should be found in an industry (the reciprocal of the Herfindahl Index).

G. The hypothesis that the degree of concentration in an industry is a reliable index of monopoly power and that a high concentration ratio is likely to be associated with undesirable monopoly behavior.

H. Prices that are relatively rigid, or changed only infrequently.

I. The offsetting power possessed by both sides of the market in a monopoly.

J. A policy tool for forcing a monopoly to behave more like a competitive firm by regulating the monopoly price so that it is equal to marginal cost.

K. An index that evaluates the gap between price and marginal cost as a measure of monopoly power.

L. The form of price regulation that allows firms a markup that is a percentage of average costs of production.

M. The normal profit that a regulated industry must earn in order to stay in business.

N. Organizations set up to control the stock of other companies through boards of trustees.

O. Firms set up for the sole purpose of owning and thus controlling other firms.

Part II

_____ 1. National Recovery Administration (NRA)

_____ 2. tying contracts

_____ 3. Hart-Scott-Rodino Antitrust Improvement Act

_____ 4. Federal Trade Commission Act

_____ 5. Clayton Act

_____ 6. Sherman Antitrust Act

_____ 7. Robinson-Patman Pact

_____ 8. predatory pricing

_____ 9. Celler-Kefauver Antimerger Act

_____ 10. Wheeler-Lea Act

A. The first federal antitrust law in the United States, passed in 1890. Section 1 of the act declared every contract, combination, or conspiracy in restraint of trade to be illegal. Section 2 made it illegal to monopolize or attempt to monopolize.

B. Federal law, passed in 1914, prohibiting the acquisition of the stock of a competing company if such an acquisition would "substantially lessen competition." It also prohibits tying contracts.

C. Agreements between producers and retailers that call for the retailer to stock certain items in return for being allowed to stock other items.

D. A federal law that amended the Clayton Act in 1936, making predatory pricing illegal.

E. The act of selling below cost to destroy competitors.

F. A federal law that strengthened the Clayton Act in 1950 by making it illegal in certain circumstances for a firm to merge with another by purchasing its assets.

G. A federal law passed in 1914 that set up the Federal Trade Commission (FTC) to police unfair and deceptive business practices.

H. A 1938 federal law amending the FTC Act to make unfair or deceptive acts or practices in commerce illegal.

I. A 1970 federal law amending the FTC Act to require firms to report mergers or acquisitions to the FTC and Department of Justice before the fact.

J. A major New Deal program that was aimed at business recovery but was anticompetitive since it allowed and encouraged agreements between firms. It was eventually declared unconstitutional.

TESTING YOURSELF

In the next three sections, you will answer questions and work problems that are based on information in the text. Master all of the terms before you begin these sections. Work each section without referring to your notes or the text, and then check your answers.

Part I: True or False

Mark each statement as true or false. Whenever you mark a statement as false, jot down a sentence stating why it is false.

_____ 1. An industry is composed of firms producing the same or highly similar products.

_____ 2. In the United States, industries are designated by the Commerce Department according to the system established by the Federal Trade Commission.

_____ 3. We would expect to find a negative coefficient of cross elasticity of demand between products made by firms in the same industry.

_____ 4. Suppose the efficient firm size is estimated to be approximately 15 percent of industry sales. If the four-firm concentration ratio is 70 percent, there are probably too many firms in this industry.

_____ 5. Antitrust activity may introduce inefficiencies into industries that have large economies of scale.

_____ 6. If a high level of concentration in an industry is illegal, *per se*, the court can restructure an industry solely on the grounds of concentration.

_____ 7. Countervailing power theory holds that the best way of measuring monopoly is by measuring the concentration of the industry.

_____ 8. Natural monopolies have constantly declining average cost curves.

_____ 9. A government can capture monopoly profits by taxing the monopoly.

_____ 10. The rule of reason was established in 1914 by the Clayton Act.

_____ 11. If one firm purchases a customer, it is a vertical merger.

_____ 12. If the government supported a policy of easing entry into concentrated industries, competitive pressure would increase in those industries.

___ 13. The primary casuality in a price war is usually the customer.

___ 14. Japan's trading conglomerates can be compared to U.S. holding companies.

Part II: Problems

1. Consider the following industry data.

Industry I		Industry II	
Firm	Sales (in millions)	Firm	Sales (in millions)
A	$200	A	$300
B	150	B	50
C	50	C	25
D	50	D	25
E	50	E	25
		F	25
Total	$500	G	25
		H	25
		Total	$500

a. What is the four-firm concentration ratio in each industry? Which is more concentrated?

b. What is the Herfindahl Index for each industry? Which is more concentrated? Why does the Herfindahl Index give a different result than the four-firm concentration ratio?

c. What is the number equivalent in each industry?

2. Use the figure below to answer the following questions.

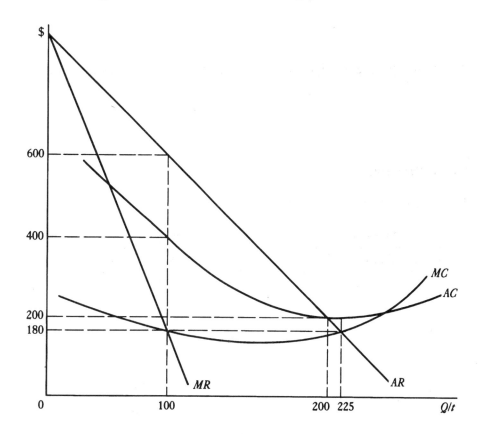

a. If the monopoly shown in the graph is not regulated, what price and quantity combination will it choose?

b. What price and quantity combination will a regulatory authority using marginal cost pricing choose? Why is this an unlikely outcome?

c. What price and quantity combination will allow the monopoly firm to earn a fair rate of return?

Part III: Multiple Choice

_____ 1. In a highly concentrated industry, we would expect to find
   a. purely competitive firms.
   b. many barriers to entry.
   c. a low Herfindahl Index.
   d. a low SIC code.

_____ 2. If an industry has a Herfindahl Index of 0.25, it has
   a. a concentration ratio of 1.
   b. a number equivalent of 4.
   c. too many firms.
   d. not enough firms.

_____ 3. Some economists prefer a Herfindahl Index to a concentration ratio because
   a. the index is more accurate, since it takes into account all the firms in an industry.
   b. the index concentrates on the top four firms in the industry.
   c. the index is easier to calculate.
   d. data are more readily available.

_____ 4. If the four largest firms in the timber business have combined annual sales of $250,000 and sales for the entire industry are $750,000, then the
   a. Herfindahl Index is 0.250.
   b. number equivalent is 5.
   c. four-firm concentration ratio is 0.667.
   d. four-firm concentration ratio is 0.333.

_____ 5. If the ideal number of firms in an industry is seven, what is the Herfindahl Index?
   a. 0.143
   b. 0.700
   c. 1.7
   d. A number that cannot be calculated with the information given

_____ 6. An industry is less differentiated when
   a. the product is more income elastic.
   b. cross elasticity between firms is negative.
   c. there are fewer digits in the SIC code.
   d. its number equivalent is high.

_____ 7. In the 1980s, U.S. corporations
   a. engaged in very little merger activity because of the Reagan administration's attitude toward mergers.
   b. were severely damaged by unorthodox merger activity by a few large firms.
   c. engaged in a huge reshuffling of corporate assets.
   d. tended to become more regional and less national.

8. The market concentration doctrine
   a. holds that only structure should be a criterion for antitrust action.
   b. is an innovative and unproven approach to evaluating monopoly power.
   c. is used more in Europe than in the United States.
   d. is the basis of the theory of countervailing power.

9. Gardiner Means found that prices in highly concentrated industries
   a. are virtually the same as in unconcentrated industries.
   b. tend to be rigid and change infrequently.
   c. fluctuate more than competitive prices.
   d. are lower than those in unconcentrated industries.

10. If a highly concentrated industry must negotiate with a strong union, the countervailing power theory would predict that
    a. consumers will benefit.
    b. consumers will be worse off than if only one monopoly were present.
    c. the monopoly profits will be shared by the industry and the union.
    d. the union will absorb all of the industry's monopoly profits, leaving it with only normal profits.

11. Suppose that a monopoly is charging a price of $25. An economist estimates that the purely competitive price for this industry would be $10. What is the Lerner Index?
    a. 2.5
    b. 1.67
    c. 0.6
    d. 0.4

12. Studies conducted by Choi and Philippatos found that
    a. the filing of antitrust cases causes restraint in pricing, but with diminishing returns.
    b. collusive firms are more profitable than noncollusive firms.
    c. stock prices are very sensitive to the filing of antitrust cases.
    d. markets in the 1980s are less concentrated than those in the 1930s.

13. The text suggests that, as an alternative to monopoly regulation, the federal government could
    a. subsidize small firms wishing to enter heavily concentrated industries.
    b. base the corporate tax structure on the degree of industry concentration.
    c. give antitrust authority to the states.
    d. dismantle artificial barriers to entry.

14. Following World War II, in dealing with Germany and Japan, the U.S. government
    a. imposed antitrust regulations intended to decrease economic efficiency.
    b. imposed antitrust regulations intended to foster pure competition and growth of the industrial base.
    c. assumed a *laissez-faire* attitude.
    d. nationalized all vital industries.

CHECKING OUT

Now that you have finished studying this chapter, you should be able to:

1. Define an industry and use the SIC system, a Herfindahl Index, and a Lerner Index to characterize the structure of an industry, interpret concentration ratios in U.S. industry, and discuss U.S. merger movements.

2. Describe the results of studies of the relationship between concentration and prices, and concentration and profits.

3. Diagram the regulation of monopoly power through price regulation and through taxation.

4. Identify and discuss the major events in the history of antitrust legislation and the economic consequences of this antitrust activity.

5. Describe the public policy debate concerning competitiveness.

6. Evaluate the alternatives in public policy toward monopoly power.

ANSWERS

Trying Out the Terms

Part I

1. F   5. I   9. M   13. H
2. K   6. L   10. G   14. O
3. C   7. D   11. J   15. A
4. N   8. B   12. E

Part II

1. J   5. B   9. F
2. C   6. A   10. H
3. I   7. D
4. G   8. E

Testing Yourself

Part I: True or False

1. true
2. false. They are designated by the Standard Industrial Classification (SIC) system, which was established by the Commerce Department.
3. false. The coefficient of cross elasticity of demand would be positive, indicating that the goods are substitutes.
4. false. The concentration ratio does not indicate an appropriate number of firms; it is simply a measure.

5. true
6. true
7. false. This is the market concentration doctrine. Countervailing power theory holds that monopolies on both sides of the market offset each other's power.
8. true
9. true
10. false. It was established by the Supreme Court in 1911.
11. true
12. true
13. false. The customer stands to gain from the lower price. The firms, particularly high-cost combatants, lose as revenues drop.
14. false. These informal associations of financial, industrial, and commerical companies could not exist under U.S. law.

Part II: Problems

1. a. Industry I = 90 percent; industry II = 80 percent. Industry I is more concentrated.
   b. Industry I = 0.280, or 2800; industry II = 0.385, or 3850. Industry II is more concentrated. The results differ because the Herfindahl Index (which sums the square of each firm's percentage of sales) gives more weight to the heavy concentration in the larger firm. The four-firm concentration ratio gives the first four firms equal weight.
   c. Industry I = 3.57, or approximately 4; industry II = 2.60, or approximately 3.
2. a. $P = \$600, Q = 100$
   b. $P = \$180, Q = 225$. It is an unlikely outcome because the firm is not earning a normal profit $(P < AC)$.
   c. $P = \$200, Q = 200$

Part III: Multiple Choice

1. b
2. b
3. a
4. d
5. a
6. c
7. c
8. a
9. b
10. c
11. c
12. a
13. d
14. a

Name _____

CHAPTER 26 EXERCISES

1. Name each of the laws described below, and give the year of its adoption.

	Act	Year	Major Provision(s)
a.	_____	_____	Made it illegal to monopolize or attempt to monopolize. Made contracts, combinations, or conspiracies in restraint of trade illegal.
b.	_____	_____	Prohibited the acquisition of the stock of another company if such an acquisition would substantially lessen competition. Prohibited tying contracts and price discrimination.
c.	_____	_____	Amendment to Clayton Act that made predatory pricing illegal.
d.	_____	_____	Amendment to the Clayton Act that made it illegal in certain circumstances for one firm to merge with another by purchasing its assets.
e.	_____	_____	Established the FTC to police unfair and deceptive business practices.
f.	_____	_____	Amendment to the FTC Act that made unfair or deceptive trade practices illegal.
g.	_____	_____	Required firms to notify the FTC and Justice Department prior to mergers or acquisitions.

2. Mark each of the following statements as true or false. Whenever you mark a statement as false, jot down a sentence stating why it is false.

_____ a. Industry studies concentrate on comparing the results given by the model of pure competition to those of monopoly industries.

_____ b. A Standard Industrial Code of 30 would represent a major industry group.

_____ c. Yale Brozen found that the rate of profit is uniformly higher in concentrated industries than in unconcentrated industries.

_____ d. One argument in favor of industry concentration is that it leads to innovation and technological advances.

_____ e. John Galbraith feels that the presence of highly concentrated industries impedes technological advances.

_____ f. If a regulated monopoly is operating at a level of output where $P < MC$, there is economic efficiency.

_____ g. From the point of view of economic efficiency, it is better to regulate the price of a natural monopoly than to tax it.

_____ h. The Lerner Index of monopoly power is the ratio of the difference in price to marginal cost.

_____ i. A state government attempting to increase competitiveness might offer tax relief to an out-of-state firm considering relocation.

CHAPTER 27

MARGINAL PRODUCTIVITY THEORY AND LABOR MARKETS

CHECKING IN

This chapter shifts the focus from product markets to resource markets. Firms are the demanders in these markets, and households are the suppliers. Income is earned in resource markets by all of the inputs. Here we discuss the labor market.

The demand for labor is derived from the demand for the final product that the labor produces. The amount of other inputs used and the level of technology also affect the demand for labor. A firm bases its demand for labor on that labor's productivity. A firm will pay a wage up to the amount that the increase in production adds to the firm's revenue; the marginal revenue product curve is a firm's demand curve for labor. A firm in a perfectly competitive product market will use more labor than a firm in an imperfectly competitive market because that firm will restrict output.

If the labor market is competitive, a firm will face a perfectly elastic supply curve of labor. It can hire as many workers as it wishes at the prevailing wage, and the marginal resource cost curve is equal to the supply curve. If the labor market is not competitive and there is a monopsonistic employer (a single purchaser of labor), the marginal resource cost curve will lie above the labor supply curve, because the firm must pay a higher wage rate as it hires more labor. This means that a monopsonistic firm will restrict employment, compared to one in a competitive labor market.

A change in the wage rate will cause a change in the quantity of labor that is employed. That change can be measured by the elasticity of demand for labor. The price elasticity of demand for the final product, the importance of labor in the production process, and the degree of input substitutability all directly affect the elasticity of demand for labor. A change in demand for the final product or a change in the use of other inputs can cause a shift in the demand curve for labor.

Individuals may attempt to become more productive by investing in human capital. One reason frequently given for the lower wages received by blacks and women is that, historically, they have invested less in human capital than have white males.

TRYING OUT THE TERMS

Match each of the following terms with its definition, and then check your answers. If you are having trouble, go back to the text and find the definition there.

____ 1. value of the marginal product of labor (VMP_L)

____ 2. marginal resource cost of labor (MRC_L)

____ 3. derived demand

____ 4. comparable worth

____ 5. monopsony

____ 6. technologically determined demand

____ 7. monopsonistic exploitation

____ 8. marginal revenue product of labor (MRP_L)

____ 9. interdependent demand

____ 10. marginal productivity theory

____ 11. backward-bending supply curve

A. Demand for a productive resource that results from demand for a final good or service.

B. Demand that depends on another type of demand.

C. Demand that depends on the techniques of production and technological progress.

D. An explanation of how the distribution of income is determined in a market system. Each input is paid according to its contribution or its marginal productivity.

E. A measure of the value of the additional output that each unit of additional labor adds to a firm's total, found by multiplying the marginal product by the price at which the firm can sell the product.

F. The amount that an additional unit of labor adds to a firm's total revenue.

G. A labor supply that slopes back to the left at the point where the income effect dominates the substitution effect.

H. The cost of each additional unit of labor.

I. A market structure in which there is a single purchase of a productive resource.

J. The difference in wages paid by a firm that has monopsony power, compared to what would be paid in a competitive market.

K. A standard for determining wages that calls for equal pay for jobs that require similar levels of training, responsibility, and skills.

TESTING YOURSELF

In the next three sections, you will answer questions and work problems that are based on information in the text. Master all of the terms before you begin these sections. Work each section without referring to your notes or the text, and then check your answers.

Part I: True or False

Mark each statement as true or false. Whenever you mark a statement as false, jot down a sentence stating why it is false.

_____   1. XYZ Steel increases employment of steelworkers because sales of domestically produced automobiles have increased. This is an example of derived demand.

_____   2. In the circular flow model, businesses are suppliers in both the product and the resource markets.

_____   3. Consumer demand determines the techniques of production.

_____   4. A profit-maximizing firm will employ or purchase a resource until $MRP = MRC$.

_____   5. A firm that takes the prices of both its inputs and its product as given is operating in perfect competition in both product and resource markets.

_____   6. A large university in a small town would be in a perfectly competitive labor market.

_____   7. A firm's demand curve for labor is labor's marginal revenue product curve.

_____ 8. The marginal resource cost curve is the supply curve for labor in imperfectly competitive resource markets.

_____ 9. The fact that a worker receives a lower wage in a monopsonistic market than a similar worker receives in a purely competitive market is evidence of an unfair labor practice.

_____ 10. An increase in the wage rate will cause the demand curve for labor to shift.

_____ 11. If $VMP > MRP$, there is imperfect competition in the product market.

_____ 12. If more labor is hired in a monopsonistic market, the wage rate will fall.

_____ 13. If salt is a very small component in the production of Max's Mighty Snack Morsels, we would expect Max's demand for salt to be very elastic.

_____ 14. The presence of reserve clauses in professional sports contracts keeps the level of payments to players lower than it otherwise would be.

_____ 15. Patty and Bob are employed as Level II electricians by the city. Since they earn the same wage, we can assume that the city is following a comparable worth policy.

Part II: Problems

1. a. Complete the table.

Units of Labor	Total Product	Product Price (P)	Marginal Product (MP)	Marginal Revenue Product (MRP)
1	8	$7	_____	_____
2	15	7	_____	_____
3	21	7	_____	_____
4	26	7	_____	_____
5	30	7	_____	_____
6	33	7	_____	_____

b. In what kind of product market is this firm operating?

c. If the firm is operating in a perfectly competitive resource market with an equilibrium wage of $30, how many units of labor will be hired?

d. If the prevailing wage rises to $40, how many units of labor will be hired?

2. Use the figure below to answer the following questions.

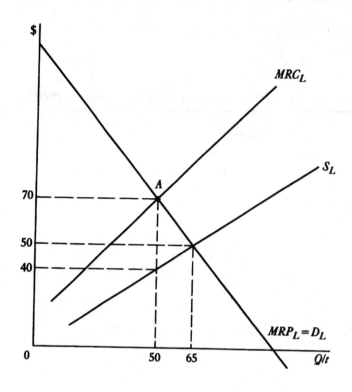

a. If this firm is operating in a perfectly competitive resource market, how many units of labor will be hired? What will the wage rate be?

b. Suppose a monopsonist enters this market. What will happen to the level of employment and the wage rate? Is there any monopsonistic exploitation?

Part III: Multiple Choice

1. Which one of the following is *not* a characteristic of the demand for labor?
   a. It is technologically determined.
   b. It is derived.
   c. It is perfectly inelastic.
   d. It is interdependent with the demand for other resources.

2. Derived demand is demand that is derived from the
   a. supply of the input.
   b. demand for the final product or service.
   c. demand for other inputs.
   d. production function.

3. When John hires the 35th worker in his box plant, he determines that the *MRC* of that worker is $5.50 and the worker's *MRP* is $7. Assuming that the market for boxes is perfectly competitive, John should
   a. lay off the new employee.
   b. hire more workers.
   c. maintain the current level of employment.
   d. obtain more capital.

4. The labor supply curve is typically upward sloping because
   a. it indicates that the firm is operating in an imperfectly competitive labor market.
   b. most people are willing to work more hours for higher wages.
   c. more people are willing to work for higher wages.
   d. higher wages induce both longer hours and more workers.

5. If a firm has a perfectly elastic labor supply curve, it is
   a. operating in a perfectly competitive resource market.
   b. operating in a perfectly competitive product market.
   c. acting as if it were an oligopsonist.
   d. making only a normal profit.

6. The value of the physical product sold
   a. is total revenue.
   b. equals price times quantity sold.
   c. equals average revenue times quantity sold.
   d. All of the above

7. A worker in John's box factory can add 100 boxes a week to total production. John can sell the boxes for $2.50 each in a perfectly competitive product market. At which marginal resource cost of labor will John maximize profits?
   a. $1.00
   b. $2.50
   c. 100/$2.50
   d. $250

8. When there is only one firm in a labor market, it is called
   a. a monopolist.
   b. a monopsonist.
   c. an oligopsonist.
   d. illegal.

9. The cost of adding a unit of labor is shown in the
   a. marginal resource cost curve.
   b. total resource cost curve.
   c. marginal revenue curve.
   d. marginal revenue product curve.

10. If a firm is operating in perfect competition in both the resource and the product market, it will have
    a. wage > MRP > MRC.
    b. wage = MRC > MRP.
    c. wage = MRP > MRC.
    d. wage = MRP = MRC.

11. If there is a monopsonistic employer, the imposition of a minimum wage may
    a. further depress the wage rate and leave employment unchanged.
    b. result in a higher wage but lower employment.
    c. result in increases in both wages and employment.
    d. increase employment while decreasing the wage rate.

12. If the demand for the final product is highly inelastic, we would expect resource demand to be
    a. relatively elastic.
    b. relatively inelastic.
    c. perfectly inelastic.
    d. unrelated to product demand.

13. Andy is tired of being a clerk in a convenience store, so he enrolls in an introductory management class at the community college. Andy is
    a. acting, in some ways, like an entrepreneur.
    b. investing in human capital.
    c. attempting to increase his lifetime earnings.
    d. All of the above

14. James P. Smith's research indicates that income differences between blacks and whites exist because
    a. of discrimination.
    b. blacks invest less in human capital.
    c. the returns to human capital investment have long lags.
    d. of the geographical concentrations of blacks in urban centers.

15. Many women should expect to earn more in the future because
    a. equal wages will be required by comparable worth legislation.
    b. human capital investments by women are reaching the same level as those by men.
    c. more men are entering low-paying occupations, such as nursing, and driving up wages in those occupations.
    d. women are investing in human capital at the same time that men are entering the low-paying occupations.

CHECKING OUT

Now that you have finished studying this chapter, you should be able to:

1. Explain what makes the demand for labor different from the demand for final goods.

2. Describe how a profit-maximizing firm in pure competition decides how much labor to employ in terms of its marginal revenue product and marginal resource cost.

3. Use a resource market diagram to illustrate and explain the difference between the use of labor under pure competition versus monopoly in the product market.

4. Define monopsony and discuss why monopsonistic exploitation may occur.

5. Determine the factors that affect the elasticity of demand for labor and describe possible causes for a shift in the demand for labor.

6. Explain how human capital relates to racial and gender differences between income levels.

ANSWERS

Trying Out the Terms

1. E
2. H
3. A
4. K
5. I
6. C
7. J
8. F
9. B
10. D
11. G

Testing Yourself

Part I: True or False

1. true
2. false. Businesses are suppliers in the product market and demanders in the resourse market.
3. false. The techniques of production are determined by engineers in a production function. Consumer preference determines what is produced.
4. true
5. true
6. false. It would be a monopsonistic employer.
7. true
8. false. The marginal resource cost curve is the supply curve of labor in perfectly competitive factor markets.
9. false. It is monopsonistic exploitation.
10. false. A change in the wage rate will cause a movement along the demand curve for labor.
11. true

12. false. It will rise. In order to hire another worker, the monopsonist must offer a higher wage to all workers.
13. false. Demand for a factor is more inelastic when the factor represents an insignificant cost of production.
14. true
15. false. Patty and Bob have the same job. Comparable worth refers to equal pay for jobs that require similar levels of training, responsibility, and skill but do not carry the same job description.

Part II: Problems

1. a.

Units of Labor	Total Product	Product Price (P)	Marginal Product (MP)	Marginal Revenue Product (MRP)
1	8	$7	8	$56
2	15	7	7	49
3	21	7	6	42
4	26	7	5	35
5	30	7	4	28
6	33	7	3	21

b. The firm is in a perfectly competitive product market; it has a perfectly elastic demand curve.
c. 4 units of labor, which is the last level of output where $MRP > MRC$
d. 3 units of labor, which is the last level of output where $MRP > MRC$

2. a. quantity of labor = 65; wage = $50
b. Employment will fall to 50, and the wage rate will fall to $40. There is $10 of monopsonistic exploitation.

Part III: Multiple Choice

1. c
2. b
3. b
4. d
5. a
6. d
7. d
8. b
9. a
10. d
11. c
12. b
13. d
14. c
15. b

Name _____

CHAPTER 27 EXERCISES

1. Complete the table.

Units of Labor	Total Product	Marginal Product (MP_L)	Product Price (P)	Total Revenue	Value of the Marginal Product (VMP_L)	Marginal Revenue Product (MRP_L)
1	20	_____	_____	$16	_____	_____
2	36	_____	_____	14	_____	_____
3	48	_____	_____	12	_____	_____
4	56	_____	_____	10	_____	_____
5	60	_____	_____	8	_____	_____

2. Graph and label the marginal revenue product curve and the value of the marginal product curve.

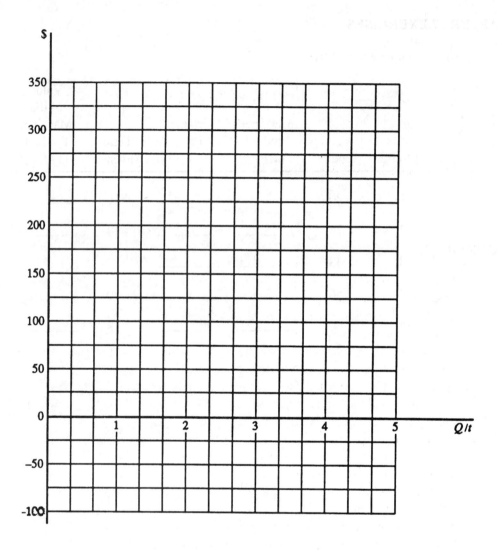

3. How do you know that the product market is not competitive? Why is *MRP* < *VMP*?

CHAPTER 28

ORGANIZED LABOR IN THE UNITED STATES

CHECKING IN

You have surveyed the theory of resource markets in the preceding chapters. In this chapter, you will examine one specific part of the labor market: labor unions. Although unions may have many objectives, such as political power and social reform, this chapter concentrates on the economic goals of unions.

Unions may be exclusive or inclusive. An exclusive union restricts membership and raises the wages of members by shifting the supply curve of labor to the left. Inclusive unions attempt to enroll all the workers in an industry and gain higher wages through negotiation and the threat of strikes. Exclusive unions are usually more successful in securing higher wages than inclusive unions.

Unions have generally been successful in gaining higher wages for their members. These increases come mainly from higher consumer prices and lower nonunion wages. Only a small portion of higher union wages come from business profits. Unions are often criticized for causing inflation and hampering the growth of productivity. There is evidence to counter both of these arguments. Unions may increase productivity by reducing employee turnover and increasing employee well-being. Long-term union contracts can actually cause union wages to rise more slowly than nonunion wages during an inflationary period.

The first unions sought political and social reform in addition to economic gain. These unions were mostly unsuccessful. The American Federation of Labor was the first business union (a union with exclusively economic goals). Unions faced hostility from businesses and the public until the election of Franklin D. Roosevelt in 1932. Since then, Congress has passed several important labor laws. The Norris-La Guardia Act and the Wagner Act encouraged the formation of unions. The Taft-Hartley Act established the rights of employers, and the Landrum-Griffin Act established rules of conduct for unions.

In recent years, the role of unions in the U.S. economy has diminished. Union membership appears to be shifting away from its original base in heavy manufacturing industries and toward service industries and the government. The Reagan administration did not provide an extremely friendly environment for unions.

Conditions in factor markets and the market for the final product can increase or decrease union power. Unions are stronger in industries with monopoly market power and an inelastic demand for labor. Unions are weakened by increased competition, right-to-work laws, increased international trade, and deregulation.

TRYING OUT THE TERMS

Match each of the following terms with its definition, and then check your answers. If you are having trouble, go back to the text and find the definition there.

Part I

____ 1. United Mine Workers (UMW)

____ 2. AFL-CIO

____ 3. featherbedding

____ 4. bilateral monopoly

____ 5. Industrial Workers of the World (IWW)

____ 6. injunctions

____ 7. Knights of Labor

____ 8. Congress of Industrial Organizations (CIO)

____ 9. inclusive union

____ 10. American Federation of State, County, and Municipal employees (AFSCME)

____ 11. yellow-dog contracts

____ 12. business union

____ 13. exclusive union

____ 14. wildcat strikes

____ 15. industrial union

____ 16. National Labor Union

____ 17. craft union

____ 18. American Federation of Labor (AFL)

A. The maintenance of jobs that management claims are unnecessary or redundant.

B. A union that restricts the supply of labor and maintains a higher-than-competitive wage for its members by excluding workers from a trade or occupation. Craft unions are examples of these.

C. A union composed of specific kinds of skilled workers, such as plumbers or carpenters.

D. A union that attempts to organize all the workers in an industry and to maintain a strong bargaining position with respect to management.

E. An inclusive union that gains power by organizing all (or a large share) of the workers in an industry.

F. A market structure in which monopolies deal with each other as buyers and sellers, such as when an inclusive union sells labor to a monopsonistic firm.

G. The first successful national union in the United States, founded in 1867 by William Sylvis.

H. Organized as a secret organization by Uriah Stevens in 1869, it won the first major strike in the United States against the railroad industry but had political reformist goals that led to its demise.

I. An exclusive union for skilled workers founded by Samuel Gompers in 1886 as the first business union.

J. According to Samuel Gompers, a union that works for economic goals without wanting to change or destroy the business organization or the political environment in which it functions.

K. The industrial union for mine workers.

L. Local strikes that are unauthorized by the national union.

M. An international union that organized U.S. steelworkers after World War I and was viewed as a socialistic organization, which contributed to its demise.

N. Contracts that require employees to agree to refrain from union activity as a precondition for employment and that allow firms to discharge workers who violate that agreement.

O. Court orders to cease some activity, such as ordering labor to stop a strike or walkout.

P. An affiliation of industrial unions that was organized when the AFL decided not to move into the mass-production industries.

Q. An organization formed by the merger of the American Federation of Labor and the Congress of Industrial Organizations in 1955, which gave labor a more unified political front.

R. A union of public employees that was one of the few unions that grew in the 1970s.

Part II

_____ 1. right-to-work laws
_____ 2. secondary boycotts
_____ 3. Landrum-Griffin Act
_____ 4. arbitration
_____ 5. Humphrey-Hawkins Act
_____ 6. union shops
_____ 7. Workplace Fairness Act
_____ 8. Taft-Hartley Act
_____ 9. National Labor Relations Board (NLRB)
_____ 10. Mediation
_____ 11. Wagner Act
_____ 12. closed shops
_____ 13. Norris-La Guardia Act

A. A law passed in 1932 that vastly strengthened the power of labor unions by limiting the court's use of injunctions in labor-management disputes.

B. A law passed in 1935 that gave employees the right to organize and bargain collectively and outlawed certain unfair labor practices by employers.

C. A board established by the Wagner Act in 1935 and empowered to investigate employer unfair labor practices and to determine the legitimate bargaining agent for labor when there are competing unions.

D. Act passed in 1947 to reverse some of the Wagner Act's favoring of labor by shifting some legal rights back to employers.

E. Firms where contract provisions require that workers must be union members before being employed.

F. Firms where union membership is necessary for a worker to remain employed.

G. State laws that allow people to hold jobs without belonging to unions.

H. Union actions to stop an employer from doing business with other firms.

I. Third-party intervention in a dispute consisting of attempts to keep the parties together and talking by offering suggestions and clarifying issues.

J. Third-party intervention in a dispute consisting of hearing the arguments of both sides, studying their positions, and rendering a decision. When this is binding, both sides must abide by the decision.

K. An act passed in 1959 and aimed at curbing union power by making unions more democratic, restricting Communist Party members and convicted felons from union leadership, and making picketing illegal under certain circumstances.

L. A 1978 amendment to the Employment Act of 1946 that set specific targets for output, employment, and prices.

M. An act that prohibits firms from permanently replacing striking workers.

TESTING YOURSELF

In the next three sections, you will answer questions and work problems that are based on information in the text. Master all of the terms before you begin these sections. Work each section without referring to your notes or the text, and then check your answers.

Part I: True or False

Mark each statement as true or false. Whenever you mark a statement as false, jot down a sentence stating why it is false.

_____ 1. The main goal of labor unions is to raise wages for all workers.

_____ 2. Unions may attempt to increase the demand for union labor by working with the firm and the government to increase the demand for the product the union firm produces.

_____ 3. If a union persuades a firm to employ an elevator operator to run a self-service elevator, the union is featherbedding.

_____ 4. A union that lobbies Congress for strict immigration controls is probably a craft union.

_____ 5. A union that has a minimum age and requires a long apprenticeship is an industrial union.

_____ 6. If workers in a monopsonistic industry organize into a union, they create a bilateral monopoly.

_____ 7. The only cost of unions' getting higher wages is lower profits to business.

_____ 8. If unions allow workers a voice in the firm and encourage workers to stay longer in one job, then unions may cause workers to be more productive.

_____ 9. When unions have long-term contracts, they exert an inflationary influence on the economy.

_____ 10. If productivity rises, wages can rise without a price increase.

_____ 11. The first successful union in the United States was the American Federation of Labor.

_____ 12. During the 1920s, firms frequently attempted to slow the growth of unions by obtaining injunctions.

_____ 13. Union growth has slowed in the last 20 years.

_____ 14. A monopoly firm is more likely to fight union organization than is a firm in perfect competition or monopolistic competition.

_____ 15. If the share of labor cost in total cost is small, demand for labor will be inelastic and a union will be stronger.

Part II: Problems

1. Each of the following graphs depicts a competitive labor market. Illustrate the given events on the appropriate graph. Label the new levels of wage and labor. Use arrows to mark the direction of change.

a. A union raises the passing grade on the examination required for full membership from 70 percent to 85 percent.

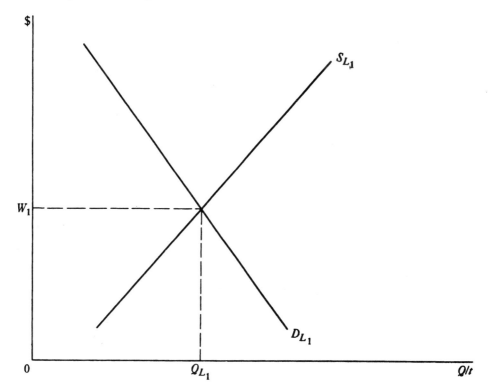

b. A firm is operating without a union in a monopsony market.

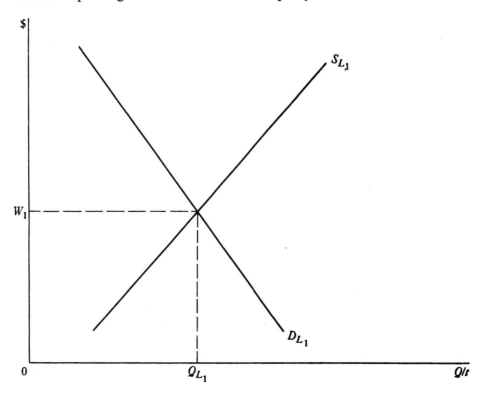

c. A union organizes all workers in an industry and threatens a strike unless wages are raised above the competitive level.

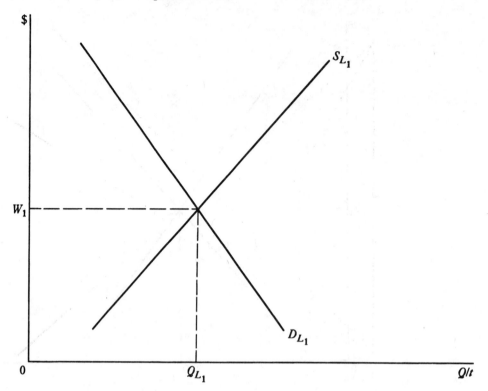

d. A union extensively advertises its product on television.

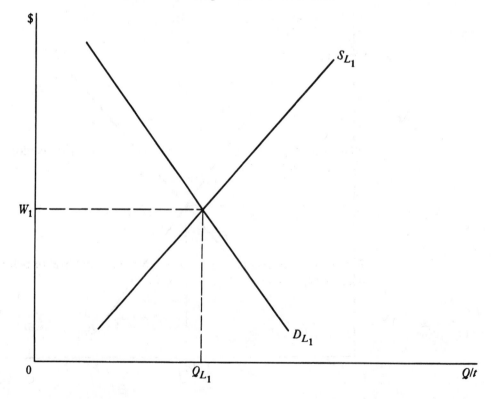

2. The graph below shows a bilateral monopoly.

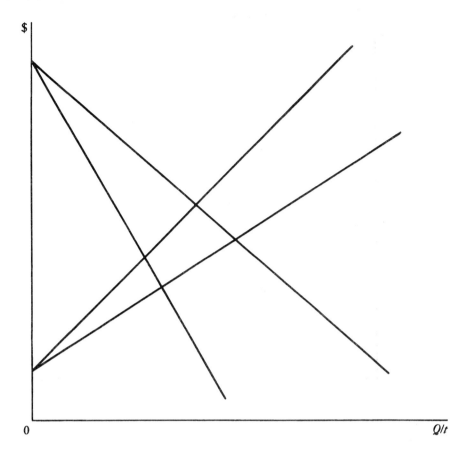

a. Label the graph correctly.

b. What is the highest wage a union would demand? Why wouldn't it ask for the highest possible wage?

c. Why is the union more likely to ask for a wage that is at or below the level associated with a monopsonist employer?

d. Over what range of wages will the level of employment be greater with a union than without one?

e. What would the wage and the quantity of labor be in a competitive labor market?

Part III: Multiple Choice

_____ 1. In order to increase wage rates in a competitive labor market, a union must
   a. increase the demand for labor.
   b. increase the price of other inputs.
   c. decrease the supply of labor.
   d. either increase the demand for labor or decrease the supply of labor.

_____ 2. Which of the following would *not* reduce the supply of labor?
   a. Child labor laws
   b. More overtime hours
   c. Shorter work weeks
   d. Lower retirement age

_____ 3. When unions raise wages, employment among union members
   a. always falls.
   b. is unaffected.
   c. falls when supply decreases.
   d. falls when demand increases.

_____ 4. A craft union
   a. is ineffective unless it has the power to strike.
   b. raises wages through negotiation.
   c. raises wages by restricting the labor supply.
   d. attempts to organize all of the workers in an industry.

_____ 5. Historically, union members have earned
   a. about the same as nonunion workers.
   b. more than nonunion workers.
   c. less than nonunion workers.
   d. twice as much as nonunion workers.

6. A union negotiated a new contract. The wage had been $7.50 an hour; the new wage per 40-hour week is $360. If nothing else changes, we would expect a
    a. decrease in the quantity of labor demanded.
    b. decrease in the quantity of labor supplied.
    c. decrease in the supply of labor.
    d. wage lower than $8 an hour.

7. If a union negotiates a 7 percent wage increase when productivity in that industry has risen by 10 percent, we would most likely observe
    a. that the increase in wages was passed on to the consumer in the form of higher prices.
    b. inflation.
    c. that the price remained the same or fell.
    d. an increase in the supply of labor.

8. The National Labor Union was
    a. a welfare union.
    b. the first successful national union in the United States.
    c. the first union to successfully strike a U.S. railroad.
    d. both politically active and the first successful national union in the United States.

9. The American Federation of Labor was
    a. the first business union.
    b. the first successful inclusive union.
    c. founded by Uriah Stevens.
    d. founded by Uriah Stevens and the first successful inclusive union.

10. Samuel Gompers thought that
    a. unions should have both economic and social goals.
    b. economic gain for union members was impossible unless the government became socialist.
    c. economic gains should be the only goal of a union.
    d. economic gains could be obtained through negotiation, and strikes were unnecessary.

11. Firms were prohibited from firing a worker who engaged in union activity by the
    a. Taft-Hartley Act.
    b. Norris-La Guardia Act.
    c. Humphrey-Hawkins Act.
    d. Landrum-Griffin Act.

12. A company must recognize and bargain with a union if
    a. a majority of the workers vote to have a union.
    b. 30 percent of the workers vote to have a union.
    c. union workers obtain an injunction ordering the firm to negotiate.
    d. the company has more than 20 employees and is engaged in interstate commerce.

____ 13. We would expect to find strong unions in industries where
   a. the demand for the final product is highly elastic.
   b. there are very few substitutes for labor.
   c. the share of labor in total cost is large.
   d. the supply of labor is elastic.

____ 14. The movement of U.S. industry from the North and Midwest to the South and West may be because of
   a. the right-to-work laws in many southern and western states.
   b. the right-to-work laws in many northern and midwestern states.
   c. many nonunion workers in southern and western states.
   d. the presence of many nonunion workers in the area as a result of the right-to-work laws.

____ 15. The deregulation of a unionized industry may
   a. strengthen the unions in that industry.
   b. present the unions with a good opportunity to strike.
   c. weaken the unions in that industry.
   d. invite new unions to compete with the existing union.

CHECKING OUT

Now that you have finished studying this chapter, you should be able to:

1. List the economic goals of unions and the ways they can be achieved.

2. Diagram and analyze the economic effects of an exclusive union and an inclusive union.

3. Discuss the effects of unions on wages and productivity.

4. Trace the history of the U.S. labor movement.

5. Analyze the economic factors that strengthen unions and weaken unions.

ANSWERS

Trying Out the Terms

Part I

1. K	5. M	9. D	13. B	17. C
2. Q	6. O	10. R	14. L	18. I
3. A	7. H	11. N	15. E	
4. F	8. P	12. J	16. G	

Part II

1. G	5. L	9. C	13. A
2. H	6. F	10. I	
3. K	7. M	11. B	
4. J	8. D	12. E	

Testing Yourself

Part I: True or False

1. false. The main goal of unions is to raise wages for *their members*.
2. true
3. true
4. false. It is more likely to be an industrial union. This type of union has a great deal to fear from an influx of new, nonunion workers.
5. false. This would be a craft union.
6. true
7. false. Most likely, higher wages will be at the expense of consumers (higher prices) and nonunion workers (lower wages), as well as profits.
8. true
9. false. Long-term contracts with set wage rates cause union wages to rise more slowly than nonunion wages.
10. true
11. false. The first successful union was the National Labor Union.
12. true
13. true
14. false. A monopolist has control over prices and can pass wage increases on to the consumer in the form of higher prices. A firm with competition cannot do this.
15. true

Part II: Problems

1. a. This is an attempt to decrease the supply of labor, which will shift supply to the left and result in a higher wage.

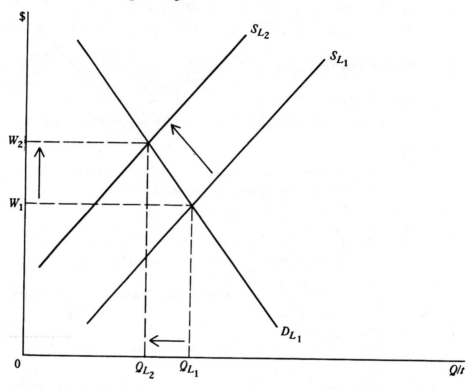

b. In a monopsony market, wages and employment will be below competitive levels.

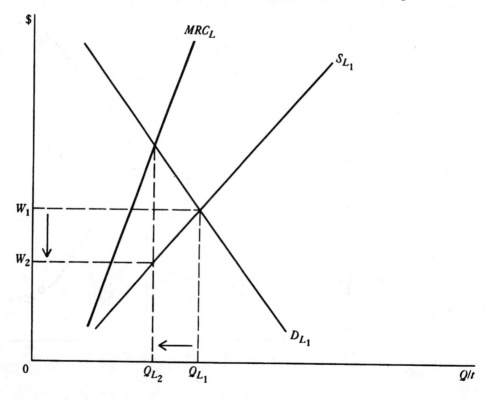

c. This situation is caused by an industrial (inclusive) union.

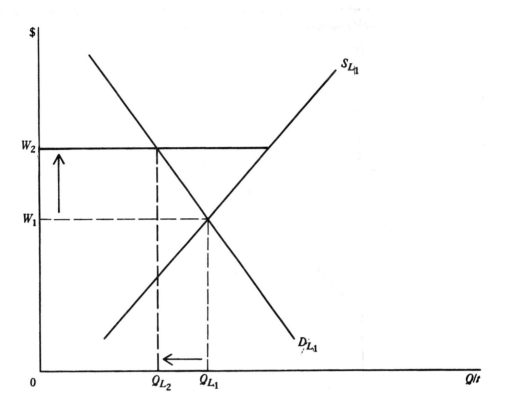

d. This is an attempt to raise wages by increasing demand for a union-made product.

2. a.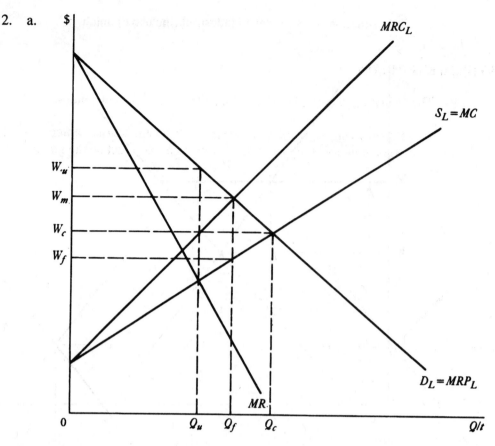

b. The highest wage a union would demand is W_u, which equates the union's marginal cost and marginal revenue. At higher wages, union gains would not be maximized.
c. At a wage at or below W_m, employment will be greater than the monopsony level. At a wage above W_m, employment will decrease.
d. Between W_m and W_f the level of employment with a union will be greater than the level of employment without a union.
e. W_c and Q_c would prevail in a competitive labor market.

Part III: Multiple Choice

1. d
2. b
3. c
4. c

5. b
6. a
7. c
8. d

9. a
10. c
11. b
12. a

13. b
14. d
15. c

Name _____

CHAPTER 28 EXERCISES

1. The following two graphs illustrate the labor markets in two industries.

   a. Suppose that the workers in industry A form an inclusive union and successfully negotiate a wage higher than W_1. Illustrate this effect on the graph for industry A.

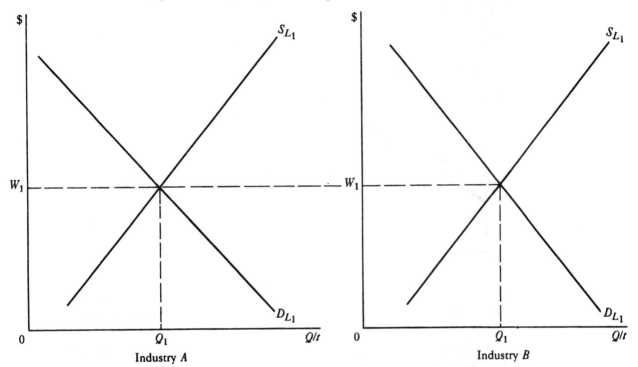

   b. What effect will this unionization have on industry B?

   c. Illustrate this change on the graph for industry B. Mark the new levels of wage and employment.

2. Trace the history of the U.S. labor movement by noting the important event(s) that occurred in each of the following years:

1867:

1869:

1886:

1932:

1935:

1947:

1959:

1977:

1978:

CHAPTER 29

RENT, INTEREST, AND PROFIT

CHECKING IN

Until now, our study of factor markets has focused on the labor market. In this chapter, we discuss the markets for land and capital and, in addition, give some consideration to the role of profits.

Land includes those factors of production that have a fixed supply. The return to the productive services of land is rent. The term *economic rent* describes a payment to a factor in excess of the amount necessary to bring that factor into production. Land is in fixed supply, and rent is determined by the level of demand. These two facts led Henry George to suggest replacing all taxes with a single tax on land. George maintained that this single tax could raise money for government without affecting economic activity or the supply of land. However, such a tax would have a negative effect on the efficient allocation of land among competing uses.

Capital is a produced factor of production. Like the other factors, it is demanded by firms because it is productive. Capital receives the payment of interest. Because the marginal revenue product curve of capital is downward sloping, less capital is acquired when interest rates rise. Government entry into the market for loanable funds can drive up the interest rate. This is called crowding out, because the higher interest rates crowd households and businesses out of the market for loanable funds.

After labor, land, and capital have been paid, any remaining revenue is profit. Profit is the residual that goes to entrepreneurs. Entrepreneurs try to increase their profits by increasing their monopoly power, taking uninsurable risks, and introducing innovations. The presence or absence of profits acts as a signal for other firms to enter or leave certain industries.

Marginal productivity theory tells us that each factor of production will be paid according to its productivity. This market-determined distribution is the natural outcome of market forces, and it may or may not be considered fair.

TRYING OUT THE TERMS

Match each of the following terms with its definition, and then check your answers. If you are having trouble, go back to the text and find the definition there.

_____ 1. capitalized value

_____ 2. roundabout production

_____ 3. functional distribution of income

_____ 4. demand-determined price

_____ 5. distributive justice

A. A price that is determined solely by changes in demand because supply is perfectly inelastic.

B. The present value of a stream of future rent payments.

C. The creation of physical capital (such as tools) that enhances productive capacity and ultimately allows increased output of consumer goods and services.

D. A normative argument for a particular distribution of income.

E. The pattern of payments to the productive resources (rent, wages, interest, and profits).

TESTING YOURSELF

In the next three sections, you will answer questions and work problems that are based on information in the text. Master all of the terms before you begin these sections. Work each section without referring to your notes or the text, and then check your answers.

Part I: True or False

Mark each statement as true or false. Whenever you mark a statement as false, jot down a sentence stating why it is false.

_____ 1. Productive resources with a supply fixed by nature are called land.

_____ 2. When the supply curve is perfectly inelastic, a change in demand will affect only price.

_____ 3. Economic rent is a payment to a productive resource equal to the amount necessary to bring that resource into production.

_____ 4. If a person earns more in one job than she could in another equally attractive occupation, the difference between the two wages is economic rent.

_____ 5. Henry George suggested that a tax on land be used to augment the existing income and property taxes.

_____ 6. George maintained that if all of the unearned income associated with land were taxed away, the supply of land would diminish very little.

_____ 7. Increasing land prices can provide an incentive to make land more productive.

_____ 8. An important economic function of the price of land is allocating land to its most highly valued economic use.

_____ 9. The object of all production is to encourage saving and investment.

_____ 10. When a monkey pulls a stick out of a tree to use in extracting ants from an anthill, the monkey is engaging in roundabout production.

_____ 11. The risk premium is the difference between the nominal interest rate and the real interest rate.

_____ 12. If the government enters the market for loanable funds, it may drive up the interest rate and discourage business and consumer borrowing.

_____ 13. An increase in government borrowing will have no effect on a firm that represents only a miniscule part of the demand for loanable funds.

_____ 14. The presence of economic profits enhances the efficiency of the market.

_____ 15. Marginal productivity theory was developed by John Bates Clark.

_____ 16. The market will generate an even income distribution.

_____ 17. The statement "Corporate profits accounted for 11.9 percent of income in 1940" refers to the market-determined distribution of income.

Part II: Problems

1. Graph A below shows the marginal revenue product of capital (demand) curve for a single firm. Graph B shows the market for loanable funds. The firm is a very small part of the entire market for loanable funds.

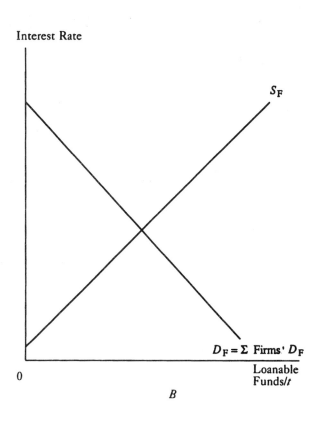

a. Draw the supply curve of loanable funds for this firm. Label the interest rate that it will pay and the quantity of funds that it will borrow.

b. Now suppose that this firm enrolls all of its factory employees in a training course that increases their productivity by 25 percent. What effect will this investment in human capital have on the firm's demand for and supply of loanable funds? Illustrate this on the graph.

2. The graphs below again illustrate the market for loanable funds for a firm and for the entire market. Suppose the government decides to fund its deficit by borrowing in the loanable funds market. What effect will this have on the market and the firm's demand for and supply of loanable funds? Illustrate these changes on the graphs.

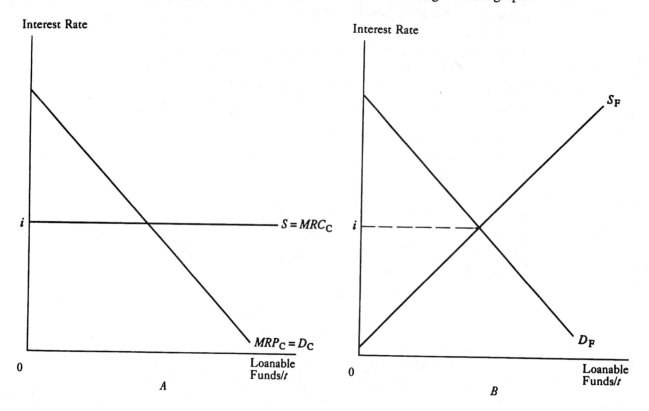

Part III: Multiple Choice

_____ 1. When people are willing to pay $15 for product Y, 200 units are sold. When people are willing to pay $6 for product Y, 200 units are sold. The price of product Y is
   a. not determined in the market.
   b. demand determined.
   c. fixed.
   d. not consistent with the law of demand.

_____ 2. The price of land is
   a. rent.
   b. surplus.
   c. the capitalized value of future rents.
   d. the capitalized value of historical rents.

_____ 3. James was earning $600 a week as a manager when he accepted a job as an investment banker for $300,000 a year. James is earning
   a. economic rent.
   b. more than his marginal revenue product.
   c. more than his marginal resource cost.
   d. an exploitative wage.

4. Mary Evans works as a secretary for $19,000 a year. She is offered a promotion to administrative assistant and a $10,000 raise. How much tax will Mary be willing to pay out of her raise if both jobs are equally attractive to her?
   a. $0.
   b. $5,000
   c. $9,999
   d. An amount that cannot be calculated from the information given

5. Henry George argued that a single tax on land would
   a. lead to greater income disparity between the rich and the poor.
   b. leave the supply of land unchanged.
   c. bring more land onto the market.
   d. encourage owners to make land more productive.

6. Economic rent
   a. serves no useful economic purpose.
   b. is paid only to land.
   c. is a short-run phenomenon.
   d. allocates land to its most highly valued use.

7. A good example of roundabout production would be
   a. hand-making a dress instead of using a sewing machine.
   b. producing goods for sale at home.
   c. making gardening tools in a factory.
   d. making dishes in a factory.

8. The market supply of loanable funds
   a. is upward sloping.
   b. comes from the personal savings of households.
   c. comes from businesses.
   d. is upward sloping and consists of funds from both businesses and households.

9. We observe a variety of interest rates because
   a. markets are imperfect.
   b. loans vary in both length and risk.
   c. both nominal and real rates are generally reported by the media.
   d. the Fed sets interest rates according to the type of market.

10. The real interest rate is the
    a. rate that is reported in the newspaper.
    b. rate given to a bank's best customers.
    c. nominal rate minus the expected rate of inflation.
    d. nominal rate plus the expected rate of inflation.

11. Whenever the government enters the market for loanable funds,
    a. private borrowing may be crowded out.
    b. the supply of loanable funds will increase.
    c. interest rates should fall.
    d. it can monopolize the market by prohibiting private borrowing.

_____ 12. All *except* which one of the following are ways an entrepreneur might seek to increase profits?
   a. Attempting to monopolize the industry
   b. Assuming only insurable risks
   c. Seeking innovative techniques and products
   d. Acquiring other firms

_____ 13. According to marginal productivity theory,
   a. income to a factor of production will increase as that factor's productivity increases.
   b. income will be distributed in proportion to the capital/labor/land ratio.
   c. profits should not be counted when income distribution is figured.
   d. income should be distributed according to law rather than market outcomes.

_____ 14. In 1990, the percentage of total U.S. income representing corporate profits was approximately
   a. 35 percent.
   b. 25 percent.
   c. 12 percent.
   d. 7 percent.

_____ 15. Since 1940, the smallest component of the functional distribution of income in the United States has been
   a. interest payments.
   b. rent.
   c. corporate profits.
   d. proprietors' income.

_____ 16. In a purely competitive factor market, the supply of and demand for productive resources will determine
   a. the functional distribution of income.
   b. a just distribution of income.
   c. the employment rate.
   d. the distributive justice rule.

TAKING ANOTHER LOOK

I.

Land can be in fixed supply even when it is underwater. Twenty-five years ago, about all you would see in the isolated waters off the coast of Maine were a few lonely lobster boats. Today, the same waters are jammed with the vessels of pleasure-seeking visitors. Moorings for boats are so scarce that some entrepreneurs are building marinas over prime lobster beds. The marina builders explain that a pleasure boater will be willing to pay $1,000 to tie up a boat for three months and that the pleasure boaters spend much more than the lobstermen. The lobstermen are angry and are calling for the city and state governments to limit the construction of marinas. If they are successful, what do you think will happen to the cost of mooring a boat in Maine for the summer?

II.

Iraq invaded Kuwait in the summer of 1990. The resulting fall in the oil supply caused the world price of oil, and gasoline, to increase dramatically. The OPEC countries faced a dilemma. They could increase the supply of oil to the world market and help maintain worldwide economic stability, or they could maintain the current level of production. Why would they want to do the latter? Because the new higher price was yielding them an economic rent (windfall profit) on each barrel of the fixed supply of oil that they chose to sell.

CHECKING OUT

Now that you have finished studying this chapter, you should be able to:

1. Describe the productive resource land and explain economic rent.

2. Explain the relationship between interest and capitalized value, crowding out, and roundabout production.

3. Itemize the sources of profit and the role that profit plays in a market economy.

4. Discuss and analyze the influences that help determine the distribution of income.

ANSWERS

Trying Out the Terms

1. B
2. C
3. E
4. A
5. D

Testing Yourself

Part I: True or False

1. true
2. true
3. false. Economic rent is a payment to a resource that is greater than the amount necessary to bring that resource into production.
4. true
5. false. He suggested that a tax on land be the only tax.
6. false. He believed that the supply of land was fixed and would be unaffected by a single tax.
7. true
8. true
9. false. The ultimate object of production is consumption.
10. true.
11. false. The risk premium is the difference between the T-bill interest rate and the interest rate to private borrowers for the same length of time.

12. true
13. false. A firm's supply curve of loanable funds is perfectly elastic (horizontal); therefore, when government borrowing causes market rates to increase, the firm's supply curve shifts up.
14. true
15. true
16. false. According to marginal productivity theory, factors are paid according to their productivity. This may produce a very unequal distribution of income.
17. true

Part II: Problems

1. a.

b. The firm's MRP_c (demand curve) will shift to the right. The firm will obtain a greater quantity of loanable funds. The interest rate will not change. This firm is such a small part of the market that the shift of its demand curve will have no effect on the market. (See the graph above.)

2. The government's demand is huge, so it will shift the market demand curve and the interest rate will rise. This in turn will shift the firm's supply curve of loanable funds. The firm will now obtain fewer loanable funds at a higher interest rate. This is an example of crowding out. (See Figure below.)

A

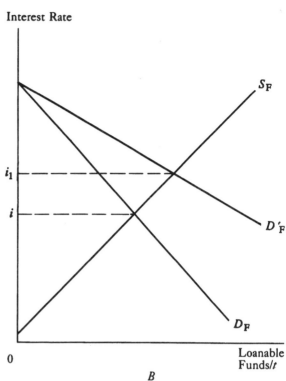
B

Part III: Multiple Choice

1. b
2. c
3. a
4. c
5. b
6. d
7. c
8. d
9. b
10. c
11. a
12. b
13. a
14. d
15. b
16. a

Chapter 29   Rent, Interest, and Profit

Name _____

CHAPTER 29 EXERCISES

The following table shows supply and demand data for a certain tract of land.

Price/Acre	S_0	D_0	D_1	D_2	D_3
$1,000	2,000	150	1,000	1,400	1,800
800	2,000	300	1,200	1,600	2,000
600	2,000	500	1,400	1,800	2,200
400	2,000	600	1,600	2,000	2,400
200	2,000	750	1,800	2,200	2,500
0	2,000	1,000	2,000	2,500	3,000

1. Graph and label the supply curve and the four demand curves.

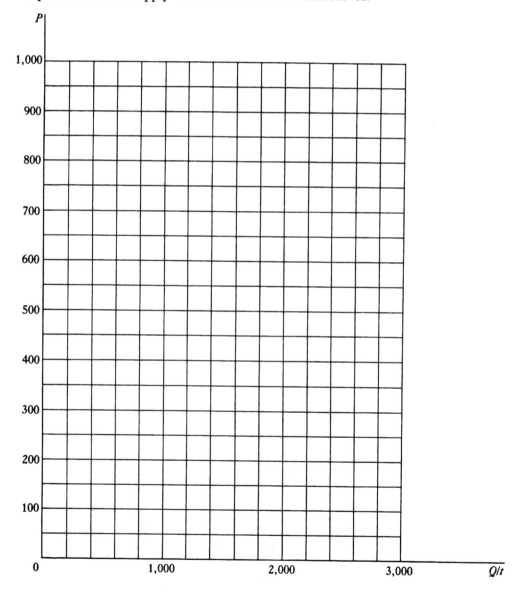

Chapter 29   Rent, Interest, and Profit   401

2. a. If the demand curve is D_0, what will the market price be?

   Will there be any economic rent?

   How much?

   b. If the demand curve is D_1, what will the market price be?

   Will there be any economic rent?

   How much?

   c. If the demand curve is D_2, what will the market price be?

   Will there be any economic rent?

   How much?

   d. If the demand curve is D_3, what will the market price be?

   Will there be any economic rent?

   How much?

CHAPTER 30

POVERTY, INEQUALITY, AND INCOME REDISTRIBUTION POLICIES

CHECKING IN

Marginal productivity theory tells us that productive resources are paid according to the value placed on their productivity. To a large extent, this is true in the United States. This chapter discusses the nation's income distribution and then examines some instances when marginal productivity theory does not hold. Discrimination may prevent certain groups from earning the amounts the theory predicts. Sometimes individuals (or the nation as a whole) find the market distribution of income unsatisfactory and seek to change that distribution in a variety of ways.

Income distribution can be measured in two ways. The preceding chapter defined the functional distribution of income as the pattern of payments to the factors of production. In the United States, most income is in the form of wages and salaries. A personal distribution of income measures how income is divided among individuals or households. Personal income distributions are often illustrated with a Lorenz curve.

Discrimination occurs when equally productive individuals or groups of individuals are paid at different rates. Sometimes, what appears to be discrimination is really due to a difference in productivity or some objective choice. The existence of discrimination not only harms the individual worker but also impairs the economic efficiency of the entire nation. Market forces often eliminate discrimination, because it is costly to entrepreneurs. Profit-seeking employers can produce at a lower cost by not discriminating.

Many people view income redistribution as a public good and believe that the government must provide it. There are many reasons people support income redistribution: they may have interdependent utility functions; they may be insuring themselves against possible future poverty; they may view poverty as a negative externality; or they may want to transfer income to themselves through the political process. The United States has many income redistribution programs. Social Security is the largest. Some programs are aimed at equality of opportunity, whereas others seek equality of results. There is concern that redistribution programs may encourage people to not work. The negative income tax has often been suggested as a program that can provide a guaranteed minimum level of income without reducing the incentive to seek employment.

TRYING OUT THE TERMS

Match each of the following terms with its definition, and then check your answers. If you are having trouble, go back to the text and find the definition there.

_____ 1. personal distribution of income

_____ 2. workfare

_____ 3. Lorenz curve

_____ 4. interdependent utility function

_____ 5. Gini coefficient

A. A measure of how total income is divided among individuals or households.

B. A graph showing the cumulative percentages of income received by various percentages of households.

C. A numerical measure of income equality equal to the area between the Lorenz curve and the diagonal divided by the area of the triangle below the diagonal on the Lorenz curve diagram.

D. Preference patterns in which the welfare of some individuals depends on the well-being of others.

E. State welfare programs requiring beneficiaries to take jobs or participate in training in order to remain eligible for benefits.

TESTING YOURSELF

In the next three sections, you will answer questions and work problems that are based on information in the text. Master all of the terms before you begin these sections. Work each section without referring to your notes or the text, and then check your answers.

Part I: True or False

Mark each statement as true or false. Whenever you mark a statement as false, jot down a sentence stating why it is false.

_____ 1. In the United States, income is primarily determined by productivity.

_____ 2. The statement "50 percent of the people in this country earn 80 percent of the income" refers to the personal distribution of income.

_____ 3. If a country's Lorenz curve lies perfectly straight along the 45-degree line, income in that country is distributed in a perfectly even way.

_____ 4. Lorenz curves contain information about the absolute distribution of personal income.

_____ 5. Between 1980 and 1991, the poverty level in the United States remained relatively constant.

_____ 6. In the United States, measures of poverty include both cash and in-kind payments.

_____ 7. Thomas Sowell maintains that, because of discrimination, the monetary returns to education are less for members of minority groups than for the population at large.

_____ 8. One way of measuring discrimination against women is to compare the earnings of single men and single women.

_____ 9. Market forces should eliminate discrimination, because firms that hire women and minorities should be more profitable.

_____ 10. In the United States, most income redistribution comes from the private sector.

_____ 11. Redistribution policies designed to increase productivity have the goal of equality of results.

_____ 12. Donations to a program that provides shoes for needy children are an example of specific egalitarianism.

_____ 13. George Stigler and Gordon Tullock argue that, because of political power, most income transfers go to the wealthy.

_____ 14. Transfers to the elderly have increased in the United States because the level of their wealth has fallen.

Part II: Problems

(The problems are based on material presented in Policy Focus.) Use the following equation in Problems 1-3:

$$W = IG - (t_n \times EI)$$

where W = welfare payment,
IG = income guarantee,
t_n = negative tax rate, and
EI = earned income.

1. Find t_n when

   a. $W = \$4,000$, $IG = \$20,000$, and $EI = \$40,000$.

   b. $W = \$10,000$, $IG = \$12,000$, and $EI = \$10,000$.

   c. $W = \$5,000$, $IG = \$8,000$, and $EI = \$5,000$.

2. Find W when

   a. $IG = \$5,000$, $t_n = 0.5$, and $EI = \$10,000$.

b. $IG = \$5{,}000$, $t_n = 0.5$, and $EI = \$5{,}000$.

c. $IG = \$12{,}000$, $t_n = 0.333$, and $EI = \$9{,}000$.

d. $IG = \$12{,}000$, $t_n = 0.333$, and $EI = \$0$.

3. Find IG when

 a. $W = \$5{,}000$, $t_n = 0.4$, and $EI = \$8{,}000$.

 b. $W = \$12{,}000$, $t_n = 0.6$, and $EI = \$15{,}000$.

 c. $W = \$10{,}000$, $t_n = 0.5$, and $EI = \$8{,}000$.

Part III: Multiple Choice

___ 1. A Lorenz curve measures the _____ income distribution.
 a. functional
 b. personal
 c. absolute
 d. age-adjusted

___ 2. The Lorenz curve of _____ would lie closest to the 45-degree line.
 a. Sweden
 b. the United States
 c. Mexico
 d. South Africa

___ 3. If the personal income distribution of the United States is adjusted for life-cycle changes,
 a. the Lorenz curve becomes a straight line.
 b. the poverty rate increases.
 c. wealth effects dominate income effects.
 d. there is a trend toward a more equal distribution of income.

4. According to Table 3 in the text chapter, in the United States the highest incidence of poverty is among
   a. all African-Americans.
   b. people over 65.
   c. households headed by African-Americans between 25 and 34.
   d. households headed by African-Americans over 65.

5. Wages may be higher in some occupations than in others if
   a. supply in the higher paying occupations is restricted by discriminatory practices.
   b. fewer workers have been channeled into the higher paying occupations.
   c. workers in the higher paying occupations are more productive.
   d. either supply in the higher paying occupations is restricted or fewer workers have been channeled into higher paying occupations.

6. Why may women and minorities earn less than white males?
   a. Less investment in human capital
   b. Channeling in specific occupations
   c. Lower productivity
   d. Discrimination
   e. All of the above

7. If paying for a foster child in New York City makes the Reynolds family of Cheyenne, Wyoming, feel better, they
   a. have interdependent utility functions.
   b. have regional interdependencies.
   c. have independent utility functions.
   d. are free riders.

8. When a person feels personal benefits from the reduction of poverty but refuses to participate to private redistribution, that person is
   a. a free rider.
   b. a general egalitarian.
   c. a specific egalitarian.
   d. irrational.

9. Private redistribution is more likely to take place if
   a. there is no public redistribution.
   b. it is done anonymously and in a large group.
   c. it is done in a small, homogeneous group.
   d. there are no externalities associated with poverty.

10. An elderly person living in poverty is more likely to benefit from a redistribution policy that
    a. seeks equality of opportunity.
    b. seeks equality of results.
    c. is based on productivity.
    d. encourages economic growth.

_____ 11. In the United States, income redistribution is carried out by
   a. the federal government.
   b. state and local governments.
   c. private organizations.
   d. all levels of government and private organizations.

_____ 12. The largest income redistribution program in the United States is
   a. Social Security.
   b. welfare.
   c. food stamps.
   d. agricultural supports.

_____ 13. Workfare programs require
   a. anyone who receives welfare to work.
   b. welfare recipients who are able to work to accept a job or enter a training program.
   c. welfare recipients to find jobs in the private sector.
   d. mothers of infants to work as day-care assistants.

_____ 14. A major attraction of the negative income tax is that
   a. it would cost less to implement than other types of distribution programs.
   b. the government could control the way recipients spend the money.
   c. it would not go to undeserving people.
   d. there is no income test involved.

_____ 15. The percentage of gross domestic product spent on social welfare programs is
   a. higher in the United States than in any other country.
   b. higher in the United States than in any other industrial country with the exception of Sweden.
   c. lower in the United States than in any other country.
   d. lower in the United States than in any other industrial country with the exception of Japan.

TAKING ANOTHER LOOK

It sometimes seems that those who live in poverty are condemned to continue there despite the best efforts of governments and individuals. Fortunately, this is not always the case; the market system and productivity-based distribution do produce happy endings—and beginnings.

In a recent *New York Times* column, Anthony Lewis recounts the story of a 10-year-old Vietnamese boy whose family arrived in the United States several years ago with only $200, which they spent on used winter coats. The family now owns a successful grocery store in Oregon, and the boy, now grown, is a graduate of Harvard Law School and clerks for Supreme Court Justice Sandra Day O'Connor.

CHECKING OUT

Now that you have finished studying this chapter, you should be able to:

1. Describe the measurement of income distribution in the United States.

2. Explain how poverty is defined and the characteristics of those most likely to be poor.

3. Analyze the effects of discrimination on wage differences.

4. Summarize the arguments for and against the redistribution of income through government policy, and discuss the advantages and disadvantages of equality of opportunity versus equality of results strategies, and redistribution in kind versus in cash.

5. Describe current government transfer programs and proposals for policy reform.

ANSWERS

Trying Out the Terms

1. A
2. E
3. B
4. D
5. C

Testing Yourself

Part I: True or False

1. true
2. true
3. true
4. false. Lorenz curves provide information about the relative distribution of personal income.
5. true
6. false. They generally do not include in-kind payments and therefore overestimate the poverty rate.
7. false. Sowell argues that returns to education are higher for minority groups.
8. true
9. true
10. false. The public sector is responsible for most income redistribution in the United States.
11. false. The goal of these programs is equality of opportunity.
12. true
13. false. They maintain that, because of political power, most income transfers go to the middle class.
14. false. Although it is true that transfers to the elderly have increased, it is also true that their accumulated wealth has increased.

Part II: Problems

1. a. $t_n = 0.4$
   b. $t_n = 0.2$
   c. $t_n = 0.6$
2. a. $W = \$0$
   b. $W = \$2,500$
   c. $W = \$9,003$
   d. $W = \$12,000$
3. a. $IG = \$8,200$
   b. $IG = \$21,000$
   c. $IG = \$14,000$

Part III: Multiple Choice

1. b	5. d	9. c	13. b
2. a	6. e	10. b	14. a
3. d	7. a	11. d	15. d
4. c	8. a	12. a	

CHAPTER 30 EXERCISES

You are given the following income distribution information for the southern and western areas of the United States in 1985.

SOUTHERN UNITED STATES

Income Class	Upper Limit for Class	Percentage of Total Income	Cumulative Percentage
Lowest fifth	$11,795	4.5	_____
Second fifth	20,100	10.5	_____
Middle fifth	30,100	16.4	_____
Fourth fifth	45,119	24.1	_____
Highest fifth	73,847	44.6	_____

WESTERN UNITED STATES

Income Class	Upper Limit for Class	Percentage of Total Income	Cumulative Percentage
Lowest fifth	$14,592	4.9	_____
Second fifth	24,572	11.1	_____
Middle fifth	35,352	16.9	_____
Fourth fifth	50,900	24.0	_____
Highest fifth	82,742	43.1	_____

Source: U.S. Department of Commerce, *Statistical Abstract of the United States: 1989* (Washington DC: U.S. Government Printing Office, 1989).

1. a. Calculate the cumulative percentage of income for each group.

b. Graph each Lorenz curve.

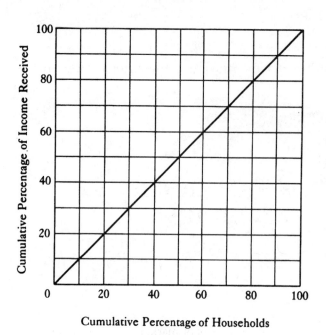

Cumulative Percentage of Households

Southern U.S., 1985

Cumulative Percentage of Households

Western U.S., 1985

2. a. In which region is there more relative poverty?

    b. In which region is there more absolute poverty?

    c. Which region will have a larger Gini coefficient?

CHAPTER 31

MARKET FAILURE AND GOVERNMENT INTERVENTION POLICIES

CHECKING IN

Markets *almost* always work. You have studied two instances of market failure: monopoly power and poverty. This chapter discusses what happens when markets don't work. Is there any way for society to produce a more desirable outcome? One way is to look to government to provide solutions. Government acts through its laws. As legislative bodies pass new laws and court decisions change existing laws, the economy is affected, sometimes intentionally, but sometimes as a side effect.

Externalities occur when some costs and/or benefits of production are not considered when economic decisions are made. Unrecognized social costs, or negative externalities, result in overproduction, whereas unrecognized social benefits, or positive externalities, result in underproduction. The Coase theorem suggests that market forces may resolve many externality problems when property rights are clearly defined and the number of people affected is small.

Because a public good is nonexcludable and nonrivalrous, the market will not provide enough of it; sometimes, the market will not provide a public good at all. Public goods are underproduced because some people, called free riders, will consume them without paying for them. Free-riding behavior means that a firm cannot expect to make a profit by producing a public good. Not all goods provided by the government are public goods; on the other hand, not all public goods are provided by the government.

The market does not solve the problems of monopoly, externalities, and public goods, so people often look to the government for solutions. The next chapter will discuss how the government deals with these situations.

TRYING OUT THE TERMS

Match each of the following terms with its definition, and then check your answers. If you are having trouble, go back to the text and find the definition there.

_____ 1. Coase theorem   _____ 6. Clean Air Act

_____ 2. social costs   _____ 7. internalization

_____ 3. externalities   _____ 8. tort law

_____ 4. property law   _____ 9. eminent domain

_____ 5. tort   _____ 10. contract law

A. Law that concerns the enforcement of property rights.

B. Law that deals with intentional and unintentional wrongs inflicted by one party on another.

C. Law that deals with the enforcement of voluntary exchanges.

D. A doctrine that gives government the right to buy property at "fair market value" if the purchase is in the public interest.

E. A wrongful action (or failure to act) that causes damage to the person or property of another individual.

F. Costs or benefits associated with consumption or production that are not reflected in market prices and fall on parties other than the buyer or seller.

G. Costs that are borne by society or some group in society without compensation.

H. The incorporation of the social costs of negative external effects into the market price.

I. The idea that well-defined property rights are sufficient to internalize any external effect that is present, when there are small numbers of affected parties.

J. Federal law passed in 1970 that empowered the EPA to set emission standards and impose standards on polluters.

TESTING YOURSELF

In the next three sections, you will answer questions and work problems that are based on information in the text. Master all of the terms before you begin these sections. Work each section without referring to your notes or the text, and then check your answers.

Part I: True or False

Mark each statement as true or false. Whenever you mark a statement as false, jot down a sentence stating why it is false.

_____   1. Market failures frequently occur when property rights are not clearly defined.

_____   2. Dandy Danny's sign reads "Money back if you are not satisfied." If Dandy Danny refuses to pay up when you are unhappy with one of his hamburgers, there may be a contract violation.

_____   3. External costs cause underproduction.

_____   4. Most economists agree that the market will eventually resolve the problems caused by externalities.

_____   5. If firms properly internalized the costs of pollution, pollution levels would fall to zero.

_____   6. Acid rain is a negative externality.

_____   7. The Coase theorem holds that production can be increased if property rights are well defined.

_____   8. If other store owners agree to pay to clean up an abandoned store front on Main Street, they are following the Coase theorem.

_____ 9. When the government imposes a tax on individuals or firms that pollute the air, it is forcing cost internalization.

_____ 10. Public goods are goods provided by the government.

_____ 11. If Janie listens to the local public radio station without sending in a contribution, she is imposing an external cost.

_____ 12. If there were no public goods, there would be no free riders.

_____ 13. Although there is no market for public goods, the demand curve for these goods can easily be determined through the political process.

_____ 14. Governments provide both public and private goods.

_____ 15. Steven Cheung found that externalities may have more negative effects than had previously been supposed.

Part II: Problems

1. The following schedules show the private demand (D_p), external benefits (EB), and supply schedule for a product with substantial positive externalities. You should be aware of two things in working this problem. First, you must sum vertically (add the relevant price for each quantity). Second, in this case external benefits are constant.

Quantity	Price/Private Demand (D_p)	Price/External Benefit (EB)	Price/Combined Demand ($D_p + EB$)	Price/Supply
2	$18	$8	_____	$10
4	16	8	_____	12
6	14	8	_____	14
8	12	8	_____	16
10	10	8	_____	18
12	8	8	_____	20

a. Complete the schedule for combined demand ($D_p + EB$), and graph all the schedules.

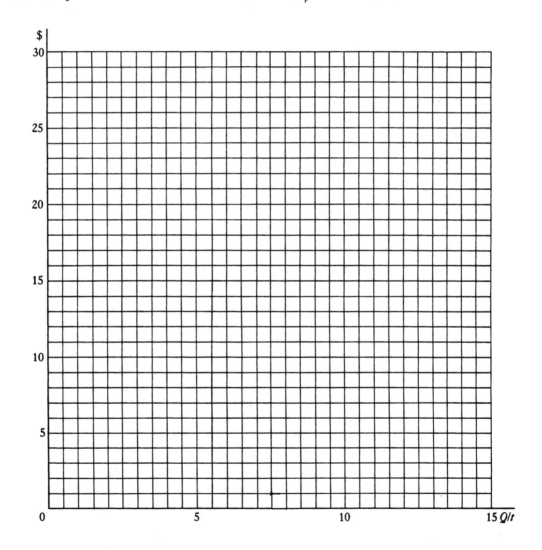

Chapter 31 Market Failure and Government Intervention Policies

b. When only private demand and supply interact, what price and quantity will prevail?

c. If external benefits are taken into account, what price and quantity will prevail?

2. The following schedules show the marginal costs (MC), the social costs (SC), and the demand for a product with substantial external costs.

Quantity	Price/Marginal Costs (MC)	Price/Social Costs (SC)	Price/Total Supply (MC + SC)	Price/Demand
0	$0	$0	$0	$40
1	5	2	_____	37
2	10	4	_____	34
3	15	6	_____	31
4	20	8	_____	28
5	25	10	_____	25
6	30	12	_____	22

a. Complete the schedule of the true supply curve (*MC* + *SC*), and graph all the schedules. Once again, you sum vertically.

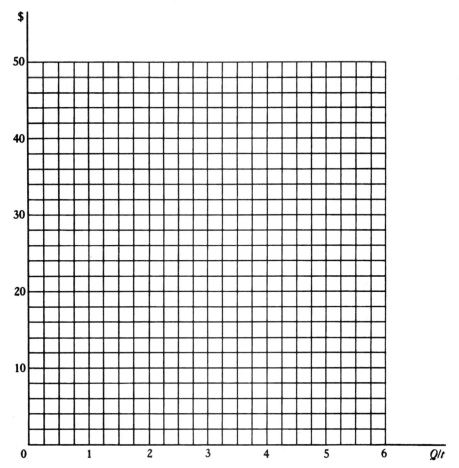

b. When only private demand and supply interact, what price and quantity will prevail?

c. If external costs are taken into account, what price and quantity will prevail?

Part III: Multiple Choice

_____ 1. Property law would be involved if
   a. a trespassing child fell into your beautiful Japanese fish pond.
   b. a careless waiter dumped orange juice down your back.
   c. a rock star failed to appear for a concert.
   d. your microwave oven wouldn't cook.

2. The inoculation of children against contagious diseases is an example of a
   a. private good with social benefits.
   b. private good with social costs.
   c. purely private good.
   d. purely public good.

3. When Mesa Petroleum built a park in front of its corporate office, it was
   a. imposing external costs on its shareholders.
   b. providing external benefits to the community.
   c. assuming some of the responsibilities of government.
   d. providing a purely public good.

4. When a negative externality is present, how do price and output compare to what they would be in an optimal solution?
   a. Price is the same, but output is too low.
   b. Price is too high, and output is too low.
   c. Price is too low, and output is too high.
   d. Price is too low, and output is the same.

5. A firm will take social costs into account if
   a. it is a good corporate citizen.
   b. the government forces it to internalize all costs.
   c. it is able to offer social benefits equal to the social costs.
   d. its product is a public good.

6. The pollution level would be reduced to zero if
   a. firms were forced to internalize their costs.
   b. the marginal social costs of pollution were equal to the marginal social benefits.
   c. the production process causing pollution was halted.
   d. either firms were forced to internalize their costs or the marginal social costs of pollution were equal to the marginal social benefits.

7. The government can force firms to internalize external costs by
   a. placing a tax on the firm equal to the external costs.
   b. charging the firm a fee equal to the external costs.
   c. paying the firm to correct the externality.
   d. either placing a tax or charging a fee that is equal to the external costs.

8. Firms impose external costs because
   a. they do not consider costs that they don't have to pay.
   b. they are unaware of them.
   c. production drops to zero if costs are internalized.
   d. All of the above

9. For the Coase theorem to apply,
   a. property rights must be clearly defined.
   b. a small number of individuals must be involved.

c. there must be no external costs.
d. property rights must be clearly defined and also only a small number of individuals must be involved.

10. State Street Jazz Club has begun having post-lunch concerts in its building next door to Happy Hours Day Care. According to the Coase theorem,
    a. Happy Hours can't do anything except switch naptime to before lunch.
    b. Happy Hours can pay State Street to switch the concert to before lunch.
    c. State Street can pay to soundproof a room for Happy Hours.
    d. the room can be soundproofed or the concert switched, but who pays depends on how property rights are defined.

11. The Coase theorem states that
    a. production will be the same, regardless of how property rights are defined.
    b. income distribution will be the same, regardless of how property rights are defined.
    c. property rights should be assigned to the party imposing the externality.
    d. costs can never be fully internalized.

12. The government is often reluctant to impose controls on externalities because
    a. it is hard to measure the true social costs.
    b. it is easy to make a mistake.
    c. enforcement is expensive.
    d. All of the above

13. The free-rider problem occurs
    a. only when people are excluded from consumption of a public good.
    b. more often in large groups than in small groups.
    c. when the government becomes involved in what is essentially a market problem.
    d. when the government makes in-kind rather than cash distributions.

14. A good is considered a public good if it is
    a. provided by the government.
    b. nonrivalrous in consumption.
    c. nonexcludable in consumption.
    d. both nonrivalrous and nonexcludable.

15. Many economists regard education as
    a. a purely private good.
    b. a purely public good.
    c. a private good with some characteristics of a public good.
    d. most efficient when it is provided by the market.

16. Welfare economics deals with
    a. normative policy prescriptions.
    b. positive approaches to income redistribution.
    c. statistically measuring levels of national well-being.
    d. finding market solutions to both positive and negative externalities.

TAKING ANOTHER LOOK

Free-riding keeps public goods from being provided by the market. Most people won't pay for something they can have at no cost. Why are most fireworks shows free? One way to avoid this problem is by tying the public good to the purchase of a private good. The fireworks show might follow a concert by a popular group. The ticket price would reflect both the performance and the fireworks. Of course, there would still be folks parked by the side of the road, but they didn't get to hear the concert.

CHECKING OUT

Now that you have finished studying this chapter, you should be able to:

1. Describe the economic and policy impact of property law, tort law, and contract law.

2. Define externalities and explain how the Coase theorem can resolve some externality problems.

3. Explain how free-riding behavior results in the underproduction of public goods.

4. Evaluate the public goods aspects of income redistribution and education.

5. Discuss welfare economics.

ANSWERS

Trying Out the Terms

1. I
2. G
3. F
4. A
5. E
6. J
7. H
8. B
9. D
10. C

Testing Yourself

Part I: True or False

1. true
2. true
3. false. External costs cause overproduction.
4. false. In the case of externalities, the majority of economists believes that there is a legitimate role for government in the market.
5. false. Pollution levels would fall to zero only if production of the good in question fell to zero.
6. true
7. false. The Coase theorem states that production will be the same regardless of who has the property rights, as long as the number of people affected is small and the property rights are clearly defined.
8. true
9. true
10. false. Public goods are goods that are nonexcludable and nonrivalrous. They are provided by government and the private sector.

11. false. She is enjoying an external benefit. She is also a free rider.
12. true
13. false. Whenever there is a public good, there will be free riders who will hide their demand for the good. It is also very difficult for individuals to place a monetary value on such public goods as defense and police protection.
14. true
15. false. In studying bees and apple orchards, Cheung found that markets work very well in correcting externalities and that there may be fewer market failures than we thought.

Part II: Problems

1. a.

Quantity	Price/Private Demand (D_p)	Price/External Benefit (EB)	Price/Combined Demand ($D_p + EB$)	Price/ Supply
2	$18	$8	$26	$10
4	16	8	24	12
6	14	8	22	14
8	12	8	20	16
10	10	8	18	18
12	8	8	16	20

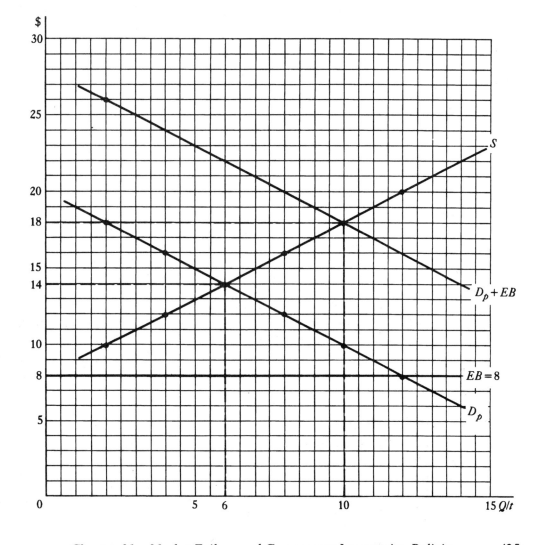

Chapter 31 Market Failure and Government Intervention Policies

  b. price = $14; quantity = 6
  c. price = $18; quantity = 10

2. a.

Quantity	Price/Marginal Costs (MC)	Price/Social Costs (SC)	Price/Total Supply (MC + SC)	Price/Demand
0	$ 0	$ 0	$ 0	$40
1	5	2	7	37
2	10	4	14	34
3	15	6	21	31
4	20	8	28	28
5	25	10	35	25
6	30	12	42	22

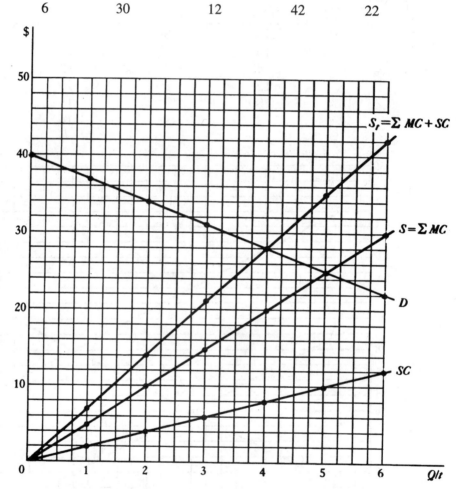

  b. price = $25; quantity = 5
  c. price = $28; quantity = 4

Part III: Multiple Choice

1.	a	5.	b	9.	d	13.	b
2.	a	6.	c	10.	d	14.	d
3.	b	7.	d	11.	a	15.	c
4.	c	8.	a	12.	d	16.	a

Name _____

CHAPTER 31 EXERCISES

Joe and Carol own the only houses on an isolated road. They are considering hiring a private security service to drive by their houses on a regular basis. The firm charges $80 for each drive-by. Joe and Carol have the following demand schedule for this service:

Price	Quantity Demanded By Carol	By Joe
$80	0	0
70	0	0
60	0	1
50	0	2
40	1	3
30	2	4
20	3	5
10	4	6

1. Clearly, neither of them will employ the service if he or she has to pay for it alone. Since they can use the service jointly (one drive-by will cover both houses), they can combine their demands. Fill in their combined demand schedule. (Note: This is rather tricky, since you are summing vertically. For each quantity, add the price Joe is willing to pay and the price Carol is willing to pay. Two entries have been made for you.)

Quantity	Price	
0		
1	100	($40 + $60)
2	80	($30 + $50)
3	_____	
4	_____	
5	_____	
6	_____	
7	_____	

Chapter 31   Market Failure and Government Intervention Policies

2. Graph their individual demand curves and their combined demand curve on the following graph.

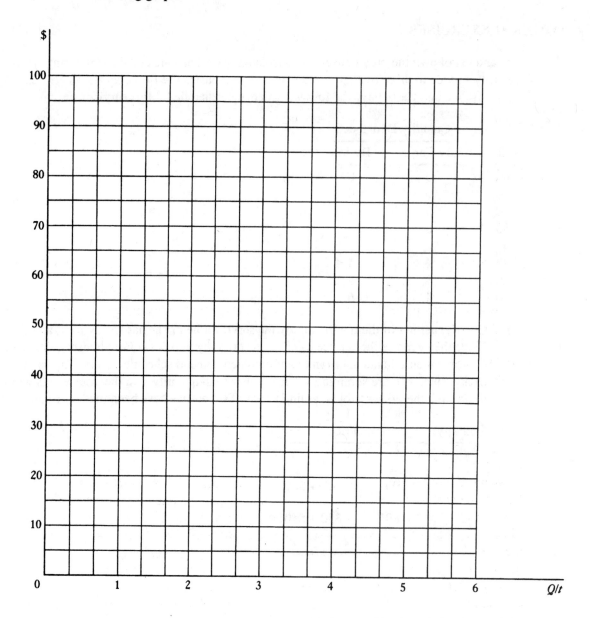

3. If they combine their demands, how many drive-bys will Joe and Carol purchase and what will their combined expenditures be?

428 *Chapter 31 Market Failure and Government Intervention Policies*

CHAPTER 32

GOVERNMENT FAILURE AND PUBLIC CHOICE

CHECKING IN

The preceding chapter discussed several ways in which markets can fail. It concluded by stating that many people look to the government to correct market failures. This chapter considers some of the ways governments attempt to correct market failures and the related costs. Public choice theory is one method of evaluating government provision of public and private goods.

When economic decisions are made through the political process, there are strong incentives for individuals and groups to attempt to affect the outcome. Rent seeking occurs when individuals or groups attempt to generate transfers to themselves. Politicians may respond by attempting to extract rent in exchange for legislation favorable to certain individuals or groups. Consumers' defense of their consumer surplus against rent seekers is called rent defending.

Many economists believe that political decision making and public provision of goods lead to an excessively large government. Logrolling, or vote trading, makes government too big, because the beneficiaries of government programs do not have to bear the entire costs of these programs. Bureaucracy and bureaucratic decision making lead to a large government because the system provides incentives to maximize budgets instead of minimizing costs. Although it is necessary to have some government involvement in a market economy, the degree of involvement varies. Sometimes a government function can be provided more efficiently by relying on the market. Privatization occurs when government activities and/or assets are transferred to the private sector.

Two additional approaches to explaining government failure come from the Austrian school of economic thought and radical economics. The Austrian economists assume that decision makers have incomplete information. They oppose economic planning by governments. Radical economics is based on the belief that government protects capitalist monopolies, which exploit workers and Third World countries.

TRYING OUT THE TERMS

Match each of the following terms with its definition, and then check your answers. If you are having trouble, go back to the text and find the definition there.

_____ 1. rent seeking   _____ 4. logrolling

_____ 2. dual labor markets   _____ 5. rent defending

_____ 3. privatization   _____ 6. median voter theorem

A. The commitment of scarce resources to capture returns created artificially.

B. Actions by consumers to keep their consumer surplus from being captured by rent seekers.

C. A theorem that predicts that under majority rule, politicians will reflect the positions of voters near the center of the political spectrum.

D. Vote trading in the legislative process.

E. The transfer of governmental activities and/or assets to the private sector.

F. The radical economists' idea that there are two labor markets because of artificial barriers that keep some workers earning low wages.

TESTING YOURSELF

In the next three sections, you will answer questions and work problems that are based on information in the text. Master all of the terms before you begin these sections. Work each section without referring to your notes or the text, and then check your answers.

Part I: True or False

Mark each statement as true or false. Whenever you mark a statement as false, jot down a sentence stating why it is false.

_____ 1. Public choice economics combines economics and sociology.

_____ 2. According to public choice theory, politicians will usually vote for programs that benefit a few and distribute costs widely.

_____ 3. William C. Mitchell argues that a proposal that taxes market efficiency stands a better chance of adoption than a proposal that rewards efficiency.

_____ 4. An important defense contractor takes a congressional representative to lunch and happens to discuss how a new contract could benefit her firm, she is extracting rent.

_____ 5. The congressional repeal of a law requiring warranties on used cars is a good example of a milker bill.

_____ 6. In W. C. Nicholson's campaign for mayor, he has taken the position that the local marina should be closed for the winter season. His opponent maintains that it should be open year round. Public opinion is mixed. According to the median voter theorem, as election day approaches, each candidate will continue to hold the same position.

_____ 7. If a senator from Arkansas votes for a bill to build a military base in Mississippi because he expects the senator from Mississippi to vote for a bill to build a new highway across Arkansas, they are conducting yellow-dog politics.

_____ 8. The efficiency of a bureau is usually evaluated in terms of some measurable output.

_____ 9. Because the U.S. economy is market-controlled, privatization is not an issue.

_____ 10. The basic premise of the Austrian school of economic thought is that markets are basically stable and operate with full information.

_____ 11. The Austrian school of economics holds that many macroeconomic problems have their roots in microeconomic political maneuvering.

_____ 12. Radical economists base some of their thinking of the works of Karl Marx.

_____ 13. Radical economists view the state as the adversary of monopoly power.

_____ 14. Low voter turnout in the United States appears to be irrational and can be attributed primarily to voter apathy.

_____ 15. Because the government grants a monopoly to the mail service, it has no competition.

Part II: Problem

1. The following graph illustrates a monopoly market that is operating without government intervention.

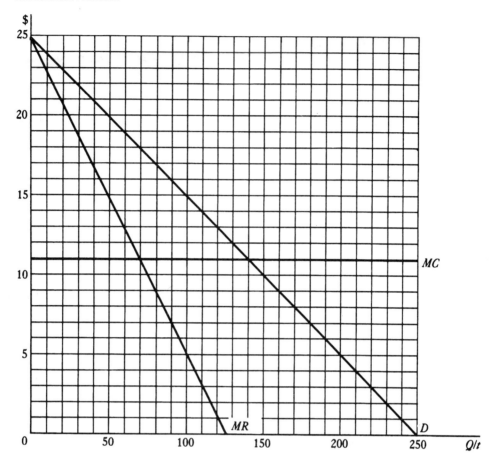

a. What price will the monopolist charge? What quantity will be sold?

b. What would the price and quantity be if this were a competitive market?

c. What would the consumer surplus be in a competitive market?

d. What would the consumer surplus be in a monopoly market?

e. If the government seeks to regulate this market, how much will the monopolist be willing to spend on rent seeking?

f. If consumers defend their consumer surplus (rent defending) and the monopolist counters with rent seeking, what is the most the two groups will spend?

Part III: Multiple Choice

1. Suppose Representative Tate proposes that the state fund college scholarships for all students who graduate from high school with an average of B or better, but that this scholarship not go into effect until the class entering first grade this year graduates (12 years from now). This proposal will have the best chance of being adopted if
    a. Representative Tate makes clear the amount of taxes that will have to be collected in order to fund the project.
    b. the proposal is accompanied by a clearly stated plan for an increase in the sales tax to fund the plan.
    c. Representative Tate suggests that the plan be funded only after the scholarships are in place, since it is difficult to predict what they will cost.
    d. the plan is contingent on funding by the school districts where the high schools are located.

2. A politician who attempts to build a coalition of rent-seeking groups by brokering transfers to those groups is
    a. rent seeking.
    b. acting like an entrepreneur.
    c. breaking the law.
    d. logrolling.

3. Consumers' use of political pressure to resist monopolies is called
    a. rent defending.
    b. rent extracting.
    c. applying the Tiebout solution.
    d. coalition monitoring.

4. Senator Jones accepts a campaign donation from the Association of Lady Bug Raisers. The next week he introduces a bill declaring the lady bug the national insect. This is called
    a. rent extracting.
    b. logrolling.
    c. pork-barrel politics.
    d. both logrolling and pork-barrel politics.

5. Chip McGuire visits the courthouse to show the county commissioners his new jail-security system and to invite them all to a barbeque at his ranch. Chip is being a
    a. yellow dog.
    b. rent seeker.
    c. rent extractor.
    d. perfect competitor.

6. Logrolling tends to create an excessively large government because
    a. it results in many projects with dispersed benefits.
    b. that is the optimal level of public output.
    c. local beneficiaries of government projects believe that someone else is paying for them.
    d. projects are determined by bureaucrats rather than by a legislature.

7. The transfers of government assets and/or activities to the private sector is called
    a. pro-market implementation.
    b. deficit financing.
    c. privatization.
    d. private sector initiative.

8. Some social critics have suggested using a voucher system for public education because it would
    a. introduce competition into public education.
    b. improve the quality of public education.
    c. increase the quantity of public education.
    d. All of the above

9. The theories of the Austrian school of economics are very close to those of
    a. public choice economists.
    b. political scientists.
    c. libertarians.
    d. classical economists.

10. All *except* which one of the following is among Hayek's arguments against government planning?
    a. Planning results in more planning.
    b. No plan can cover all details.
    c. High morale destroys the planning process.
    d. Planning often leads to a dictatorship.

11. Economists of the Austrian school think that
    a. most problems can be solved by market forces.
    b. the economy would be improved by industrial restructuring.
    c. orthodox economic analysis is too narrow.
    d. All of the above

Chapter 32   Government Failure and Public Choice

_____ 12. Radical economists maintain that individuals in a capitalistic society
   a. feel alienated because they are prevented from purchasing a high level of consumption goods.
   b. are not able to participate in a dual labor market.
   c. feel alienated because they have little control over their own destinies.
   d. waste money on consumer goods because they are unemployed and have nothing else to do.

_____ 13. The most serious weakness of the modern radical critique is that
   a. industrial capitalism does not exist in the United States.
   b. their proposals for change are very costly.
   c. their proposals for change would lead to high levels of unemployment.
   d. they point out weaknesses without suggesting solutions.

_____ 14. In analyzing third-world development, radical economists
   a. follow traditional Marxist theory.
   b. assert that industrial capitalists export excessively complex technology to underdeveloped countries.
   c. assert that industrial capitalists drain capital from underdeveloped countries.
   d. oppose exporting luxuries to underdeveloped countries.

_____ 15. The theory of dual labor markets holds that
   a. marginal productivity theory mirrors reality.
   b. capitalists intentionally hold down the pay of certain groups.
   c. pay should accurately reflect the level of investment in human capital.
   d. markets provide different levels of pay arbitrarily.

TAKING ANOTHER LOOK

Behavior that supports the median voter theorem can be observed in the marketplace as well as the voting booth. Many times consumers are referred to as voters, with firms competing for their dollar "votes." Firms sometimes face the dilemma of having to choose between advertising to women who are full-time homemakers and advertising to women who are employed. Some believe that to target one group is to risk putting off the other. According to a *Wall Street Journal* article, some markets resolve the dilemma by portraying women in their ads in a manner suggestive of either a professional women or a homemaker. For example, they might show a woman holding both a dust cloth and a cellular telephone. This attempt to avoid either extreme is similar to the political maneuvering described in the text.

CHECKING OUT

Now that you have finished studying this chapter, you should be able to:

1. Examine the implications of self-interested behavior in the public sector (public choice) as a cause of government failure.

2. Develop the concept of rent seeking.

3. Analyze the effects of rent defending.

4. Explain why government grows in terms of logrolling and bureaucratic incentives and why regulation creates a bias against new products and new technology.

5. List some of the methods of privatization.

6. Identify the contributions of the Austrian school and radical economics to understanding governmental failure.

ANSWERS

Trying Out the Terms

1. A
2. F
3. E
4. D
5. B
6. C

Testing Yourself

Part I: True or False

1. false. Public choice economics combines economics and political science.
2. true
3. true
4. false. She is rent seeking. The congressional representative may be extracting rent.
5. true
6. false. By election day they should both have moved toward the center. Mr. Nicholson will say it shouldn't be closed all season, and his opponent will suggest it not be open all the time.
7. false. They are logrolling.
8. false. Because bureaus produce activities rather than goods, they are usually evaluated on the basis of the size of expenditures on these activities.
9. false. Many goods and services provided by the government are candidates for privatization.
10. false. The Austrian school holds that individuals make economic decisions in a state of partial ignorance.
11. true
12. true
13. false. In the radical view, the state protects big business and monopolies.
14. false. Low voter turnout can be seen as a result of the determination by rational voters that the costs of voting outweigh the benefits.
15. false. The postal service is selling communication. While it may have a monopoly on one means of distribution, it still suffers competition from the telephone, faxes, and private delivery services.

Part II: Problem

1. a. price = $18; quantity = 70
   b. price = $11; quantity = 140
   c. Consumer surplus is $980, which is the area of the triangle formed by the price axis above the competitive price, the demand curve, and the competitive quantity.
      $1/2[(\$25 - \$11) \times 140] = \$980$
   d. Consumer surplus is $245, which is the area of the triangle formed by the price axis above the monopoly price, the demand curve, and the monopoly quantity.
      $1/2[(\$25 - \$18) \times 70] = \$245$
   e. $\$490 = (\$18 - \$11) \times 70$
   f. $\$1,470 = \$735 \times 2$. The area of rent defense is the surplus consumers stand to lose without regulation:
      $[(\$18 - \$11) \times 70] + 1/2[(\$18 - \$11) \times 70] = \$490 + \$245 = \$735$

Part III: Multiple Choice

1. c	5. b	9. a	13. d
2. b	6. a	10. c	14. a
3. a	7. c	11. a	15. b
4. a	8. d	12. c	

CHAPTER 32 EXERCISES

Recently, newspapers have reported that some drug addicts are so desperate for treatment that they commit crimes just so they can be sentenced to prison, where they can receive treatment. The reason they are doing this is that government-funded drug treatment centers are full and have long waiting lists, and these people do not have the money for private treatment.

Suppose the government decides to privatize the existing government-funded drug treatment centers in order to provide more efficient treatment. The text lists seven methods that governments can use to privatize a government service. Consider each of them, then select three of these methods that you think might provide a feasible solution. Give an example of how each could be implemented, and list some potential problems that might crop up.

1.

2.

3.

CHAPTER 33

POLICY STUDIES: CITIES, THE ENVIRONMENT, AND HEALTH CARE

CHECKING IN

The two preceding chapters discussed a number of economic theories that address the problems of market and government failures. In this chapter, you will examine closely three areas in which such failures often occur: cities, the environment, and health care.

Cities come in an assortment of sizes. They are established and grow or stagnate because of the benefits and costs of living in groups. These benefits and costs are called economies of agglomeration and diseconomies of agglomeration, respectively. The best size for any particular city will be that size where the difference between the benefits and the costs of agglomeration is greatest.

One function of local government is to provide public goods of a local nature, such as police and fire protection. Often the correct level of services is difficult to determine because the benefits of the local public good may spill over into another jurisdiction that is not paying for it. Local governments may attempt to charge nonresidents user fees. Another solution, suggested by Tiebout, may be competition between adjacent cities, which will cause people to move to the location with the most desirable combination of taxes and services.

When a resource is a common access resource—one that is jointly owned by many people—it is often overused. The owners consider the benefits but not the cost of consuming it. This situation is called the tragedy of the commons. Overfishing of certain varieties of ocean fish and the disappearance of the American buffalo are examples of this situation. Governments can avert such tragedies by assigning property rights to the resource or by establishing regulations for the use of the resource. This problem is compounded when the resource is a global common, such as the oceans held in common by many nations.

In the past two decades, the health care industry has grown at an astonishing rate. Increasing costs coupled with increases in demand have created spiraling prices, which absorb an alarming share of GDP. The issue has become one of national importance and debate.

TRYING OUT THE TERMS

Match each of the following terms with its definition, and then check your answers. If you are having trouble, go back to the text and find the definition there.

_____ 1. tragedy of the commons _____ 4. economies of agglomeration

_____ 2. diseconomies of agglomeration _____ 5. common access resource

_____ 3. Tiebout hypothesis _____ 6. user charges

    A. The cost savings that individuals enjoy when enough of them locate close together in or near a large city.

    B. The additional costs that individuals must pay when too many of them locate in one city (thus creating negative external effects for one another).

    C. Fees that cover part or all of the cost of a public service.

    D. The idea that competition among local governments as suppliers of local public services will force them to offer the desired combination of spending and taxing to voters, who will migrate to those jurisdictions that produce that combination.

    E. A resource that is not owned by any individual but is available for all to use.

    F. The overuse of common access resources.

TESTING YOURSELF

In the next two sections, you will answer questions that are based on information in the text. Master all of the terms before you begin these sections. Work each section without referring to your notes or the text, and then check your answers.

Part I: True or False

Mark each statement as true or false. Whenever you mark a statement as false, jot down a sentence stating why it is false.

_____ 1. The many discount outlets clustered along interstate highways, such as I–75 in Georgia and Florida, are an example of economies of agglomeration.

_____ 2. Optimal city size is best determined by local zoning boards.

_____ 3. When small towns lose population, they are usually able to maintain their downtown business and shopping districts.

_____ 4. When significant spillovers are present, crime prevention will be underprovided.

_____ 5. Revenue sharing is not effective in correcting interjurisdictional externalities.

_____ 6. The Tiebout hypothesis suggests that people will express their preference for local public goods by moving about until they find communities that offer what they are looking for.

_____ 7. Based on the example of mass transit, it appears that it is easier to measure the costs of providing a positive externality than to measure the benefits of that externality.

_____ 8. When shrimpers in the Gulf of Mexico continue to catch shrimp, even though they know they are exhausting the population, they are attempting to run the competition out of business.

_____ 9. Because the Brazilian rain forests represent a global commons, one approach to maintaining them would be for other countries to pay Brazil to restrict deforestation.

_____ 10. The use of high-sulfur coal in electrical generation is a source of acid rain.

_____ 11. Most hazardous waste problems are the result of surreptitious dumping.

_____ 12. In the United States, spending on health care tripled between 1985 and 1995.

_____ 13. The increasing cost of health care would have been even greater had not supply increased as demand increased.

_____ 14. Improved levels of health care should lead to a fall in demand for health care because people are heathier.

_____ 15. Under the Clinton plan, rich people will pay more for health care and poor people won't pay at all.

Part II: Multiple Choice

_____ 1. The growth of suburban governments surrounding large cities may
   a. cause needless duplication of government services.
   b. make governments more sensitive to voter demands.
   c. contribute to the free-rider problem.
   d. both make governments more sensitive to voter demands and contribute to the free-rider problem.

_____ 2. Fiscal conservatives argue against grants from higher levels of government to lower levels on the grounds that
   a. they are an ineffective method of transferring income between jurisdictions with different levels of wealth.
   b. cities would not provide positive externalities to surrounding suburbs with this funding.
   c. local politicians find it easier to spend money when they don't have to pay for it by raising taxes.
   d. they lead to diseconomies of agglomeration.

_____ 3. Spruce City has the only swimming pool in the county, and many county residents who do not pay city taxes swim there. How can Spruce City discourage these free riders?
   a. It can charge everyone who comes to the pool an admission fee.
   b. It can charge only nonresidents an admission fee.
   c. It can have special hours for nonresidents.
   d. It cannot overcome the free-rider problem.

4. Marshall and Agatha recently retired; they are very concerned about health care and security. The Tiebout hypothesis suggests that they
   a. will have to choose between health care and security.
   b. should arrange for private provision of health care.
   c. will move to a community that provides both and pay the higher taxes involved.
   d. will move closer to an urban center.

5. Proponents of public mass transit systems argue that these systems
   a. have many characteristics of public goods.
   b. will not be provided unless the government does it.
   c. will eliminate many areas of high population density.
   d. have negative externalities that only the government can correct.

6. When resources are held in common, users will
   a. use the resources on a rotation basis.
   b. overuse the resources.
   c. underuse the resources.
   d. assign property rights to the resources.

7. The tragedy of the commons can be averted by
   a. allowing market forces to replace government regulation.
   b. having government assign property rights to the common resource.
   c. having government impose regulations on the use of the resource.
   d. having government either assign property rights or impose regulations.

8. The problem of acid rain is distinctive because
   a. the source of the pollution is fairly easy to identify.
   b. there are no spillovers associated with acid rain.
   c. pollution associated with acid rain is mainly a local problem.
   d. we do not understand the source of acid rain.

9. When a local government imposes a fine on households that refuse to recycle their newspapers and aluminum cans, that government is
   a. using the Tiebout hypothesis.
   b. using a market incentive to regulate a local common resource.
   c. circumventing a market solution.
   d. privatizing garbage collection.

10. Past problems with hazardous waste were the result of
    a. a refusal by local governments to accept responsibility for a national problem.
    b. a lack of information and government regulation.
    c. too much regulation.
    d. a failure to employ adequate user fees.

_____ 11. Which of the following did *not* cause the demand curve for health care to shift to the right over the last three decades?
   a. Technological advances in medical treatment
   b. Higher income for U.S. citizens
   c. Government- and employer-provided health insurance
   d. Longer life expectancies.

_____ 12. As a result of rising incomes during the 1960s and 1970s,
   a. the supply curve of physicians shifted to the right.
   b. the quantity of physicians supplied increased.
   c. medical school applications began to increase during the 1980s.
   d. the law of supply was violated.

_____ 13. Under the Clinton health plan,
   a. employers and employees would split the cost of health care.
   b. employers would pay 80 percent of health costs and employees would pay 20 percent.
   c. employers would pay all of the cost of health care.
   d. employees could choose between employer-paid care and paying for their own insurance.

_____ 14. In the United States, 25 percent of spinal injuries are the result of
   a. medical malpractice.
   b. automobile accidents.
   c. automobile accidents involving drinking drivers.
   d. assaults.

_____ 15. Which group would *not* be against the Clinton health care plan?
   a. Trial lawyers
   b. The tobacco lobby
   c. Major insurance companies
   d. Small insurance companies

TAKING ANOTHER LOOK

What can a small town do when the merchants move out to the regional mall? Some folks in Havana, Florida, used economies of agglomeration to turn their town around. They persuaded three antique dealers to move into vacant downtown stores. Soon, several other dealers opened shops, and one entrepreneur moved into an old house to house her expensive antiques. Before long, there were two art galleries, a rare book dealer, several restaurants, and bed and breakfast inns. Then some out-of-town dealers got together and opened an antique mall housing about twenty boutiques in the closed Ford dealership. Now Havana is a popular North Florida weekend destination instead of a town to speed through on the way to Panama City or Atlanta.

CHECKING OUT

Now that you have finished studying this chapter, you should be able to:

1. Explain optimal city size in terms of economies and diseconomies of agglomeration, and demonstrate how the provision of local public goods is complicated by spillovers.

2. Use housing and transportation to explore various blends of private and public roles in the provision of urban services.

3. Explain the role of the tragedy of the commons, inadequate information, and sovereignty issues in making some kinds of environmental issues difficult to address and solve.

4. Identify the economic issues in the health care crisis.

5. Evaluate the Clinton proposal for policy reform of health care.

ANSWERS

Trying Out the Terms

1. F
2. B
3. D
4. A
5. E
6. C

Testing Yourself

Part I: True or False

1. true
2. false. It is best determined by the individuals who live in the city.
3. false. Even when small towns are not losing people, the shopping may be largely abandoned as regional malls serving several towns spring up.
4. true
5. false. It is very effective because it offers external funding to assist in solving a local problem.
6. true
7. true
8. false. They are enacting the tragedy of the commons. They realize that if they don't go out and catch the shrimp, other shrimpers will.
9. true
10. true
11. false. Most hazardous waste problems stem from dumping in the past, when there was less knowledge about its dangers.
12. true
13. false. One reason health care costs are so high is that supply fell at the same time that demand was increasing.

14. false. Improved health care means more people grow up and live longer, and old people have more health problems; demand will increase.
15. false. Under this plan everybody, even the poor, pay something.

Part II: Multiple Choice

1. d
2. c
3. b
4. c
5. a
6. b
7. d
8. a
9. b
10. b
11. a
12. b
13. b
14. d
15. c

Name _____

CHAPTER 33 EXERCISES

Each of the following statements is false. In the space provided, rewrite each statement so that it is true.

1. Economies of agglomeration cause urban firms to face higher average cost curves.

2. The optimal size for a U.S. city is a population between 500,000 and 800,000.

3. Barbara Boggs Sigmund believes that the growth of new suburbs may offer the solution to many urban problems.

4. A city can determine the optimal level of crime prevention by vertically summing the demand curves of its citizens. This eliminates the demand of nonresidents.

5. The Reagan administration encouraged cities to solve the spillover problem by offering them intergovernmental grants.

6. The Tiebout hypothesis calls for federal standards for local public goods.

7. The Local Initiative Support Corporation provides low-cost housing, using only private funds.

8. Proponents of public mass transportation maintain that an adequate system reduces population density.

9. User charges are not effective in controlling spillovers because they are hard to collect.

10. Because they involve common access resources, pollution problems can never be solved by rigid assignment of property rights.

11. Scientists are able to predict where the greenhouse effect will be harmful but not when.

12. The tragedy of the commons represents a market failure.

13. Because people only go to the doctor when they have to, an increase in third-party payments will not cause an increase in demand for health care.

14. Life expectancy is lower in the United States than in many other countries because medical care is not as good as it is in those countries.

15. The present system of medical care in the United States is a purely market-based system.

CHAPTER 34

TRADE AMONG NATIONS

CHECKING IN

Most countries engage in substantial trade with other nations. In the United States, international trade accounts for between 10 and 12 percent of GNP. The percentage is much higher in many other countries.

Trade between two countries is very much like trade between two individuals. It occurs when both parties benefit from the exchange. International trade is based on comparative advantage. A country produces those goods with low opportunity costs and exchanges them for goods with higher domestic opportunity costs. Such specialization increases total output with the same amount of resources. Other benefits from trade are increased competition and economies of scale.

In spite of the advantages international trade can bring to a nation, it is often opposed by many groups that are hurt by imports. For example, producers and workers in domestic industries that compete with imports often seek protective legislation. Tariffs, quotas, and nontariff barriers are all ways of interfering with free trade. For most of its history, the United States had high tariffs. However, since 1934, U.S. tariffs have been dramatically reduced. Advocates of protectionism have several arguments supporting their case. Although most of these arguments (balance of payments, employment, and cheap foreign labor) have weak economic foundations, the infant industry and national defense arguments are valid under certain restricted circumstances. The optimal tariff argument and the theory of the second best are more sophisticated rationales for protectionism. Nevertheless, the goal of most calls for protection is really income redistribution.

Multinational corporations operate in many countries. These firms may either increase or decrease competition, depending on the specific circumstances. They increase the transfer of technology between countries. If the company is very large and the country is small, the company may have too much power compared to the government of the host country.

TRYING OUT THE TERMS

Match each of the following terms with its definition, and then check your answers. If you are having trouble, go back to the text and find the definition there.

___ 1. gains from trade
___ 2. consumption possibilities curve
___ 3. terms of trade
___ 4. multinational corporation
___ 5. nontariff barriers
___ 6. tariff
___ 7. trade creation
___ 8. absolute advantage
___ 9. product cycle
___ 10. trade diversion
___ 11. commercial policy
___ 12. quota
___ 13. comparative advantage
___ 14. common market
___ 15. free trade area
___ 16. tariff quota
___ 17. fair trade

A. The increase in economic well-being resulting from specialization and trade.

B. The ability to produce something using fewer resources than other producers use.

C. The ability to produce something at a lower opportunity cost than other producers face.

D. The ratio at which one product is exchanged for another.

E. A line showing the consumption combinations attainable through trade.

F. A series of stages, from development to standardization, through which a new product passes.

G. A tax on imported goods or services.

H. A limit on the amount of a good or service that can be imported during a given time period.

I. Trade restrictions other than tariffs and quotas.

J. The set of actions that a country undertakes to deliberately influence trade in goods and services.

K. An agreement between two or more countries to eliminate tariffs and other trade barriers on trade among themselves, while each country maintains its existing trade barriers to outside countries.

L. A free trade area with a common external tariff, free movement of capital and labor, and harmonization of social and economic policies.

M. Shifting from a higher-cost supplier to a lower cost supplier as a result of forming a free trade area or common market.

N. Shifting from a lower cost supplier to a higher cost supplier as a result of forming a free trade area or common market.

O. A combination of a quota and a tariff that allows a certain amount of a good or service to be imported without paying a tariff and imposes the tariff on further imports.

P. A firm with headquarters in one country and plants in one or more subsidiaries in other countries.

Q. The idea that the United States should impose trade barriers equivalent to those that its trading partners place on U.S. exports.

TESTING YOURSELF

In the next three sections, you will answer questions and work problems that are based on information in the text. Master all of the terms before you begin these sections. Work each section without referring to your notes or the text, and then check your answers.

Part I: True or False

Mark each statement as true or false. Whenever you mark a statement as false, jot down a sentence stating why it is false.

_____ 1. Trade will take place if one party to the transaction gains from the trade.

_____ 2. Mercantilists discouraged imports and encouraged exports.

_____ 3. A country with an absolute advantage in a product should produce that product for export.

_____ 4. If all countries specialized and traded, world output would increase without an increase in the use of resources.

_____ 5. A country's comparative advantage is fixed and will not change over time.

_____ 6. The production of low-cost cotton textiles is concentrated in England.

_____ 7. Trade increases the number of choices available to consumers.

_____ 8. If the U.S. government imposes a $6 import fee on every lamb imported from New Zealand, it has imposed a specific tariff.

_____ 9. No one gains from protectionist policies.

_____ 10. If a quota is in place, an increase in demand will cause both price and quantity to increase.

_____ 11. Dumping can be a form of price discrimination.

_____ 12. The Smoot-Hawley Act enacted the highest tariff ever imposed in the United States.

_____ 13. Political support for protectionism should come from an alliance of consumers and exporters.

_____ 14. If market externalities distort opportunity costs, then the theory of the second best holds that a tariff may be appropriate.

_____ 15. Strict immigration laws are a form of employment protection.

Part II: Problems

1. Each of the states in the following table is using one-half of its resources on the production of each good.

	Output/Hour	
	Bread	Cheese
Kansas	150	300
Missouri	300	900

    a. If these states specialized in the production of either cheese or bread, how much could each produce?

    b. Which state has an absolute advantage in bread and in cheese?

    c. What is the opportunity cost of cheese in Kansas and in Missouri?

    d. What is the opportunity cost of bread in Kansas and in Missouri?

    e. Which state should specialize in bread?

2. The country of Arcadia represents a very small part of the world market for cut flowers. The figure below shows the demand and supply curves for Arcadia.

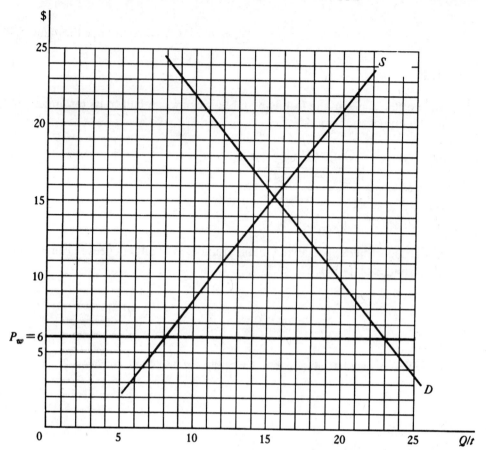

a. If there is free trade, how many boxes of flowers will be bought and at what price?

How many will be produced domestically?

How many will be imported?

b. If Arcadia imposes a tariff of $5 on each box of flowers, what will happen to the price and quantity?

How many will be produced domestically?

How many will be imported?

c. What size quota would Arcadia have to impose to achieve the same results?

Part III: Multiple Choice

_____ 1. In the United States, trade represents about _____ percent of GDP.
   a. 3 to 5
   b. 10 to 12
   c. 15 to 18
   d. 25 to 30

_____ 2. International trade occurs
   a. for the same reasons that domestic trade occurs.
   b. only between countries in the same common market.
   c. even when there is no opportunity for profit.
   d. only when exchange rates are flexible.

For Questions 3–6, use the following information: In one hour, Lester can peel 10 potatoes or make 50 cookies. In one hour, James can peel 15 potatoes or make 60 cookies.

_____ 3. Lester has an absolute
   a. advantage in cookies.
   b. advantage in both potatoes and cookies.
   c. disadvantage in both potatoes and cookies.
   d. advantage in potatoes.

_____ 4. For Lester, the opportunity cost of 1 potato is
   a. 1 cookie.
   b. 5 cookies.
   c. 10 cookies.
   d. 50 cookies.

_____ 5. James has
   a. a comparative advantage in cookies.
   b. a comparative advantage in potatoes.
   c. an absolute advantage in both potatoes and cookies.
   d. a comparative advantage in potatoes and an absolute advantage in both potatoes and cookies.

_____ 6. If they are going to specialize,
   a. James should peel potatoes.
   b. James should make cookies.
   c. Lester should make cookies.
   d. James should peel potatoes and Lester should make cookies.

7. If Canada can produce 1 steer for 6 bushels of corn and France can produce 1 steer for 8 bushels of corn, then
   a. the two countries will not trade.
   b. Canada will be willing to trade 1 steer to France for 6 bushels of corn.
   c. France will be willing to trade 1 bushel of corn to Canada for one-eighth of a steer.
   d. the terms of trade will be somewhere between 1 steer for 6 bushels and 1 steer for 8 bushels.

8. If one nation's productivity or potential level of output for a certain product is greater than that of another nation, it has
   a. an absolute advantage.
   b. a comparative advantage.
   c. a productive advantage.
   d. excess capacity.

9. The first nation to produce a product is likely to
   a. maintain the comparative advantage in that product if the world market is large.
   b. maintain the comparative advantage in that product if the world market is small.
   c. lose the comparative advantage quickly, even if it has the technology and skills needed in production.
   d. be immune to the product cycle.

10. When a tariff is imposed,
    a. the total quantity sold increases, while the quantity imported decreases.
    b. both the quantity sold and the quantity imported decreases.
    c. the quantity produced domestically increases.
    d. the quantity sold and the quantity imported decrease and the quantity produced domestically increases.

11. If a quota is imposed, the winners are
    a. the producers and workers in the country that is exporting.
    b. the exporter, producers, and workers in the country that is importing.
    c. the government of the importing country, since a quota works like a tax.
    d. the importer and the producers and workers in the country that is importing.

12. Domestic preference laws act as
    a. a tariff.
    b. a quota.
    c. a nontariff barrier.
    d. free-trade legislation.

13. An infant industry argument for protection may be economically valid if the industry
    a. will eventually be able to compete in the world market.
    b. generates substantial external benefits.
    c. is financed with imported capital.
    d. will eventually be able to compete in the world market or generates substantial external benefits.
    e. generates substantial external benefits and is financed with imported capital.

_____ 14. The national defense argument for protection
   a. is more valid now than it was before World War II.
   b. would be valid if an extensive nuclear war was anticipated.
   c. would be valid if a nonnuclear war of attrition was anticipated.
   d. has no economic validity.

_____ 15. The concept of fair trade calls for
   a. arbitrary tariffs.
   b. a "level playing field."
   c. across-the-board tariff reductions.
   d. the abolition of all nontariff barriers.

_____ 16. A country that is poor in raw materials, capital, or skilled labor
   a. has no comparative advantage.
   b. cannot gain from trade.
   c. can import inputs and produce its own final goods.
   d. can import but not export.

CHECKING OUT

Now that you have finished studying this chapter, you should be able to:

1. Describe the benefits of free trade based on comparative advantage.

2. Analyze the effects of tariffs, quotas, and other trade restrictions.

3. Evaluate the arguments for tariff protection.

4. Discuss the costs and benefits of forming free trade areas and common markets.

5. Evaluate the impact of immigration and direct foreign investment.

ANSWERS

Trying Out the Terms

1. A	5. I	9. F	13. C	17. Q
2. E	6. G	10. N	14. L	
3. D	7. M	11. J	15. K	
4. P	8. B	12. H	16. O	

Testing Yourself

Part I: True or False

1. false. Both parties must gain from trade.
2. true

3. false. A country should specialize in and export products in which it has a comparative advantage.
4. true
5. false. Comparative advantage may change if there is a change in resources or technology.
6. false. It is concentrated in countries with low-cost, low-skill labor, though it was developed in England.
7. true
8. true
9. false. Domestic producers, their workers, and their suppliers gain, but consumers and workers in export industries lose.
10. false. Only price will increase, since the quantity is fixed by the government.
11. true
12. true
13. false. These groups should support free trade.
14. true
15. true

Part II: Problems

1. a. Kansas could produce either 300 units of bread or 600 units of cheese. Missouri could produce either 600 units of bread or 1,800 units of cheese.
   b. Missouri has an absolute advantage in both bread and cheese.
   c. The opportunity cost of cheese in Kansas is 1/2 unit of bread. In Missouri, it is 1/3 unit of bread.
   d. The opportunity cost of bread in Kansas is 2 units of cheese. In Missouri, it is 3 units of cheese.
   e. Kansas should specialize in bread.
2. a. Twenty-three boxes of flowers will be bought at $6. Eight boxes will be produced domestically. Fifteen boxes will be imported.
   b. Nineteen boxes of flowers will be bought at $11. Twelve boxes will be produced domestically. Seven boxes will be imported.
   c. Arcadia would have to impose a quota of seven boxes to have the same results.

Part III: Multiple Choice

1. b	5. d	9. b	13. d
2. a	6. d	10. d	14. c
3. c	7. d	11. d	15. b
4. b	8. a	12. c	16. c

Name _____

CHAPTER 34 EXERCISES

Mark each statement as true or false. If you mark a statement as false, write a sentence that makes the statement true.

_____ 1. If Chile can produce a maximum of 25 units of grapes or 30 units of beef and Argentina can produce a maximum of 25 units of grapes or 35 units of beef, Chile should produce grapes and trade with Argentina for beef.

_____ 2. Specialization and trade can result in an increase in total world output without an increase in the use of world resources.

_____ 3. The theory of comparative advantage was set forth by John Stuart Mills.

_____ 4. Gains from trade are always equal.

_____ 5. According to the product cycle, when the market for a product is strong, wealthy countries will produce it, but when the market begins to weaken, only developing nations will produce it.

_____ 6. A quota is a tax on imported goods.

_____ 7. A tariff quota is a tariff placed on imports above a fixed quantity or quota.

_____ 8. Most economists prefer tariffs to free trade.

_____ 9. A monopolist is likely to be in favor of international trade.

_____ 10. Foreign competition is unpopular with owners of resources only when the competition is in the resource market.

_____ 11. The increased output from comparative advantage is the sole benefit of international trade.

_____ 12. The United States puts fewer restrictions on the inflow or outflow of capital than most other countries.

_____ 13. Organized labor generally opposes liberal immigration legislation.

_____ 14. Multinational firms impede trade.

CHAPTER 35

INTERNATIONAL FINANCE AND EXCHANGE RATES

CHECKING IN

International trade, which you studied in the preceding chapter, involves not only the exchange of goods and services but also the exchange of payment. This exchange can be complicated, because most countries have their own currencies. This chapter discusses the financing of international transactions.

Currencies are exchanged in foreign exchange markets. The demand for foreign exchange is a reflection of the demand for foreign goods, services, and financial assets that must be paid for in the foreign currency. The supply of foreign exchange is determined by the desire of foreigners to buy domestic goods, services, and financial assets. The foreign exchange market can involve a lot of risk. Participating in the forward market is one way to reduce the risk of foreign exchange.

As in all markets, the supply and demand curves for foreign exchange will shift when something other than price changes. Changes in relative prices, incomes, interest rates, tastes, population, technology, and input cost and availability may cause these curves to shift. Surpluses and shortages often occur in foreign exchange markets. One way to eliminate these surpluses and shortages is to change the price, but it is also possible to shift supply and demand curves, ration foreign exchange, or draw on accumulated reserves.

The United States summarizes the transactions between its residents and foreigners in its balance of payments. This statement is composed of four accounts: the current account, the capital account, a statistical discrepancy, and the settlement account. The sum of the current and capital accounts and the statistical discrepancy is the balance of payments surplus or deficit. The settlement account shows how this surplus or deficit was financed.

There are four different international monetary systems. Under the gold standard, all currencies can be redeemed for a fixed amount of gold. The movements of gold ensure balance of payments equilibrium. This flow of gold between countries leaves a nation with little power to control its money supply. This is a major drawback of the gold standard.

Between 1945 and 1973, the Bretton Woods system governed international transactions. It provided fairly stable exchange rates and relied on international reserves to settle deficits. This system failed because it was too dependent on the U.S. dollar as a reserve.

Since 1973, most foreign exchange markets have depended on floating rates that are set by the interaction of supply and demand. Under floating rates, changes in the value of currency solve the deficit problem. Countries can control their own money supplies separately from the foreign exchange market. Floating rates can be very volatile.

Under exchange control, all foreign exchange passes through the government. This system gives government the power to ration foreign exchange. The government may also have different rates for different uses of foreign exchange. Black markets for currency usually develop under an exchange control system.

TRYING OUT THE TERMS

Match each of the following terms with its definition, and then check your answers. If you are having trouble, go back to the text and find the definition there.

_____ 1. statistical discrepancy   _____ 11. capital account

_____ 2. appreciation   _____ 12. speculators

_____ 3. balance of payments   _____ 13. current account

_____ 4. gold standard   _____ 14. balance of trade

_____ 5. International Monetary Fund (IMF) _____ 15. balance of payments deficit

_____ 6. European Monetary Union (EMU) _____ 16. hedgers

_____ 7. foreign exchange market   _____ 17. real exchange rate

_____ 8. depreciation   _____ 18. Bretton Woods System

_____ 9. trade weighted dollar   _____ 19. international monetary reserves

_____ 10. forward market   _____ 20. key currency

A. Difference between the value of a country's merchandise exports and imports.

B. The foreign currency exchange rate after adjustment for changes in relative price levels.

C. An annual summary of transactions between residents of one country and residents of the rest of the world.

D. The part of the balance of payments that summarizes transactions in currently produced goods and services.

E. The currency that serves as a major reserve asset and is used in transactions between third-party nations.

F. The part of the balance of payments that summarizes purchases and sales of financial assets.

G. The part of the balance of payments that reflects unrecorded transactions and inaccurate estimates of spending by tourists.

H. An excess of a country's foreign spending over its foreign earnings for a given year.

I. The network of banks and financial institutions through which buyers and sellers exchange national currencies.

J. The market in which contracts are made for future deliveries of specific amounts of a currency at a specified price.

K. A price index for the dollar that measures changes in its value in terms of a market basket of currencies of major trading partners.

L. The pool of gold and major currencies created under the Bretton Woods system, from which countries could borrow to settle deficits and replenish from surpluses.

M. The international monetary system in effect from 1945 to 1973, based on infrequent changes in currency prices, ample reserves, and the dollar as key currency.

N. People who try to reduce their risk by buying or selling contracts in the forward market for currency.

O. People who asssume risk in the forward market for currency in return for a chance of a profit.

P. A market-determined increase in a currency's price.

Q. A market-determined decrease in a currency's price.

R. An international monetary system in which currencies were defined in terms of gold, money supplies were linked to gold, and balance of payments deficits were settled in gold.

S. The agency that supervised the operation of the Bretton Woods system and maintained a reserve pool, and which continues to assist countries with currency and monetary management problems.

T. A currency area of members of the European Community in which exchange rates are fixed among members within narrow bonds, but float together with respect to other currencies; broke up in 1993.

TESTING YOURSELF

In the next three sections, you will answer questions and work problems that are based on information in the text. Master all of the terms before you begin these sections. Work each section without referring to your notes or the text, and then check your answers.

Part I: True or False

Mark each statement as true or false. Whenever you mark a statement as false, jot down a sentence stating why it is false.

_____ 1. A balance of payments deficit puts downward pressure on the price of a nation's currency.

_____ 2. A transaction that involves a payment from someone in the United States to someone in another country will be recorded as an addition to the U.S. balance of payments.

_____ 3. In recent years, foreign investment in the United States has decreased.

_____ 4. The recent increase in the statistical discrepancy in the balance of payments accounts indicates that there may have been an increase in unrecorded capital inflows into the United States.

_____ 5. If Americans decide to invest more in Brazil, the demand for Brazilian cruzados (currency) will increase.

_____ 6. Interest rates are the most significant determinant of demand for foreign exchange.

_____ 7. If the United States imposed a tariff on sweaters imported from Peru, the demand for Peruvian soles (currency) would increase.

_____ 8. If a country that is experiencing inflation increases its imports, this will have a dampening effect on the inflation.

_____ 9. If Morris, Inc. buys a forward contract for Colombian pesos in June to pay for the coffee delivery it will accept in December, it has avoided the risk of fluctuating exchange rates.

_____ 10. The forward markets were more active in the 1950s and 1960s than they are today.

_____ 11. When a government interferes in a foreign exchange market with floating exchange rates, there is a dirty float.

_____ 12. If there is a balance of payments deficit in a country operating on the gold standard, gold will flow into the country.

_____ 13. Operating on the gold standard gives a nation more control over its macroeconomic policy tools.

_____ 14. Under the Bretton Woods system, exchange rates were neither fully fixed nor truly floating.

_____ 15. Exchange control inhibits free international trade.

Part II: Problems

1. The following graphs show the foreign exchange market for Danish kroner in equilibrium. Show the effect that each of the following events would have on the market.

   a. Denmark begins to subsidize the Danish cheese industry.

   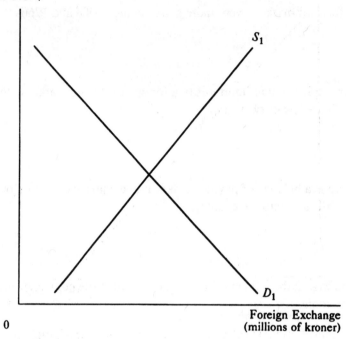

   b. Prices in the United States fall, relative to prices in Denmark.

   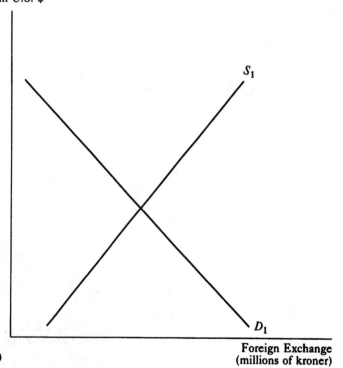

468   Chapter 35   *International Finance and Exchange Rates*

c. The price of wool used in Danish-made sweaters increases.

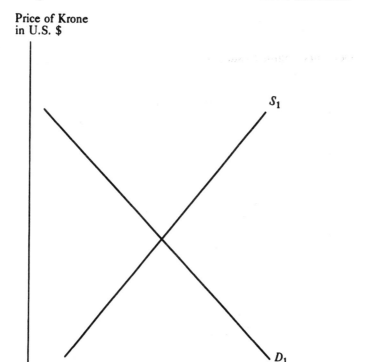

d. Danish interest rates fall, relative to those in the United States.

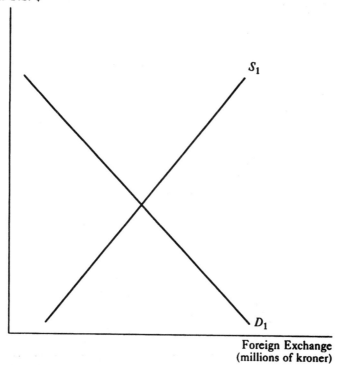

2. The graph below shows the foreign exchange market for Swiss francs.

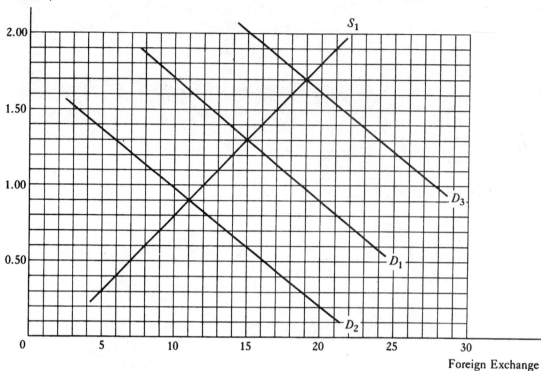

a. If the market reflects S_1 and D_3 and exchange rates are floating, what is the exchange rate? How many francs will be exchanged for dollars?

b. If the market reflects S_1 and D_3 and the exchange rate is fixed at $1.30, will there be a surplus or a shortage of francs? How large?

c. If the market reflects S_1 and D_2 and the exchange rate is fixed at $1.30, will there be a surplus or a shortage of francs? How large?

d. If the exchange rate is allowed to float between $1.10 and $1.50 and the demand curve shifts from D_1 to D_2, what will happen to the exchange rate and the quantity of francs exchanged?

470   Chapter 35   *International Finance and Exchange Rates*

e. If the exchange rate is allowed to float between $1.10 and $1.50 and the demand curve shifts from D_3 to D_1, what will happen to the exchange rate and the quantity of francs exchanged?

f. If the exchange rate is allowed to float between $1.10 and $1.50 and the market reflects S_1 and D_1, what will happen to the exchange rate? Will there be a surplus or a shortage of francs? How large?

Part III: Multiple Choice

1. A U.S. balance of payments surplus would be decreased by all *except* which one of the following?
   a. Mexican citizens buy condominiums in Texas.
   b. U.S. residents spend their vacations in Cancun.
   c. A U.S. factory buys a new lathe from Poland.
   d. A U.S. developer builds a shopping center in Montreal.

2. Which of the following would be included in the balance of trade?
   a. Investment by foreign citizens in U.S. corporations
   b. A dividend from a French firm received by a U.S. citizen
   c. The sale of a large machine to an Italian corporation by a U.S. firm
   d. Unreported income from drug smuggling

3. If the dollar price of the Venezuelan bolivar (currency) decreases, there will be
   a. an increase in the supply of U.S. dollars.
   b. a decrease in the supply of the bolivar.
   c. an increase in the bolivar price for dollars.
   d. a decrease in the bolivar price for dollars.

4. Suppose the price of the Canadian dollar is $0.80. What is the price of the U.S. dollar in Canadian dollars?
   a. $8.00
   b. $1.25
   c. $0.80
   d. An amount that cannot be determined.

5. If interest rates in the United States rose relative to those in the rest of the world, we would expect
   a. the supply of dollars to increase.
   b. the demand for dollars to increase.
   c. foreign investment in the United States to increase.
   d. U.S. investment abroad to increase.
   e. the demand for dollars to increase as foreign investment in the United States increased.

6. Which of the following would *not* cause the demand curve for Mexican pesos to shift?
   a. A change in the U.S. tariff structure
   b. A change in export subsidies in Mexico
   c. A change in population in the United States
   d. A change in preferences of Mexicans for U.S.-made goods

7. A country has a dirty float when
   a. black markets develop under exchange control.
   b. the government announces different exchange rates for industrial firms and individuals.
   c. the government enters the exchange market when rates are not fixed.
   d. a country with fixed rates unexpectedly devalues its currency.

8. Which of the following is a goal of an ideal international monetary system?
   a. Stable exchange rates
   b. Control over macroeconomic policy tools
   c. A self-correction mechanism for balance of payments surpluses and deficits
   d. All of the above

9. When a country is on the gold standard,
   a. its exchange rate is determined in market exchanges with other currencies that are also tied to gold.
   b. balance of payment deficits will be corrected as gold leaves the country.
   c. monetary policy is made stronger.
   d. exchange rates are flexible within a narrow range.

10. One drawback to the gold standard is that
    a. no one really knows what gold is worth.
    b. the money supply cannot be determined by the government.
    c. there is not enough gold in the world to support the U.S. money supply.
    d. gold cannot serve as an international reserve.

11. Under the Bretton Woods system, each country
    a. agreed to let its exchange rate float in the world market.
    b. set a par value for its currency in gold.
    c. agreed to buy and sell its own currency in gold alone.
    d. set a fixed rate for its currency in either U.S. dollars or British pounds.

12. Under the Bretton Woods system, a country that ran consistent balance of payments deficits could
    a. borrow from the international reserves at the International Monetary Fund.
    b. change the price of its currency.
    c. agree to let its currency float against the key currencies.
    d. either borrow from the international reserves at the IMF or change the price of its currency.

13. The Bretton Woods system failed because
    a. it did not provide enough acceptable international reserves.
    b. Great Britain refused to let the British pound serve as a key currency.
    c. higher prices brought a great deal more gold onto the market and the value of all currencies depreciated.
    d. the International Monetary Fund closed its "gold window."

14. Floating exchange rates work
    a. because the IMF guarantees a minimum level for key currencies.
    b. by curing the problem of overshooting.
    c. on the principles of supply and demand.
    d. because it is possible for foreign exchange markets to sustain a prolonged equilibrium.

15. Exchange control is practiced
    a. only when exchange rates are fixed.
    b. primarily by less developed countries.
    c. primarily by the highly industrialized nations.
    d. primarily by the International Monetary Fund.

CHECKING OUT

Now that you have finished studying this chapter, you should be able to:

1. Identify the components of the balance of payments accounts and discuss the uses of balance of payments information.

2. Explain the relationship between the foreign exchange market and the trade and capital flows on the balance of payments.

3. Explain how the foreign exchange market works and how the market for currencies is different from other kinds of markets.

4. Discuss the operation of floating rates since 1973.

5. Analyze the advantages and disadvantages of various types of fixed exchange rate systems, including the gold standard, Bretton Woods, and the European Monetary Union.

ANSWERS

Trying Out the Terms

1. G	5. S	9. K	13. D	17. B
2. P	6. T	10. J	14. A	18. M
3. C	7. I	11. F	15. H	19. L
4. R	8. Q	12. O	16. N	20. E

Testing Yourself

Part I: True or False

1. true
2. false. It will be a deduction.
3. false. It has increased.
4. true
5. true
6. false. Changes in relative price levels are the most significant determinant.
7. false. The demand would fall as importers bought fewer of the now more costly sweaters.
8. true
9. true
10. false. Forward markets are more active when exchange rates float, as they have in the United States since 1973.
11. true
12. false. Gold will flow out. People will exchange domestic currency for gold, which they will then use to buy foreign currency.
13. false. A nation loses control of these tools on the gold standard.
14. true
15. true

Part II: Problems

1. a. Cheese becomes cheaper and exports increase; the demand for kroner increases.

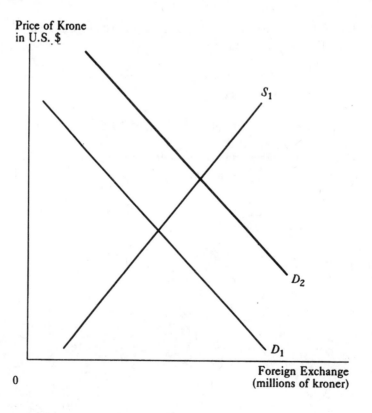

b. U.S. citizens buy fewer Danish imports; the demand for kroner decreases. At the same time, Danes demand more dollars to purchase U.S. goods; the supply of kroner increases.

c. Sweaters become more expensive and fewer are exported; the demand for kroner decreases.

d. Danes want to purchase more dollars to invest in the United States; the supply of kroner increases.

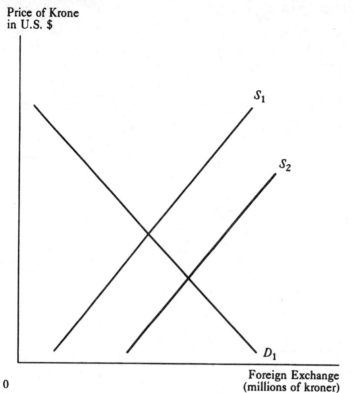

2. a. The exchange rate will be $1.70; 19 million francs will be exchanged.
   b. There will be a shortage of 9 million francs.
   c. There will be a surplus of 9 million francs.
   d. The exchange rate will be $1.10; there will be a surplus of approximately 4 million francs.
   e. The exchange rate will be $1.30; 15 million francs will be exchanged. The market will clear, so there will be neither a shortage nor a surplus.
   f. The exchange rate will be $1.30; 15 million francs will be exchanged. The market will clear, so there will be neither a shortage nor a surplus.

Part III: Multiple Choice

1. a
2. c
3. c
4. b
5. e
6. d
7. c
8. d
9. b
10. b
11. b
12. d
13. a
14. c
15. b

CHAPTER 35 EXERCISE

Correctly arrange the following entries in a hypothetical balance of payments statement (next page) for the United States. Calculate the value of the balance of trade, the current account, the value of the capital account, and the statistical discrepancy.

U.S. private investment abroad	−46,172
Service transactions (net)	+2,400
Foreign private investment in the U.S.	+152,376
Merchandise imports	−315,235
Investment income, (net)	+11,294
Change in U.S. government assets abroad	−1,758
Transfers, public and private	−10,331
Change in foreign government asset in U.S	+17,974
Merchandise exports	+185,105

U.S. BALANCE OF PAYMENTS (HYPOTHETICAL)
(millions of dollars)

CURRENT ACCOUNT

    Balance of trade   _____

    Balance on current account   _____

CAPITAL ACCOUNT

    Balance on capital account   _____

STATISTICAL DISCREPANCY

CHAPTER 36

ECONOMIES IN TRANSITION

CHECKING IN

All countries must contend with similar economic problems. Opportunity costs and the law of demand exist under all economic systems. However, economic systems operate in a variety of ways. This chapter describes the most prevalent economic systems and examines the economies of several countries. Economists use comparative economics to analyze various institutions and determine how they affect economic outcomes.

Economic systems are often classified by ideology. Most economic systems fall into the categories of capitalism or socialism. These categories are so broad, however, that the usefulness of this approach is limited. Communist countries belong in the category of socialism. These countries all considered themselves Marxist, yet their economic systems were quite different. Many of these countries developed their economic systems under dominant leaders Lenin, Stalin, Mao, and Castro.

All economies engage in planning, but different systems plan at different levels. If planning takes place at a high level (as in many socialist countries), much more information is required by the planners. Central planning is the determination of national output. The Soviet Union experienced high industrial growth in the early twentieth century because of a central decision not to produce consumer goods. Plans have to be implemented. Workers and managers must be provided with adequate incentives if planned production levels are to be reached.

During the past twenty years, the Soviet Union and other Eastern and Central European countries began to adopt economic reforms leading toward a market system. These reforms have accelerated with the dissolution of the Soviet Union. The transition to a market economy is made more difficult by the lack of basic capitalistic institutions such as banking systems and stock markets.

Economic reforms have occurred in other parts of the world as China, too, has moved to a stronger reliance on markets and Mexico has restructured its economy, reducing its strong reliance on government market activities.

TRYING OUT THE TERMS

Match each of the following terms with its definition, and then check your answers. If you are having trouble, go back to the text and find the definition there.

____ 1. socialism

____ 2. capitalism

____ 3. perestroika

____ 4. privatization

____ 5. communism

____ 6. glasnost

A. An economic system in which private individuals own the means of production and are free to use them in response to economic incentives.

B. An economic system in which the nonhuman means of production are owned by the state.

C. The final stage of social evolution according to Marx, in which the state has withered away and economic goods are distributed according to need.

D. Political reforms involving free speech and tolerance of dissent in the former Soviet Union in the Gorbachev era.

E. Economic reforms in the former Soviet Union in the Gorbachev era.

F. Transferring assets from public to private ownership in order to increase the share of economic decisions made through the market.

TESTING YOURSELF

In the next two sections, you will answer questions that are based on information in the text. Master all of the terms before you begin these sections. Work each section without referring to your notes or the text, and then check your answers.

Part I: True or False

Mark each statement as true or false. Whenever you mark a statement as false, jot down a sentence stating why it is false.

____ 1. The process which enables societies to answer the basic economic questions is determined by the ownership of productive resources and the political organization of the society.

____ 2. The percentage of GDP passing through the government is a good measure of the degree to which government is involved in economic decision making.

_____ 3. Tax systems can be designed to encourage or discourage particular economic activities.

_____ 4. Government intervention does not occur in a capitalist economy.

_____ 5. Marx predicted that communism would be established first in industrialized countries.

_____ 6. In Marxist theory, socialism is the final stage in historical development.

_____ 7. Lenin's model for revolution has been fulfilled in several countries, such as Vietnam and Cuba.

_____ 8. The development of socialism in Yugoslavia was carried out under the direction of Stalin.

_____ 9. Under the five-year plans, money did not exist in the Soviet Union.

_____ 10. Between the 1930s and the 1970s, the Soviet Union enhanced its growth by borrowing ideas and technology.

_____ 11. By using internal rate of return calculations, the Soviet Union was able to achieve an efficient allocation of capital.

_____ 12. Gorbachev introduced the socialist solution to the Soviet Union.

_____ 13. Privatization is observed only as socialist countries move toward market decision making.

_____ 14. As nations move from socialism to capitalism, there is a marked increase in income inequality.

_____ 15. Since 1976, China has greatly expanded trade with the rest of the world.

_____ 16. Reformed production incentives allowed Chinese enterprises to increase production of consumer goods.

_____ 17. The recent growth in Mexico is at least partially attributable to increased public spending to create employment opportunities.

_____ 18. In Japan, taxes are considerably higher than they are in the United States.

_____ 19. Under Castro, Cuba remained reliant on agriculture.

_____ 20. F.A. Hayek demonstrated that properly estimated shadow prices will allow a planned economy to reach the same level of efficiency as a market system.

Part II: Multiple Choice

_____ 1. An essential similarity between capitalism and socialism is
   a. the ownership of nonhuman resources.
   b. the ownership of human resources.
   c. the determination of income distribution.
   d. None of the above

_____ 2. Under socialism, the decision-making process centers on
   a. the private property owner.
   b. the owners of capital.
   c. a planning organization.
   d. elected officials.

_____ 3. Marx predicted that all *except* which one of the following would occur under communism?
   a. An end to scarcity
   b. A new social order
   c. Increased class conflict
   d. The withering away of the state

_____ 4. Countries that consider themselves Marxist
   a. believe that capitalism exploits workers.
   b. deplore the presence of profits in an economy.
   c. tend to have strong-willed leaders.
   d. All of the above

_____ 5. During the period of the New Economic Policy
   a. planning was instituted for all sectors of the Soviet economy.
   b. parts of the economy operated with markets and other parts operated with economic planning.
   c. many industries in the Soviet Union were nationalized.
   d. planning was instituted for all sectors of the Soviet economy and many industries in the Soviet Union were nationalized.

_____ 6. Forced collectivization and rapid industrialization occurred in the Soviet Union during
   a. the Cultural Revolution.
   b. the period of five-year plans.
   c. perestroika.
   d. the New Economic Policy.

_____ 7. Under the leadership of Gorbachev, the Soviet Union
   a. moved into a more solidly Marxist stance.
   b. placed planning on a local level rather than a national level.
   c. moved away from central planning and toward market solutions.
   d. became an economic ally of China.

_____ 8. The simplest enterprises to privatize are
   a. farms.
   b. utilities.
   c. retail establishments.
   d. manufacturers.

_____ 9. Countries that have been most successful in either development or rebuilding have
   a. relied mainly on domestic savings.
   b. received substantial loans from industrialized countries.
   c. developed export subsidies to attract foreign capital.
   d. reduced reliance on imported technical aid.

_____ 10. The revolution in China under the leadership of Mao
   a. took place at the direction of Stalin.
   b. followed the model established by the Soviet Union.
   c. occurred just after the Korean War.
   d. preceded the period of War Communism.

_____ 11. The Cultural Revolution was based on the
   a. radical restructuring of the economy.
   b. emphasizing the role of the worker.
   c. revolutionary values of Mao.
   d. All of the above

_____ 12. During the reforms led by Deng in China,
   a. economic incentives were offered in the form of higher wages.
   b. more consumer goods were produced.
   c. international trade was discouraged.
   d. economic incentives were offered in the form of higher wages and more consumer goods were produced.

_____ 13. In Mexico, the revenues from privatization were used to
   a. pay benefits to displaced workers.
   b. subsidize exports.
   c. reduce the budget deficit.
   d. enforce environmental standards.

_____ 14. Japan's recent economic success is due in part to
   a. the devastation of World War II.
   b. a changing social structure.
   c. high rates of saving.
   d. All of the above

_____ 15. In Cuba, after the establishment of the Castro regime,
   a. the economy became dependent on Soviet aid.
   b. market capitalism was used for consumer goods and central planning was used for heavy industry.
   c. industrialization was the first national priority.
   d. the principle of self-reliance was the foreign policy rule.

_____ 16. Lange argued that a socialist economy could be as efficient as a competitive economy if
   a. there were centrally established shadow prices.
   b. local managers were allowed to keep a percentage of the profits.
   c. there was a combination of central and local decision making.
   d. all economic calculations were rational.

CHECKING OUT

Now that you have finished studying this chapter, you should be able to:

1. List the factors used to classify economies as market-oriented, socialist, and hybrid.

2. Distinguish among capitalism, socialism, and communism as theoretical economic systems and discuss the advantages and disadvantages of each.

3. Describe the events leading up to the collapse of communism in the former Soviet Union and Central Europe.

4. Discuss the process of transition from a centrally planned to a market economy and the difficulties being encountered in Eastern and Central Europe.

5. Evaluate the changes currently taking place in China, Japan, and Mexico as examples of economies in transition.

ANSWERS

Trying Out the Terms

1. B
2. A
3. E
4. F
5. C
6. D

Testing Yourself

Part I: True or False

1. false. The two factors determining how the economic questions are answered are ownership of resources and locus of economic decision making.
2. false. In many countries this pass-through may be a transfer of income with decision making being retained in the private sector.
3. true
4. false. Government intervention usually occurs to some degree in all economies.
5. true
6. false. Socialism is an intermediate stage; communism is the final stage.
7. true
8. false. Stalin's direction was in the Soviet Union.
9. false. Money played a small role, but it did exist to permit payment for consumer goods and wages.
10. true
11. false. Although there were some internal rate of return calculations, they were poor approximations of market rates; allocation of capital was inefficient.
12. false. Gorbachev introduced *glasnost* and its economic reform program, *perestroika*.
13. false. Privatization is an important move toward a market economy, but it has also taken place in Western industrial countries such as France and the United States.

14. true
15. true
16. true
17. false. The transition is mainly due to reduced public spending and increased privatization.
18. false. They are much lower.
19. true
20. false. Hayek maintained that central planning would always be less efficient than a market system since it deflects many resources into information creation.

Part II: Multiple Choice

1. d
2. c
3. c
4. d
5. b
6. b
7. c
8. c
9. a
10. b
11. d
12. d
13. c
14. d
15. a
16. a

Name _____

CHAPTER 36 EXERCISES

Mark each statement as true or false. Whenever you mark a statement as false, jot down a sentence stating why it is false.

_____ 1. All economies are mixed, although the degree may vary.

_____ 2. The general pattern is the lower the income of a country the higher the degree of government consumption.

_____ 3. Planning does not occur in capitalist economies.

_____ 4. Capitalism and communism are the extremes of economic systems.

_____ 5. Capitalistic countries tend to be politically democratic.

_____ 6. Any economic system must depend on wages, prices, and profits to provide incentives.

_____ 7. Under the New Economic Policy, the Soviet Union virtually eliminated the market system.

_____ 8. In the last fifteen years, Western (nonsocialist) countries have moved toward a higher degree of centralization.

_____ 9. One benefit of private ownership of resources is the presence of incentives, such as profit, that reward efficiency.

_____ 10. Perestroika represented efforts to reorganize planning and produce more consumer goods.

_____ 11. The usual measure of national economic performance is per capita GDP.

_____ 12. The current inflation in the former Soviet Union is largely due to consumers spending their new, higher wages.

_____ 13. The Cultural Revolution emphasized education and a move to a freer market system in China.

_____ 14. Mexico's economic success has been accompanied by a move from communism to a market economy.

_____ 15. Since 1990, Japan's rapid economic growth has become the Japanese "miracle."